THE CHANGING POLITICS OF HUNGER

HUNGER 1999

Ninth Annual Report
on the State of World Hunger

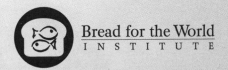

Bread for the World
INSTITUTE

1100 Wayne Avenue, Suite 1000
Silver Spring, Maryland 20910
USA

Printed on recycled paper.

Bread for the World Institute

President
David Beckmann

President Emeritus
Arthur Simon

Director
Richard A. Hoehn

Editor
James V. Riker

Co-Editor
Elena McCollim

Design
Dennis and Sackett Design

© 1998 by Bread for the World Institute
1100 Wayne Avenue, Suite 1000
Silver Spring, MD 20910-5603, USA
Telephone: (301) 608-2400 Fax: (301) 608-2401
E-mail: institute@bread.org
WWW: http://www.bread.org

Printer: HBP, Hagerstown, MD

Cover Photo: Margie Woodson Nea

Cover Quotation: "Universal Declaration on the Eradication
of Hunger and Malnutrition," United Nations, 1974.

Manufactured in the United States of America
First edition published November 1998
ISBN 1-884361-07-2

TABLE OF CONTENTS

1 **Foreword**
David Beckmann

2 **Introduction**
Richard A. Hoehn

6 Women and Children Last? – Kristy Manuliak

11 Fifty Years Is Not Enough: The Right to Food – Marc J. Cohen and John Teton

13 The Right-to-Food Resolution

14 Reflections on Christian Faith and Citizen Action – Arthur Simon

16 Legacy of *"Diet for a Small Planet"* – Frances Moore Lappé

20 **Chapter 1 – The Changing Politics of Hunger in the Poor Countries**
Paul Nelson

24 The Politics of Famine in North Korea – Kavita Pillay

29 "The Stomach Is Preferred to the Child" – Craig Cohen

34 Effects of Civil Conflict on Development – Anthony Edwin Koomson

36 **Chapter 2 – North-South Politics in the Global Economy**
Patti L. Petesch

39 International Decision-making Rules and Realities – Patti L. Petesch

40 *La Línea* – Sam Nickels and Cindy Hunter

46 Citizen Advocacy Reduces Debt – Kathleen A. Selvaggio

50 **Chapter 3 – The Global Communications Revolution**
James V. Riker

56 **Chapter 4 – The Politics of Hunger in the United States**
Leon Howell

62 Can't We Begin to See through the Eyes of a Poor Child? – Jim Shields

66 Campaign Finance Reform – Rebekah Jordan

69 Anti-Hunger Leaders Make a Difference – Shohreh Kermani Peterson

70 Bread for the World: Twenty-Five Years – Elena McCollim

72 **Chapter 5 – The Changing Politics of U.S. Welfare Policy**
Lynette Engelhardt

74 From Homelessness to Citizen Action – Peggy Thomas

76 Coalitions Catalyze Change – Hunger Task Force of Milwaukee

80 Recollections of a Child on Welfare – Janice A. Cardaro

82 **Chapter 6 – Update on the State of World Hunger**
Kristy Manuliak and Elena McCollim

85 The Politics of Hunger in Canada – Kristy Manuliak

88 Asian Financial Crisis Means Hunger in Indonesia – Kavita Pillay

90 **Chapter 7 – Political Strategies to End Hunger**
James V. Riker and Paul Nelson

92 *Africa: Seeds of Hope* – Anatomy of a Legislative Campaign – Don Reeves

95 Bishops Trigger Ouster of President in Malawi – Lisa Ferrari

98 Lobbying Brings Change – Marc J. Cohen

100 **Appendix**

100 **Tables on World Hunger**

100 Global Hunger – Life and Death Indicators

104 Food, Nutrition and Education

107 Hunger, Malnutrition and Poverty

110 Economic and Development Indicators

113 Economic Globalization

116 Global Communications

119 U.S. National Hunger and Poverty Trends

120 United States – State Hunger and Poverty Statistics

121 **Sources for Tables**

122 **Abbreviations**

123 **Glossary**

126 **Notes**

131 **Sponsors and Co-sponsors**

ACKNOWLEDGMENTS

We are deeply grateful for the valuable insights provided by sponsors, cosponsors and colleagues at two consultations related to this report and in response to drafts. Those who provided comments include:

Laurie Aomari, American Dietetic Association; Rick Augsburger, Church World Service; Manfred Bardeleben, Friedrich Ebert Foundation; Geza Bekele, U.S. General Accounting Office; Lynn Brantley, Capital Area Community Food Bank; Lisa Brendel, RESULTS; Bill Byron, Georgetown University; Carol Capps, Church World Service/Lutheran World Relief; Edward J. Chesky, economic consultant; Marc J. Cohen, IFPRI; David Crocker, University of Maryland; Carol Fennelly, Sojourners; Lisa Ferrari, Hamilton College; Rob Fersh, Consultant; Tracy Fox, American Dietetic Association; Bill Gahr, Consultant; Lisa Galloway, Citizens' Network for Foreign Affairs; Mona Hammam, World Food Programme; James Hug, Center of Concern; Evariste Karangwa, InterAction; Ellen Levinson, Coalition for Food Aid; Peter Mann, World Hunger Year; Peter Matlon, UNDP; Martin McLaughlin, Center of Concern; Lynn McMullen, RESULTS; Joe Mettimano, U.S. Committee for UNICEF; Betty Meyer, Christian Children's Fund; Paul Montacute, Baptist World Aid; Cheryl Morden, ICRW; John Morrill, Congressional Hunger Center; Robert Nieman, Public Citizen/Global Trade Watch; Haven North, Consultant; Matthew Onek, Share Our Strength; Walter Owensby, Presbyterian Church USA; Janet Poppendieck, Hunter College/CUNY; Atiqur Rahman, IFAD; Andrew Rice, International Development Conference and United Nations Association of the USA; Klaus Rieth, Brot für die Welt; Veena Siddharth, Oxfam International; Alexandra Spieldoch, Center of Concern; Ellen Teller, FRAC; Phil Thomas, General Accounting Office; Paul Thompson, MAP International; Jim Weill, FRAC; Steve Weissman, Public Citizen; Michael Wiest, Catholic Relief Services; Maurice Williams, Overseas Development Council; Mary Wright, Campaign for Human Development; Pat Young, U.S. National Committee for World Food Day.

We appreciate the assistance of the following people and institutions in obtaining data: Shirley Atchison, U.S. Department of Agriculture; Gul Tanghe Gulluova, UNDP; Peter Matlon, UNDP; Robert G. Patterson, Food and Agriculture Organization of the United Nations; Tessa Wardlaw, UNICEF; World Bank Development Data Group.

The following Bread for the World members and Bread for the World/Bread for the World Institute board members and staff provided comments and assistance: Ray Almeida, Mai Bull, Kimberly Burge, Janice Cardaro, Sara Grusky, Donna Hodge, Larry Hollar; Barbara Howell, Diane Hunt, Nellie Kamau, Margaret Cohen Lipton, Henry Maingi, Jim McDonald, Susan Kay Park, Kathy Pomroy, Nathan Raybeck, Michael Rubinstein, Stephanie Seidel, Niloufer De Silva, Katherine Simmons, Carole Southam, Lynora Williams and Dolly Youssef.

Kavita Pillay prepared the statistical tables.

David Fouse was copy editor.

THEMES OF ANNUAL REPORTS ON THE STATE OF WORLD HUNGER

Bread for the World Institute

Hunger 1990: A Report on the State of World Hunger

Hunger 1992: Ideas that Work

Hunger 1993: Uprooted People

Hunger 1994: Transforming the Politics of Hunger

Hunger 1995: Causes of Hunger

Hunger 1996: Countries in Crisis

Hunger 1997: What Governments Can Do

Hunger 1998: Hunger in a Global Economy

FOREWORD

The Changing Politics of Hunger argues that the time is ripe and urgent for making the necessary political changes at all levels to overcome hunger in the United States and worldwide. The report highlights the significant progress that has been made in fighting hunger over the past 25 years and analyzes the opportunities and challenges that remain in order to eliminate widespread hunger. The post-Cold War period presents new challenges, but also opportunities – a dynamic economy, powerful means of communication and the spread of democracy.

Bread for the World Institute is associated with Bread for the World, a Christian citizens' movement against hunger that was founded in 1974. As we approach our 25th anniversary as a faith-based organization committed to ending hunger at home and abroad, it is important to reflect on the lessons we have learned for solving hunger in the twenty-first century.

We have learned that the key to overcoming hunger is changing the politics of hunger. This requires educating and empowering people at all levels of society, including hungry and poor people. By mobilizing as individuals and collectively, we can reorient political structures and influence powerful institutions. We have seen again and again that ordinary people who care really can make a difference.

Today's citizens could be the generation that ends mass hunger in the United States and around the world – but only if we respond, charitably and politically.

David Beckmann
President, Bread for the World and
Bread for the World Institute

INTRODUCTION

BY RICHARD A. HOEHN

T he end of hunger is within reach. The effort it would take to end
hunger and malnutrition worldwide by the year 2015 is quite
modest. The World Food Summit of 1996 suggested cutting
hunger in half by 2015, and the nations of the world are making only a
feeble effort to meet that complacent goal. It is now time to close the door
on one of recent history's more sordid stories – continuing hunger in a
world of plenty.

The number of people who have died of starvation has declined fairly
consistently since the 1950s and 1960s due to economic growth and social
programs, especially improved health care.

Over the past 25 years since the first World Food Conference and the
founding of Bread for the World in 1974, tremendous progress has been
made toward eliminating hunger. The proportion of the world's hungry
people has dropped from one-third to one-fifth since 1970. Though the

Figure 1 **Net Global Starvation Deaths, in Millions, per Decade**

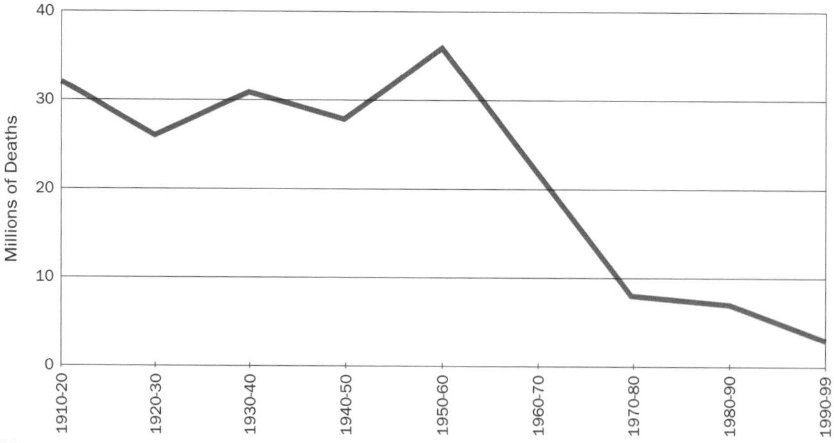

Source: Steven Hansch, "How Many People Die of Starvation in Humanitarian
Emergencies," Center for Policy Analysis on Refugee Issues, Refugee Policy Group,
June 1995. Data compiled by the author from information gathered from journals and
government publications.

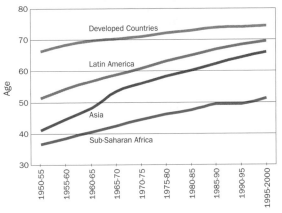

Figure 2 **Life Expectancy, by Regions, 1950-2000**

Source: James Fox, "Gaining Ground: World Well-Being 1950-95," USAID Evaluation Special Study No. 79, June 1998, 17.

world's population has increased by 2 billion people over this period, the number of malnourished people has declined from 918,000,000 to 841,000,000 in the developing world.

The quality of the average human life has improved (see Figures 2–4).

These gains are a result of human choices and efforts. They do not "just happen." They are socially created.

When the human community decided around 1974 to make overcoming hunger a higher priority, charities, governments and United Nations' (U.N.) agencies mustered funds and built an infrastructure – institutions and early warning programs – to anticipate and respond to natural disasters that lead to mass starvation. The International Fund for Agricultural Development (IFAD) of the United Nations has, since 1978, been very effective in loaning $5.6 billion for rural poverty and hunger alleviation projects in 111 countries.[1]

We still see stick-thin children in the news – the Dinkas in Sudan, North Korean school children – and the death of even a few is tragedy enough (see "Effects of Civil Conflict on Development", pp. 34-35, and "The Politics of Famine in North Korea," pp. 24-25). People are still threatened with the possibility of famine and starvation, but fewer die because organizations now have a capacity to respond. When people do die, it is often because of politics gone wrong – civil conflict and despotic governments.

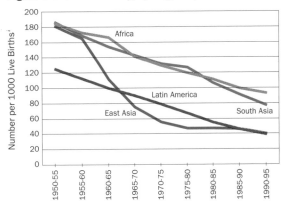

Figure 3 **Infant Mortality, by Regions, 1950-1995**

Source: James Fox, op. cit., 16.

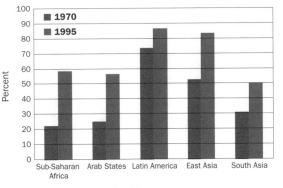

Figure 4 **Literacy, by Developing Country Region, 1970 and 1995**

Source: James Fox, op. cit., 17.

World Bank/Curt Cannemark

When tragedy is averted, either by long-term sustainable development or through crisis management, it is usually because of good political decisions.

Because malnutrition is less visible and dramatic than starvation, public media, and thus citizens and politicians, pay less attention. While both the number and percentage of people who are malnourished has been reduced, they remain at unacceptable levels. Children's lives

Not until the creation and maintenance of decent conditions of life for all people are recognized and accepted as a common obligation of all people and all countries – not until then shall we, with a certain degree of justification, be able to speak of mankind as civilized. — ALBERT EINSTEIN

can be permanently damaged by poor nutrition in their early years. Potential moral leaders, artists and physicians waste away, searching for something to fill their stomachs. And even full bellies, when stuffed with tree roots and straw, do not convert into classroom alertness (if classrooms exist), or healthy, productive and active lives. I once knew a man from Appalachia whose mother, in the 1950s, was reduced to filling her children's stomachs with dirt sandwiches. Not peanut butter, dirt sandwiches! The time for change is not only ripe, it is urgent.

The Changing Politics of Hunger: Hunger 1999 takes roughly the past 25 years as a context. Bread for the World was founded in 1974 with a certain view of how politics works. Huge changes have occurred. We have taken a fresh look at the politics of hunger on the cusp of a new century.

Because this is Bread's anniversary, *The Changing Politics of Hunger* says more about Bread for the World than has been typical of volumes in this annual series. We are particularly pleased that Arthur Simon, founder of Bread for the World, and Frances Moore Lappé, author of *Diet for a Small Planet,* have provided 25-year retrospectives (pp. 14-17).

For the first time in history it is possible to end hunger, and that, rather quickly. The world has the resources, knowledge and structures. The world's fields, livestock and oceans produce enough food. The world's economies provide sufficient wealth.

The key to overcoming hunger, in this era, is changing politics and empowering hungry and poor people. More specifically, we have identified seven imperatives, that, in combination, could rid the world of hunger early in the next century.

Shockingly, hunger persists in some industrial countries such as the United States and Canada (see Chapters 4, 5, and 6). In the United States, 11.8 million households, comprising 34 million persons, experience food insecurity. About 2 million persons live in households experiencing severe hunger, and 9 million persons live in households with moderate hunger. The other 23 million typically choose poor quality food to make ends meet.[2] Many turn to food pantries.

Despite a strong economy and low unemployment, Lutheran Social Services, Catholic Charities, the Salvation Army, Second Harvest (the national association of food banks) and allied agencies are reporting sharp increases in requests for emergency food.

Never doubt that a small group of committed citizens can change the world. Indeed, it is the only thing that ever has. — MARGARET MEAD

According to Second Harvest, of the 26 million people who receive emergency hunger assistance in the United States, 62 percent are female, 16 percent are older citizens and 38 percent are children. Many of the people who come to food pantries and soup kitchens have jobs, but receive low wages and lack health insurance.

Under these circumstances, it is difficult to imagine that progress against hunger is really possible. But past progress in the United States and in many very poor countries is reason for hope.

Also, several post-Cold War changes in the structure of politics could open opportunities to develop political will to end hunger. These same trends can be hard on hungry people. The challenge is for people of goodwill to use these trends for good. They are too powerful to resist, but could be flipped, judo style, in the direction of progress against hunger.

With the shifting of power relations in a post-Cold War world order, three key global trends now shape the possibilities and political strategies for alleviating hunger early in the 21st century. The fundamental reality is that hunger is a political condition. That is to say, politics (not just poverty or scarcity) is the root cause of, and holds the solution to, hunger at this time in history.

Over the past 70 years, *Time* magazine has featured the most important person on its "Man of the Year" cover. The person of the half-century in 1949 was Winston Churchill. The person of the decade of the 1980s was Mikhail Gorbachev. The person or group chosen typically symbolize larger historical events, for example, King Faisal and the rise of the Organization of Petroleum Exporting Countries (OPEC) in the early 1970s. Nearly two-thirds of those covers have been devoted to political figures. Politics makes the world go round. The key to overcoming hunger is changing the politics of hunger.

The first major trend affecting the politics of hunger in the post-Cold War world is the *spread of democracy*, the growth of civil society and one of its chief manifestations, the worldwide movement to empower poor people, especially women.

TO CHANGE THE POLITICS OF HUNGER

1 **Recognize the timeliness, and recover the moral and religious urgency, of ending hunger.** Because significant progress against hunger has been achieved and the world has sufficient resources, ending hunger is both timely and a fundamental moral and religious obligation. The chief enemy is not lack of food, but political apathy.

2 **Support the empowerment efforts of poor people.** Hunger will not end until poor people are empowered to participate meaningfully in political and economic processes.

3 **Hold social, economic and political institutions accountable to the common good and especially to the well-being of hungry and poor people.** Each institution and sector of society – private as well as public – has a unique role and function, but all should be held accountable.

4 **Promote participation in fair, democratic, participatory structures at all levels of private and public life.** Participation influences outcomes, but requires an appropriate political and economic infrastructure – the right to vote, the right to organize, fair financing of elections.

5 **Utilize the power of the mass media to portray the depth of, and causes and solutions to, hunger.** Modern communications have a significant impact in shaping public consciousness on hunger issues.

6 **Forge collaborative political alliances to bring effective changes at all levels – community to international.** Individuals, organizations and even governments can be more effective in their efforts to overcome hunger and poverty when they work together.

7 **Think creatively and actively learn about policies that can contribute to overcoming hunger.** The advent of the global economy calls for a revised policy agenda for combating hunger. In the information age, we need to educate ourselves about hunger and its solutions.

Amartya Sen, renowned hunger expert and economist at Harvard and Cambridge Universities, argues "that there has never been a serious famine in a country – even an impoverished one – with a democratic government and a free press."[3] Two key elements that go together are communication and democracy. When people know that others may die of starvation and when they have the power to affect political outcomes, they do something about it!

BY KRISTY MANULIAK

The worldwide women's movement is a key part of the global trend toward democracy, and the trend toward more rights for women is reshaping the world.

The 1975 Mexico City conference launching the U.N. decade for women highlighted the unmeasured and undervalued economic contribution of women, and hence the importance of gender in long-term sustainable development.

In the 1980s, women's role in food production was increasingly recognized as the "backbone of the rural food system,"[1] especially in Africa (see "Africa Seeds of Hope," pp. 92-94.) The 1990s

Celia Escudero-Espadas

have also seen new attention to girls and the importance of their education.

Today, 25 years later, the worldwide women's movement has been gaining ground at the grassroots level, for example in the founding of groups like the Self-Employed Women's Association in India in the 1970s.

While a 1987 conference speaker could raise cheers with an exhortation to help "the African farmer *and her husband*," over a decade later women and children still suffer first and most from hunger and poverty. How women and children are treated is a measure of the success of public policies. They must be first in line for our attention. Too often, they remain last.

> The tragedy of childhood malnutrition is rooted in part in the discrimination and disempowerment so many women endure. What endangers women endangers children too...and full commitment to the rights of

women is one of the best ways of protecting children's well-being and nutritional development.[2]

Women grow up to 90 percent of all food for home consumption in developing countries. They produce half the world's food, but own only 1 percent of its farmland. When women lack control over important resources and decision-making power, food security is threatened. Landholding laws, lack of access to credit, disenfranchisement and certain cultural practices keep women from securing enough food for themselves and their families.

> Discrimination against women and girls is an important basic cause of malnutrition. The very high rates of child malnutrition and low birthweight throughout much of South Asia are linked to such factors as women's poor access to education and their low levels of participation in paid employment.[3]

Since women usually make their children's well-being a priority, the 67 million children who are underweight or wasted is one measure of the effects of women's relative powerlessness.[4] Of the nearly 12 million child deaths under age 5 each year, 55 percent can be attributed either directly or indirectly to malnutrition.[5]

The deck is stacked against these children from before birth. Sixty percent to 80 percent of the women of childbearing-age in the developing world do not receive the minimum caloric requirements for good health. No wonder so many babies are undernourished.

Chronic undernutrition during the formative years can lead to stunting, the failure to grow to normal height. Of all the children under age 5 living in developing countries, 226 million, or 40 percent, suffered stunting.[6]

Nutritional deficiencies delay mental development, lower immunity to disease and can lead to death. Anemia plays a major role in 20 percent to 23 percent of all post-partum maternal deaths in Africa and Asia. And anemia in infancy and early childhood thwarts development, both physical and mental.[7]

Women face barriers in industrial countries, too. They are more likely than men to have primary responsibility for child care and for balancing conflicting job and family demands. When families break up, women often have the added challenge of providing adequate, nutritious meals

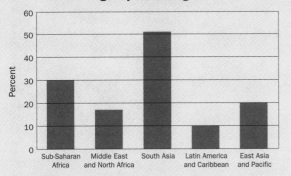

Figure 5 **Percent of Children Under 5 Who Are Underweight by World Region**

Source: UNICEF, 1997.

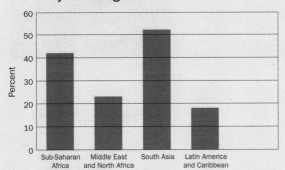

Figure 6 **Percent of Children Under 5 Who Are Stunted by World Region**

Source: UNICEF, 1997.

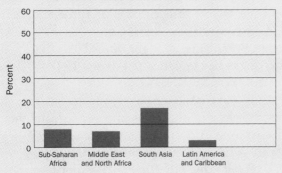

Figure 7 **Percent of Children Under 5 Who Are Wasted by World Region**

Source: UNICEF, 1997.

on single salaries. Janice Cardaro describes the harsh family effects of her father's departure (see pp. 80-81). Close to 60 percent of families headed by single women live in poverty.

When economies prosper, gender discrimination is less pernicious. The Asian financial crisis dramatizes how different treatment of women and girls in normal economic times turns into

disaster during an economic downturn – not just for the women and girls, but ultimately for the larger society. In Indonesia, "the impact on women and girls is just catastrophic," according to Linda Tsao Yang, American representative to the Asian Development Bank, headquartered in Manila. She reports that "As a result of the financial crisis, women are disproportionately losing their jobs, and families are pulling their daughters out of school or even selling them to brothels."[8]

Even before the crisis, in Indonesia girls were six times as likely as boys to leave school before the fourth grade; now, dropout rates for both genders have doubled, with girls in the majority.[9] In eastern Indonesia, 8 year-old Juliana Aoetpa had to leave school and spend her time fetching water and gathering food. Said her mother: "School is free. But the children have to buy a uniform [only less than two dollars] and we just couldn't afford it."[10] With medical costs rising, women are also more apt to neglect their care.

Putting women and children first means making the education of girls and the political and economic empowerment of women, a very high priority.

KRISTY MANULIAK, a project associate with Bread for the World Institute, was sponsored by the United Nations Association in Canada and the Canadian Department of Foreign Affairs and International Trade.

[1] Margaret Snyder, "Women: The Key to Ending Hunger," *The Hunger Project Papers*, Number 8, August 1990, 3.

[2] United Nations Children's Fund, "Child Malnutrition and Women's Rights," In: *The State of the World's Children 1998*, New York: Oxford University Press.

[3] United Nations Children's Fund, "Malnutrition," In: *The State of the World's Children 1998*, New York: Oxford University Press.

[4] Wasting is a condition in which a person is seriously below the normal weight for her or his height due to acute undernutrition or a medical condition. Underweight is a condition in which a person is seriously below normal weight for her or his age. United Nations Children's Fund, "Child Malnutrition and Women's Rights," In: *The State of the World's Children 1998*, New York: Oxford University Press.

[5] United Nations Children's Fund, "Malnutrition: Causes," In: *The State of the World's Children 1998*, New York: Oxford University Press.

[6] Ibid.

[7] Ibid.

[8] Nicholas D. Kristof, "The Human Crisis: Asian Crisis Deals Setbacks to Women," *New York Times*, June 11, 1998.

[9] Ibid.

[10] Ibid.

The gender revolution has a democratizing influence, as do movements for fairness and equality in race relations. Many governments and some international institutions such as the World Bank are attempting to be more democratic – responsive, transparent and accountable. Responding to citizen pressure, governments have also become more effective in delivering services.

The past 25 years have seen a huge rise in the number of civic groups, social service and public interest groups. While individual citizens can influence public outcomes through their activities as consumers as well as citizens, they are most effective when they join efforts and strategize together. The same is true for organizations. If each seeks only its own self-interest,

> *Peace – that is all that is required of Africa…My country is almost permanently drought-stricken, but because there is so much peace, so much democracy – and the government is one of the most incorruptible on the continent – no one has ever died from starvation.* — Legwaila Joseph Legwaila, Botswana's representative to the United Nations[4]

it is difficult to mobilize a power base to affect outcomes. Social-issue interest groups, who work on different issues sometimes join forces to elect candidates. And, small businesses with separate products but shared problems, are doing the same.[5]

It is critical that individuals, organizations and governments forge collaborative political alliances to bring effective changes. Chapter 1 links the national-level politics of hunger to poverty and economic injustice, and asks how the politics of hunger is changed and who can do it.

Today, ordinary people have more opportunity to shape government policies and corporate practices, and strategies to overcome hunger now can and should put more emphasis on empowerment. On the other hand, the majority of a population often does not support policies that may be needed by very poor people. And, so

"They shall beat their swords into plowshares."

the burden of educating the public, especially through the powerful means of modern communications, lies ever more heavily on those who seek justice for all.

The second trend is the rise and spread of the *global market economy*. It interweaves with every part of our lives. As people in the United States decorated their Christmas trees, they probably did not realize that China produced the $2 billion worth of artificial Christmas trees, lights, ornaments, dolls and stuffed toys that merchants had imported to fill their 1997 Christmas shelves.

Cold War goals once shaped superpower politics. Now capitalism reigns uncontested, and the global economy is fundamentally redefining states' social contract with their citizens. *Hunger in a Global Economy: Hunger 1998* argued that it is impossible to understand either domestic or international politics apart from global economics; or to understand elections without reading the business pages of the newspaper. Governments, at all levels, now have less say over internal and external outcomes, as they compete for jobs and capital.

The global market economy has played a major role in reducing hunger worldwide and

The world is run by those who show up. — PABLO EISENBERG, CENTER FOR COMMUNITY CHANGE

offers the opportunity for increased economic growth and with it jobs and a rising standard of living. The global market economy has helped create a situation where ending hunger is not just a vague hope or idealistic vision. Ending hunger is a realistic possibility. The market economy could help even more if we insisted that it be responsible to such things as labor rights provisions in trade agreements, investments in education and health care for all and promote opportunities for participation of poor people in the decisions that affect their lives.

Since *Hunger 1998* focused on the global economy, Chapter 2 takes a more focused look at the politics behind key international development initiatives important for reducing hunger and poverty worldwide. It examines North-South decision-making in trade, finance and aid and the power dynamics underpinning international policy-making.

The *global communications revolution* (see Chapter 3) is the third major force affecting the politics of hunger. Modern communications make the global economy possible, shape political culture and thus political elections, help individuals and anti-hunger organizations understand issues and monitor the performance of public figures.

People have more access to information and venues to express their opinions, more cheaply and regularly by computer, than at any time in history. Costs are declining and while the playing field is far from even, it is leveling, at least in the developed world. The average 12 year-old with a computer can access more information than likely existed 50 years ago.

The Internet played a central role in citizen mobilization for the International Campaign to Ban Landmines, which grew from an idea to the signing of an international treaty by 120 countries (albeit not the United States) and a 1,000 organizational members in over 60 countries, and receiving the Nobel Peace Prize in less than six years.[6]

At the same time, the media constantly reinforce images of consumerist culture such as upscale advertisements and sitcoms that shape the way people think. Owning the latest model, the new toy, can become more important, at an unconscious level, than eliminating hunger. And the 20-second sound bite lends itself to often empty or misleading rhetoric.

The media have done a reasonable job of presenting natural and human disasters, including famine, and environmental problems, but have lacked the patience and will to tackle the long-term problems of malnutrition, education and depoliticization. Funded by corporations, they have not found it in their interest to publicize the increasing commercialization of culture. Addicted to the theory that only bad news is real news, the media are more interested in the $1 million misspent by a government than the $1 billion well spent.

Without the advent of television, the dramatic events of the civil rights movement in the United States – police dogs and tear gas, killing of children in a bombed church – might not have evoked so much sympathy and the legislation that followed. Body bags on nightly television fueled demonstrations that dragged the United States out of Vietnam.

Modern communications have a significant impact in shaping public consciousness on hunger issues and bear some responsibility to portray the depth of, and causes, and solutions to hunger. Moreover, hunger advocates need to make better use of the media to get their message across.

Most of the chapters mention rising inequality worldwide. So, what is so bad about inequality as long as the bottom continues to rise? It is, after all, the people on the bottom of the income scale who are most likely to suffer from malnutrition. And, is not inequality inevitable? We are not born equal in our ability to be concert pianists, to lead nations or to win Olympic medals.

A measure of inequality is inevitable, but gross poverty is not. It is well known that people with higher incomes in just about any country have lower death and illness rates. More important, however, a study of 282 U.S. metropolitan areas reports that sharp inequality, "is associated with increased mortality."[7] The size of the income gap, not just income level, leads to more disease and earlier death.

Sharp inequality also affects politics. History is the story of the winners who typically won because they marshaled more resources. Financial and other assets fuel political campaigns. The day this was written, a gubernatorial candidate dropped out for lack of campaign funds. Sharp inequality in resources leads to sharp inequality in the ability to shape political outcomes. Elites with resources play the tune while the rest dance, if, well nourished, they have the energy.

Promoting participation in fair, democratic, participatory structures at all levels of private and public life is one crucial step toward ending hunger long term. Poor people especially need to

Broad political participation is a prerequisite for ending hunger and poverty.

UN/DPI Photo

THE SEVEN SOCIAL EVILS

Wealth Without Work

Pleasure Without Conscience

Knowledge Without Character

Commerce Without Morality

Science Without Humanity

Worship Without Sacrifice

Politics Without Principles

– GANDHI

be empowered (see Chapters 1, 2, 3, 5, and 7). Emergency, charitable and welfare programs can and should feed people today. But unless people are empowered and supported in getting an education and job, raising families (e.g., child and health care) and participating in political life, they will remain dependent, and victims. Janice Cardaro (see pp. 80-81) describes the indignities her family suffered in the charity/welfare system, reminding us that the psychological scars and stigma of assistance may be difficult to overcome.

Political and economic power most often win the day – for good and for ill. But moral and religious voices sometimes prevail. It was not just violence on television that led to changes in civil rights, or self-interest that led to changes in how women are treated, but the widespread notion that discrimination is wrong, combined with grassroots organizing by committed people.

A clear moral voice can make a difference. Bread for the World and Germany's Brot für die Welt, which observes its 40th birthday in late 1998, are deeply rooted in morality; itself rooted in religion. Lisa Ferrari recounts positive changes that occurred when Roman Catholic bishops in Malawi raised their voices in moral protest (see p. 95). The first major activity Bread for the World undertook was to convince Congress to pass a Right-to-Food Resolution (see p. 13) that reads as well today as it did two decades ago.

In 1974 at the first World Food Conference in Rome, 134 nations gathered in solemn assembly, sobered by recent famines, declared that "Every man, woman, and child has the inalienable right to be free from hunger," and "that within a decade no child will go to bed hungry, that no family will fear for its next day's bread, and that

BY MARC J. COHEN AND JOHN TETON

Fifty years ago, the United Nations General Assembly adopted the Universal Declaration of Human Rights, to establish "the foundation of freedom, justice, and peace in the world."[1] The Declaration elaborates both civil and political rights (security of the person, freedom of expression and association, government based on popular consent) and economic, social and cultural rights, including the right to food and other basic necessities. The preamble echoes U.S. President Franklin Roosevelt's Four Freedoms speech in characterizing these rights as interdependent and indivisible.

Civil and political rights are indispensable to communities struggling for food security. At the same time, as President Carter's Commission on World Hunger asserted, without the right to food, "the protection of other human rights becomes a mockery for those who must spend all their energy merely to maintain life itself."[2]

With one of every seven people worldwide (and one of five people in developing countries) lacking access to adequate food, the Declaration's vision of a world that recognizes "the inherent dignity and... the equal and inalienable rights of all members of the human family" has yet to be realized. But that vision is the moral basis for efforts to eliminate hunger. Moreover, the United Nations continues to evolve as an effective human rights institution, as seen, for example, in the recent establishment of war crimes tribunals. And, as a prominent legal scholar argues:

> Having law never guarantees that all will obey it, but the existence of law does modify behavior. Legally binding rights to food can contribute to world food security by prescribing and proscribing certain national and international actions.[3]

The United States has signed, but not yet ratified, the International Covenant on Economic, Social and Cultural Rights (ICESCR) of 1966, which further elaborates the rights to adequate food and freedom from hunger. Nevertheless, the United States has generally supported the many subsequent international reaffirmations of these rights, from the 1974 World Food Conference through the 1995 Fourth World Conference on Women.

In 1976, Bread for the World used its first "Offering of Letters" to gain congressional passage of the Right to Food Resolutions (see "Bread for the World: Twenty-Five Years," pp. 70-71). Both houses of Congress unanimously concluded that "the United States reaffirms the right of every person in this country and throughout the world to food and a nutritionally adequate diet."[4]

The Rome Declaration on World Food Security, unanimously adopted at the 1996 World Food Summit, again reaffirmed this right. The summit's Plan of Action calls upon the U.N. High Commissioner for Human Rights:

> to better define the rights related to food... and to propose ways to implement and realize these rights as a means of achieving the commitments and objectives of the World Food Summit, taking into account the possibility of formulating voluntary guidelines for food security for all.[5]

In a major disappointment to anti-hunger advocates, the United States insisted at the World Food Summit that the idea of a right to food did not create "international obligations," and rejected efforts to create new guidelines. That was a step back from the U.S. position at the World Food Conference of 1974. U.S. officials subscribed only to the "aspira-

Hold social, economic and political institutions accountable to the common good and especially the well-being of hungry and poor people

tional goal" of freedom from hunger, not guarantees. They expressed concern that endorsing the right to food would fuel domestic litigation over new restrictions on food stamp eligibility. Ironically, it was at the insistence of the United States that the summit endorsed the view that food security rests upon universal enjoyment of the full range of fundamental rights and individual freedoms.[6]

U.S. dissent stemmed largely from a misunderstanding of the ICESCR, which does not require governments to feed everyone. It includes provisions on the rights to work, just compensation, training and freedom from employment discrimination, suggesting that these are the main channels for fulfilling basic needs. Governments must *respect* the right of everyone within their borders to have access to adequate food; *protect* that right from encroachment by others; *facilitate* opportunities by which that right can be enjoyed (for example through land reform or food safety regulations); and only in the last instance *fulfill* the right to food for those unable to do so by themselves.[7]

Bread for the World and other U.S. nongovernmental organizations (NGOs) have pressed the U.S. government to reiterate its past support for the right to food. As of the spring of 1998, this dialogue was ongoing. Meanwhile, the U.S. government has stayed on the sidelines of efforts to follow through on the summit plan.

continues on next page

South Africa's post-*apartheid* constitution enshrines rights to access to food, as well as basic nutrition for children. The constitution also explicitly incorporates government obligations to "respect, protect, promote, and fulfill" these rights. The country faces daunting challenges in making these rights a reality. But the constitution recognizes that new-found political equality can only become meaningful in a context of social and economic justice, including food security.

International NGOs have elaborated a code of conduct on the right to food.[8] Although not legally binding, it sets out standards for the behavior not only of governments, but of international organizations, NGOs and private enterprises. The code has attracted widespread NGO support from both the industrial and developing worlds, and has been discussed at a number of U.N. forums. Bread for the World is among the supporters of the Code of Conduct.[9]

Given the growing sense that existing covenants and declarations have proven inadequate to define the right to be free from hunger in international law, or to protect it, the International Food Security Treaty (IFST) is addressed only to governments. The treaty aims to establish enforceable international law guaranteeing the right to be free from hunger, and to oblige states to establish and implement their own related national laws.[10]

The IFST spells out the legal responsibilities of nations to prevent starvation and malnutrition, with enforcement provisions to insure they are carried out.[11] An example of legally prohibited activity would be the deliberate use of starvation as a weapon, a tactic that led to the simultaneous famines in Bosnia and Somalia several years ago. The IFST also calls for the creation of a global food reserve to assure adequate emergency food aid, and allows both individuals and NGOs to bring complaints to U.N. bodies when governments fail to uphold the right to food. Complaints could trigger U.N. investigation and, if necessary, intervention.[12]

The IFST, at less than 700 words, is much more narrowly focused than the Code of Conduct, concentrating on the immediate objective of codification and enforcement of human rights law to eliminate malnutrition. By contrast, the Code of Conduct casts a far wider net around food security issues, and because it does not demand legally binding commitments, it is advancing within governmental circles at a much faster pace.

The challenge ahead for the anti-hunger movement is considerable: prevailing on governments to review how their laws and policies respect, protect, facilitate and fulfill the right to food; to adopt the voluntary code of conduct; and eventually to agree to be bound by "hard law" along the lines of the IFST. The U.S. government needs to be at the table for the tough discussions that lie ahead.

DR. MARC J. COHEN, former editor of Bread for the World Institute's annual reports on world hunger, represented the organization at the World Food Summit. He is currently special assistant to the director general at the International Food Policy Research Institute. E-mail: m.j.cohen@cgnet.com

JOHN TETON, director of the International Food Security Treaty Campaign, participated in the NGO Forum at the World Food Summit, and served as coordinator of the 1998 International Conference on Consensus Strategy for the Right to Food in Law. E-mail: treaty@worldnet.att.net

[1] The Declaration was adopted as U.N. General Assembly Resolution 217 A (III) on December 10, 1948. The full text is accessible at <www.unhchr.ch/html/menu3/b/a_udhr.htm>.

[2] *Overcoming World Hunger: The Challenge Ahead, Report of the Presidential Commission on World Hunger,* Washington, DC: U.S. Government Printing Office, 1980, 3.

[3] Donald Buckingham, "Legal Obligations and Rights to Food: What's New from Rome?," *Canadian Journal of Development Studies*, January 1998.

[4] The Right-to-Food Resolution, as passed by the U.S. Senate (S. Con. Res. 138) on September 16, 1976.

[5] *World Food Summit Plan of Action*, Paragraph 61 (e), accessible at <www.fao.org>.

[6] U.S. General Accounting Office, *Food Security: Preparations for the 1996 World Food Summit*, GAO/NSIAD-97-44, November 1996.

[7] Asbjorn Eide, "Human Rights Requirements to Social and Economic Development," *Food Policy* 21:1 (1996): 23-39.

[8] They include the FoodFirst Information and Action Network (FIAN), the Institute Jacques Maritain International and the World Alliance for Nutrition and Human Rights.

[9] The Code is available by electronic mail from: <fian-is@oln.comlink.apc.org>.

[10] The IFST Principles were first circulated by the U.S.-based International Food Security Treaty Campaign in 1993 and subsequently developed in partnership with the Centre for Studies in Agriculture, Law and the Environment at the University of Saskatchewan and the North American Right-to-Food Working Group, a coalition of NGOs (including Bread for the World), in consultation with anti-hunger leaders from North and South America, Africa, Asia and Europe.

[11] The Treaty text is accessible at <www.treaty.org>.

[12] Supporters of this approach include Chilean U.N. Ambassador Juan Somavia (Coordinator of the 1995 U.N. World Summit on Social Development), David MacDonald (former Canadian Secretary of State and Emergency Coordinator for the African Famine) and former U.N. Assistant Secretary General Robert Muller.

no human being's future and capacities will be stunted by malnutrition."

It was not a new idea then, and it is not an old idea now.

The right to food is more basic than almost any other human right (see "Fifty Years is Not Enough," p. 11). Food is usually the last thing people will give up when they have to make economic decisions. It's a bottom line, a *sine qua non* of existence. No food, you die (see "The Stomach Is Preferred to the Child," p. 29). Insufficient food to sustain an active life leads to shriveled bodies and minds. The right to food is a no-brainer.

Individuals have rights, but also responsibilities; and we can only hope that someday the world moves beyond "rights" to the larger notion of "responsibilities." Statements about human rights are just documents unless people take responsibility to implement them. Rights can speak about minimum conditions for social existence – the right to vote, the right to free speech, the right to food. But none of these guarantee that people will actually vote, speak out or have an adequate food supply unless they take responsibility to vote, speak out and assure that food needs are met; in short, to take responsibility to see that abstract rights become concrete realities.

Businesses, nongovernmental organizations and governments have responsibilities toward people. And, individuals have responsibilities to hold social, economic and political institutions accountable to the common good and especially to hungry and poor people. The right to food has to be guaranteed, in part, by those who already have food and who have the responsibility to build economic, social and political systems that are just.

Moral and religious voices need to be raised in the public square to proclaim the urgency of ending hunger. We must recapture the moral urgency of 1974.

The end of the century and a millennium is a time for reflecting on policies and practices that work and on those that do not; on values that are only partially realized but could be more fully expressed early in a new era.

THE RIGHT-TO-FOOD RESOLUTION

As passed by the U.S. Senate (S. Con. Res. 138) on September 16, 1976. The U.S. House of Representatives passed a similar resolution on September 21, 1976.

Resolved by the House of Representatives (the Senate concurring), that it is the sense of Congress that:

(1) the United States reaffirms the right of every person in this country and throughout the world to food and a nutritionally adequate diet; and

(2) the need to combat hunger shall be a fundamental point of reference in the formulation and implementation of United States policy in all areas which bear on hunger including international trade, monetary arrangements, and foreign assistance; and

(3) in the United States, we should seek to improve food assistance programs for all those who are in need, to ensure that all eligible recipients have the opportunity to receive a nutritionally adequate diet, and to reduce unemployment and ensure a level of economic decency for everyone; and

(4) the United States should emphasize and expand its assistance for self-help development among the world's poorest people, especially in countries seriously affected by hunger and malnutrition, with particular emphasis on increasing food production and encouraging more equitable patterns of food distribution and economic growth; and such assistance, in order to be effective, should be coordinated with expanded efforts by international organizations, donor nations, and the recipient countries to provide a nutritionally adequate diet for all.

That which is half done, can be completed. Pollyanna scenarios are irresponsible. But there is hope. As Kavita Pillay says (see p. 25), "The hope remains that future generations will one day be able to speak of hunger through historical anecdotes, and like smallpox or the Black Plague, we will know of this scourge only in the past tense."

DR. RICHARD A. HOEHN is director of Bread for the World Institute. Email: rhoehn@bread.org

BY ARTHUR SIMON

To reflect even briefly on hunger advocacy from a faith perspective over the last 25 years is to be amazed at how much has changed and how much has stayed the same since Bread for the World was launched as a U.S. Christian citizens' movement against hunger in May 1974.

The Cold War is history, and today the overarching international fact of life is the global economy. We have seen the collapse of communism and the coronation of capitalism. Hunger has diminished substantially as a proportion of the world's population, and even slightly in absolute numbers – though the Asian economic crisis could change that. In contrast to 1974, advocates for reducing hunger are now well organized, but not yet on a scale that can bring about the end of hunger.

If much has changed, much has stayed the same. The factors that cause hunger look strikingly familiar. The way out of hunger and poverty

RECOGNIZE THE TIMELINESS, AND RECOVER THE MORAL AND RELIGIOUS URGENCY, OF ENDING HUNGER

has not changed. The political will to end hunger remains a crying need. Moreover, we still have the technical capacity and economic means to end hunger.

Some things have not changed but are much clearer than they were a generation ago. The world has gained considerable wisdom from numerous experiences in development efforts, so we know better than ever what works and what does not. We see more clearly the relationship between environmental sustainability and poverty reduction. We have conclusive evidence that economic growth alone does not guarantee less hunger (witness the United States), and that investment in the education and health of people contributes to economic growth. This knowledge, along with global gains against hunger, has made it even more apparent that hunger can be overcome when the will to do so is combined with effective politics and practices. Because hunger is so demonstrably unnecessary and has been for at least a generation, we are justified in saying that hunger is a scandal.

The scandal of hunger is a particular challenge to people of faith. Those of us who started Bread for the World thought so 25 years ago, which explains why we launched it as a faith-based movement. Mounting evidence that hunger can be overcome, placed alongside the suffering of 841 million hungry people, compels us to face a great contradiction: that what we could do toward ending hunger, and what our faith commits us to do, we are *not* doing. Christians are especially well positioned in terms of numbers, education, wealth, influence and geographic spread to weigh in against hunger. And many are responding in significant ways. But Christians have not, for the most part, even begun to use their influence to insist that their own churches and their own countries lead a worldwide campaign to end hunger. So hunger is a scandal – not only in the sense of moral outrage, but also as a failure to give evidence of God's love, and this failure leaves many feeling hopeless and alienated from God.

For me the contradiction between what we could do and what our faith calls us to do, on the one hand, and the continuation of hunger on a vast scale, on the other, is not based on some new, fashionably designed or socially skewed theology, but on the word of life spoken by the prophets, incarnate in Jesus Christ and professed by the church throughout the ages. That is, we are not appealing to some fringe thinking in the church, not asking people to consider some alien or secularized gospel, but inviting them to take seriously the faith proclaimed in the Bible and passed down through the centuries. It is *this* faith that is scandalized by the vast persistence of hunger. But the same faith also offers us the undeserved gift of God's forgiveness so we can focus not on our failure, but on God's goodness, and celebrate God's love by resolving that our lives shall make a difference for those who hunger.

Has Bread for the World made mistakes along the way? No reason to doubt it. I think there was a tendency in our early years to be less critical of some of the more humane forms of socialism in developing countries than we should have been, although it is now clear that they did not serve those countries well. We sometimes failed to criticize misguided policies or practices in poor countries, because we realized how much their leaders struggled against the odds; yet on reflection it is easy to see in this a condescension that is all too frequent in the West. Concerning hunger and poverty in the United States, we did not focus consistently and strongly enough on jobs and ways to get people off welfare, and as a result the initiative was ultimately taken by people who acted rashly.

But on the whole, Bread for the World was on the right track. Organizing citizens to "lobby" on a few key hunger issues each year has proven to be a remarkably effective strategy. We sought to avoid ideologies and bring people of various political persuasions together around practical steps to reduce hunger, and to do so by appealing to a faith in which a great many people have rooted their lives. The faith that motivates them also provides staying power during times of discouragement.

Now the challenge is to build on what we have learned and enlist tens of thousands of new advocates largely from the ranks of the young and of those who are already directly assisting hungry people in some way, until the momentum generated becomes a worldwide campaign to end hunger.

Hunger can be overcome when the will to do so is combined with effective politics and practices.
— ARTHUR SIMON

The REVEREND ARTHUR SIMON is founder and president emeritus of Bread for the World. His book, *Bread for the World*, won the National Religious Book award in 1976. His forthcoming book, co-authored with David Beckmann, is entitled *Grace at the Table: Ending Hunger in God's World*.

BY FRANCES MOORE LAPPÉ

Twenty-seven years ago, when I was 27, I had just finished writing a book claiming there was enough food in the world to feed everybody. "We cannot blame nature," I said. "Hunger is human made!" In the months before the book's release, I was terrified.

What if I was wrong? After all, the experts were saying just the opposite. They – with their Ph.D.'s and university research centers, government and international agencies behind them – had concluded that humankind was overrunning the earth's capacity to provide. I, on the other hand, had just been following my nose, as I waded through statistics in the basement research library at the University of California at Berkeley.

In August of 1971, *Diet for a Small Planet* was published. I waited. I wondered how the world would receive its heretical message.

Then, a big sigh of relief. No "expert" argued with my numbers.

Soon I realized that I had absorbed a lesson for the rest of my life – the virtue of fresh eyes.

Those schooled in the institutions of the *status quo* are typically not encouraged to do what I did – to challenge the questions that frame their disciplines. In the world of international agriculture and food, the framing question had long been: How do we produce more? Resource scarcity was the pervasive paradigm.

Unschooled, however, I was free to ask: "What do we do with what we already produce?" And in so asking, I learned that indeed nearly half of global grain production went not to people but to livestock, able to return to humans only a small fraction of the nutrients the animals consumed. And, I was able to ask the square-two question as well: Why? Only to grasp that a "protein factory in reverse" was being created on a global scale because the millions of people who were hungry were too poor to make "effective demand" in the marketplace for the food they needed.

In such a world, feeding millions of tons of grain to livestock made perfect economic sense. But that system was rather a symptom of an irrational order we human beings had built and of blindness to our own capacities to create something more life-serving.

As *Diet* readers have come to share that insight, part of the book's legacy is the realization that lay people can apply their common sense to arrive at insights lost on those limited by their profession's blinders.

The book's legacy has also been highly personal. In 1971 I expected my book to appeal to some few thousand souls who, like me, had begun to question how our food is produced and

PROMOTE PARTICIPATION IN FAIR, DEMOCRATIC, PARTICIPATORY STRUCTURES AT ALL LEVELS OF PRIVATE AND PUBLIC LIFE

distributed – the ethics of eating, if you will. (Only my dad believed it had a bigger future!) Instead, over the next 20 years more than 3 million people have bought *Diet* in English and some untold number in six other languages. At first I was stunned in the discovery that I was not alone.

In a world of increasingly enormous concentrations of economic power and mind-boggling feats of technological power, millions of people were seeking evidence that as individuals we still retain personal agency. Our choices do matter. *Diet* said "yes," we can make real choices, food choices based on a logic formed by our values and knowledge rather than by the irrationality of impersonal systems.

This discovery, that what we put into our mouths has meaning of global significance, has provided millions with a daily, intimate reminder of our connectedness to all life.

But the central legacy of *Diet for a Small Planet* has only become clear in mid-life.

From the beginning I hoped that readers would experience an "ah-ha" moment: Not that eating less meat will reduce world hunger directly, but rather that our global economic system actively creates scarcity from plenty. Seeing the magnitude of the waste and suffering built in, I hoped their "ah-ha's" would spark determination to challenge the prevailing notion of automatic laws of the marketplace beyond our control. They would be eager to see how we humans can ensure that economic rules conform to deeper values – respect for life and the environment. And for many people, the "ah-ha" has been just that.

More recently, I have become convinced that for this legacy to be realized something else must be occurring. We humans must first regain belief in our capacities to deliberate together to arrive at solutions – belief in ourselves as co-creators of our societies. And that requires nothing less than a new vision of democracy well beyond a definition limited to formal political structures.

Hunger is *not* caused by a scarcity of food but a scarcity of democracy. Those who go hungry are those without voice in their societies. But a narrow structural definition of democracy is not good enough either. It has left not just the hungry but most of us voiceless in determining the shape of our communities and nations, including the economic givens that leave so many lives stunted.

The legacy of *Diet* has pushed me to devote the rest of my life to the question of democracy itself, to ask what it takes to build our collective confidence and capacities to participate in democratic problem-solving. I now see democratic, community initiatives emerging among even the most apparently powerless here and around the world. Perhaps we are witnessing the first glimmering of a new stage in the history of democracy – democracy becoming a living practice inclusive and vital enough to eliminate hunger.

Twenty-seven years ago the burning question "Why hunger in a world of plenty?" led me to peel away layer after layer of causation. I hope *Diet* nudges others also to peel away until they hit the bedrock question of democracy. Can it become more than a structure of government? Can we each take part of transforming democracy into a rewarding way of life, a living practice in which all citizens gain voice?

FRANCES MOORE LAPPÉ, author of *Diet for a Small Planet*, co-founded the Institute for Food and Development Policy in 1975. She currently is co-founder of the Center for Living Democracy in Brattleboro, VT. Web site: <http://www.livingdemocracy.org>

*Hunger is **not** caused by a scarcity of food but a scarcity of democracy. Those who go hungry are those without voice in their societies.*

– FRANCES MOORE LAPPÉ

70s

1970	1971	Early 1970s	1970s	1972	1973
	U.S. moves off gold standard; Britain in 1972; France in 1974	Civil war and famine strike Bangladesh		First Sudanese civil war ends	Oil prices soar Sahel famine peaks
Oxfam, FRAC, Campaign for Human Development, Food for the Hungry founded	*Diet for a Small Planet* published	Concerts for Bangladesh	U.S. national nutritional safety net expands: food stamps, WIC, child nutrition programs	Africare and NETWORK founded	

80s

1980	1980–1982	1981	1980s–'90s	1980s	1983
			World Bank and IMF lend for stabilization and structural adjustment		War breaks out in Sudan
	Global recession hits	Deep cuts made in U.S. anti-poverty programs	*August '82:* Mexico threatens default – debt crisis begins	Wars start in the Horn of Africa Wars erupt in Central America	Famine strikes in Ethiopia and other parts of Africa

90s

1990	1991	1992	1993	1994	Mid-1990s
Global 2000: Report to the President published Commission recommends United States make elimination of hunger a foreign policy priority	U.S. National Committee for World Food Day founded			Universal elections held in South Africa U.S.: "Contract with America" leads to deep cuts in social services	
	U.S./Iraq fight Gulf War Ethiopian civil war ends	Civil war and famine erupt in Somalia; Operation Restore Hope deemed inconclusive; United States pulls out	Eritrea wins independence Uruguay Round of the GATT concludes		U.S. economy begins long expansion

Medford Declaration targets U.S. hunger (see p. 91)		Rigoberta Menchú awarded Nobel Peace Prize U.N. Conference on Environment and Development held in Rio de Janeiro International Conference on Nutrition held in Rome	U.N. Human Rights Conference held in Vienna	U.N. Social Summit in Copenhagen World Bank increases pace of reforms	The Salaya Statement on Ending Hunger, Thailand (see p. 91)

HUNGER: 1970–1999

1974

Severe recession hits U.S. and Europe

World Food Conference held in Rome

UNCTAD calls for New International Economic Order

Bread for the World founded

1975

Vietnam war ends

Angola and Mozambique win independence

Bread for the World published

Institute for Food and Development Policy established

FAO institutes famine early warning system

IFAD and IFPRI founded

Second Harvest established

U.N. Decade for Women begins, Mexico City

Late 1970s

Debts balloon among Southern countries

1976

U.S. Congress adopts Bread for the World's Right-to-Food Resolution

October '87: U.S. stock market crashes

1977

Grain reserves formed in United States

Brady Plan ameliorates Latin American debt

1979

Second oil shock hits

U.S. Presidential Commission on World Hunger begins

Famine breaks out in Cambodia; Vietnamese invasion occurs

Berlin Wall falls: End of the Cold War

Nelson Mandela released from prison

1984

U.S. House of Representatives Select Committee on Hunger established

Live Aid concert held

World responds to Ethiopian famine

Famine emerges in North Korea

1985

United States imposes sanctions on South African government; 11 nations follow suit

U.N. Decade for Women ends, Nairobi

U.S. welfare reform signed into law

1986

Corazón Aquino elected president of Philippines

Food First Information and Action Network (FIAN) founded

Famine persists in North Korea

July '97: Asian financial crisis begins

1987

Famine hits Sudan

Late 1980s

1989

International community forms Operation Lifeline Sudan

Bellagio Declaration targets world hunger (see p. 91)

1995

U.N. Population Conference held in Cairo

U.N. Women's Conference held in Beijing

World Trade Organization formed

1996

World Food Summit: Rome Declaration sets goal of halving number of malnourished people by 2015

World Bank and IMF launch debt relief for Heavily Indebted Poor Countries

Jubilee 2000 launched in the United Kingdom

1997

Jubilee 2000 USA launched

1998

Jubilee 2000 launched in Africa, Latin America

November '98: 40th Anniversary of Brot für die Welt, Germany

December '98: 50th Anniversary of Universal Declaration of Human Rights

1999

25th Anniversary of Bread for the World

Bread for the World publishes *Grace at the Table*

The Universal Declaration of Human Rights 1948-1998

CHAPTER 1

THE CHANGING POLITICS OF HUNGER IN THE POOR COUNTRIES

BY PAUL NELSON

Introduction

Sociologist Peter Berger's 1976 *Pyramids of Sacrifice* analyzed the ways that societies on two radically different development paths – China and Brazil – were sacrificing a generation of lives to their visions of development.[1] Berger used the haunting image of the pyramids to capture the experience of the world's largest socialist and a leading capitalist development experiment sacrificing a generation of their people to build monuments to ideology. Twenty-five years later, we are still piling up bodies and diminishing lives in the name of various theories and plans – efficiency, plan, state, market, nation and development itself.

This sacrifice is organized, or at least sanctioned, by our political institutions, local, national and international. Their workings structure the politics of hunger: the way public institutions, including governments and other institutions that are part of public life, create, manage and respond to hunger, poverty and inequality. From the point of view of excluded, hungry people, the politics of hunger could be defined this way: how are poor people able to create and sustain change from public institutions?

The last decade offers signs of hope and change, and now is a good time to take a fresh look at strategies for political change. When long-time political prisoners such as South Africa's Nelson Mandela and South Korea's Kim Dae Jung are elected heads of democratic governments, their images give us hope for a new politics of justice. Their movements challenging the politics of hunger and oppression are heirs to a generation or more of popular struggle.[2] When women such as Wangari Maathai of Kenya, Aung San Suu Kyi of Burma and Rigoberta Menchú of Guatemala lead movements of hungry and oppressed people toward self-reliance, dignity and political power, they remind us of the power of grassroots organizing and the new potential for international links among people, organizations and continents in the struggle for justice.

The economics of hunger have changed rapidly as well. Trade and investment in Latin America and Asia have created new employment opportunities and new arenas of political action, as decisions affecting poor communities increasingly are taken in the board rooms of international corporations. International organizations governing trade, investment and finance have taken on more influential roles in policy decisions that affect national policy and politics (see Chapter 2, pp. 36-49).

Hunger and the politics of hunger remain dominant realities for the majority of people living in the world's poor countries. This chapter links the national-level politics of hunger to poverty and economic injustice in several cases. We trace three episodes of change in the politics of hunger, and ask who changes the politics of hunger and how? Finally, we explore how citizens of the industrial countries did, and can, help support the change.

Politics of Hunger, Economics of Injustice

The politics of hunger prop up the multi-faceted economics of injustice. Political arrangements fix in place the unequal and highly profitable access to capital, information, land, technology and the wealth that they produce. Political arrangements have sometimes sustained gross inequalities in the face of economic growth; elsewhere they have stifled both justice and economic progress.

In Guatemala, notoriously unequal distribution of land, high rates of poverty among ethnic Mayan peoples in the country's highlands, and a pattern of migrant labor and of cheap labor in plantations and factories are all aspects of a complex economics of injustice. Close ties among the landed oligarchy and high officers of

"Organization and solidarity build community." Children in a new community built by returned refugees, El Salvador.

the military have produced decades of *de facto* military rule, with occasional elected governments, crushing labor and guerrilla movements ruthlessly.

In India, the rigid caste system and extreme economic discrimination against women mark the clearest dividing lines between those who benefit from industrial growth and trade, and those who do not. Social and political inequality is encoded in a political system that limits voting and ownership rights for women and people of lower castes, and that obliges young women to marry at a very early age. Researchers in several poor countries have found that adolescent pregnancy sharply increases health and nutritional risks for the baby (low birthweight) and mother (infection, anemia, peri-natal mortality and other factors).[3]

South Africa's *apartheid* laws, separating and privileging White over Black and mixed-race populations, were renounced in 1994 elections that completed decades of struggle for a new political system. Nowhere was the politics of hunger more stark: income in South Africa was as unequal as in the most skewed of the Latin American countries, including Brazil and Guatemala. A legal and political structure governed labor, ownership, residence, travel and political participation by the country's Black majority. A democratic, non-racial government now struggles to undo the enduring economic effects of gross inequality and indignity.

Elsewhere in Africa, governments oversee discrimination against certain ethnic groups. In Nigeria, an economy built around lucrative oil exports is ruled with an iron hand by a government that concentrates oil profits among a few while polluting the lands of ethnic minorities living near oil fields. Nigeria led the campaign in Africa against South African apartheid, but it practices a form of economic and cultural apartheid among its ethnic groups that leaves many of its 111 million people in health and nutrition conditions worse than all but the very poorest African countries.[4]

South Korea's development strategy used land reform, early industrialization in steel and other products, and a political guarantee of lifetime job tenure to combine authoritarian politics with an inclusive, dynamic economy. The democracy deficit – limited social and political rights – was often defended as the cost of the country's growth, and its success in distributing the benefits of economic growth broadly. Now financial crisis has brought an end to the lifetime job guarantee, and the implied political agreement is shaken.

The changing politics of hunger

The global politics of hunger have changed since Berger wrote. One major shift is that the global economy now shapes the possibilities for development. New technologies, investment strategies and corporate structures have made investment capital instantly mobile, able to exploit quick speculative gains or to benefit from cheap labor or products. New factories created under free trade agreements have provided economic opportunities for workers (see "La Línea," pp. 40-41), even as they make exploitation profitable for companies that can often move their plants to enjoy low wages and tax and tariff benefits. Free trade, export promotion and less government have been promoted worldwide, and governments in the late 1990s are much less able to control, regulate or even tax international investment than a generation ago.

International corporations now play an increasing role in the economies of all nations. In some developing countries single companies or single industries hold great influence because of the importance of their presence. Examples include Shell Oil in Nigeria, Texaco in Ecuador, and garment and textile industries in much of Central America and in Bangladesh. International food marketing itself is increasingly controlled by a small number of firms. Cargill and five other companies now control more than 95 percent of U.S. corn and wheat exports and a major share of the grain traded by Argentina and Europe.[5]

A second major political change is the spread of democracy and the growth of civil society in a number of developing and transitional countries. After a generation of closed, authoritarian politics in many of these countries, many national political systems have embraced democratic forms of governance and are now more open to citizen participation.[6] In the last 15 years, democratically elected governments have emerged coupled with expanded political space available to organized groups in countries, including South Africa, Zimbabwe, Mali, Uganda, the Philippines, South Korea, Brazil, Chile, Guatemala, Paraguay, Haiti and most of the countries of the former Soviet bloc.

In these countries as in others where authoritarian governments remain entrenched – China, Indonesia, Mexico, Cuba – civil society organizations have strengthened their monitoring of, and advocacy on, human rights, environmental and labor issues. Public scrutiny by international networks of nongovernmental organizations (NGOs), churches and unions has helped strengthen national movements for change. Indonesian NGOs have organized with European, Asian and North American NGOs, with initial guidance and support from the Dutch NGO NOVIB, to meet in parallel to the annual meeting of governmental aid donors for the country. The NGOs' and donors' close

Figure 1.1 **Index of Democracy by World Region, 1960-1994**

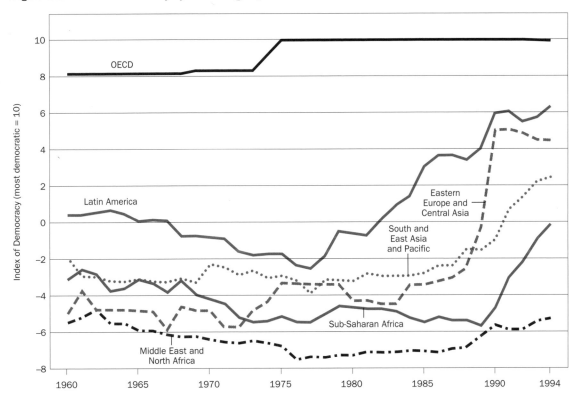

Source: World Bank, *World Development Report 1997*, New York: Oxford University Press, 172; based on Keith Jaggers and Ted Robert Gurr, "Transitions to Democracy: Tracking Democracy's Third Wave with the Polity III Data," *Journal of Peace Research*, 32:469-482, 1995.

monitoring have contributed to expanding opportunities for political action for sustainable development and civil and political rights.[7] Mexican NGOs and opposition groups use international contacts as protection against government reprisals as they monitor government corruption, aid projects and local and national elections.

Changes at international development and relief aid agencies have also shaped the changing politics of hunger. Principles – participation, gender equity, environmental sustainability and decentralization – that were once spoken of only among a few small agencies peripheral to the main flows of development finance, are now official policy of major aid agencies such as the U.S. Agency for International Development (USAID) and the World Bank.[8]

International aid agencies have become more open in applying political standards and conditions to their aid. USAID conditions aid to some extent on human rights performance. The World Bank makes loans for good governance and discusses corruption issues with borrowing government officials, subjects that were not part of international lenders' agenda a decade ago.[9] This leverage may help promote openness in some governments' policy-making processes, but it can also compel governments to be increasingly accountable to aid agencies, not necessarily to their own citizens.

The global communications revolution has also helped facilitate the spread of democratic and human rights values worldwide. The advent of new communication technologies has exposed people to new ideas and principles, provided tools for information sharing and advocacy, and led to increased international scrutiny of the policies and practices of international financial institutions, governments and corporations (see Chapter 3).

BY KAVITA PILLAY

In a hospital in a remote eastern province of North Korea, an emaciated patient clutches his dirty mattress, writhing in pain from an operation conducted without anesthesia; in the open courtyard of a school, a group of listless children have gathered not for class but to receive food rations; in a nation tradition-bound to its elders, grandparents place themselves at risk of starvation so that a new generation might live.

As one of the most closed societies in the world, much of what is known about the current crisis in North Korea is anecdotal, yet while estimates of the magnitude of the situation has varied widely, the very existence of a famine is undeniable. With at least 2.4 million people dead, North Korea today is comparable to Ethiopia in 1984 and Somalia in 1992; making it, relative to a national population of 23 million, one of the worst famines in the 20th century. Yet while Ethiopia and Somalia benefitted from a steady stream of stark media images, the North Korean situation has been exacerbated by closed borders, controlled information, an inflexible economic system and the dominance of political myth. The North Korean famine dramatically demonstrates what happens when a country lacks a free press, venues for citizen action and elected officials who are held accountable to the people.

The socialist government of the Democratic People's Republic of Korea (DPRK) has operated for decades on the principle of *juche* (self-reliance), thereby making an open admittance of serious internal problems almost impossible. Accordingly, the 1996 floods followed by the 1997 drought contributed to the famine, but have also served as the convenient scapegoat. The true beginnings of North Korea's problems coincide with the downfall of its long-time patron, the Soviet Union. Coupled with over 40 years of isolationist policy and domestic mismanagement, this once impenetrable country is now at the mercy of nations with which it is still technically at war.*

Though North Korea has been the target of much criticism for maintaining a standing army of 1 million while millions more in the general populace subsist on 100 grams of grain each day, the DPRK has been unable to purchase much needed food stocks on the international market due to a degenerated industrial sector, a valueless currency and a poor international credit rating. Fearing that food aid could be potentially channeled toward the mammoth military or other privileged groups, public and private donors alike have shied away from fulfilling the current food needs of a nation that has operated under a constant food deficit since its current borders were first drawn at the end of World War II. Contrary to such apprehensions, signs of improvement due to international assistance have been noted by relief workers: School attendance has skyrocketed from 20 percent to over 90 percent in less

But among these changes there are unchanging realities. Poor people still bear the brunt of disasters, wars and environmental degradation. Famine and a severe food crisis threaten large numbers of people in the old hard-line socialist states of North Korea and Cuba (see "The Politics of Famine in North Korea," above).[10] In civil wars in Ethiopia and Eritrea, Angola, Bangladesh, Biafra/Nigeria, Bosnia, Sudan (see "Effects of Civil Conflict on Development," pp. 34-35) as in environmental disasters in Bhopal, India and the forests of the Philippines, poor people are the principal victims. They are the least able to escape fighting or natural disaster, often located nearest to dangerous or unsanitary sites. They often depend directly on natural resources for their daily sustenance. And, they have little margin of security. They draw the lowest wages and benefits, and are the least heard by government authorities. Amid new technologies, pyramids of sacrifice are still being erected. Mobilizing and sustaining public action on injustice and hunger requires reclaiming the moral urgency for changing the politics of hunger.

Who Changes the Politics of Hunger?

Who changes the politics of hunger, and how? International agreements or changes in the institutional arrangements for trade, investment or for financing development sometimes create subtle or dramatic changes in the politics of

These children in a nursery in North Korea are three and four years old.

than one year thanks to in-class food distribution, the number of severely malnourished children has dropped and recovery rates in hospitals have improved. At the same time, more North Koreans are expected to die this year from famine-related diseases rather than starvation. The 1998 harvest is expected to provide sufficient food only through the spring of 1999 and construction of a nuclear power facility remains a contentious issue in North Korea's international dealings. How the DPRK plans to safeguard against future famines remains to be seen.

Food alone cannot heal what ails this starving nation. Indeed, famine is never wholly due to a lack of food or to the caprices of nature, rather, famine is the result of the interplay between the political and economic system that governs a given region and the role that a nation in need of

foreign assistance plays in the international arena. An ultimate solution to the North Korea conundrum lies with fundamental changes to the system, the best hope for which lies with quelling tensions on the Korean peninsula and furthering peaceful relations across the 38th parallel. Toward this end, countries with a vested interest in the stabilization of North Korea must use aid to facilitate the rehabilitation process, rather than as a weapon against its withered Stalinist regime.

Given the essentially political, and thus human-made nature of famine, we must look beyond the question of "how can famine be prevented" to "why are famines allowed to occur." The hope remains that by integrating the lessons of recent history with the understanding that famine is first and foremost a political construct, famine alleviation efforts will one day no longer be necessary, future generations will be able to speak of famine through historical anecdotes, and like smallpox or the Black Plague, we will know of this scourge only in the past tense.

KAVITA PILLAY, a Mickey Leland Hunger Fellow with the Congressional Hunger Center, is serving a policy placement with Bread for the World Institute. E-mail: kpillay@bread.org

* The agreement drawn between North and South Korea in 1953 marked only an armistice, not an end to the war. Technically the Korean War is still being waged.

hunger in much of the underdeveloped world. Such changes are the subject of Chapter 2. Chapter 1 focuses on how individuals and institutions have produced change in three countries.

Local, national and regional political changes have modified and even dramatically changed the politics of hunger. There have been a few decisive victories, many ambiguous shifts and some terrible setbacks. They have come through electoral changes in government, new policy, new information, the appeals of moral leaders (see "Bishops Trigger Ouster of President in Malawi," pp. 95), local self-help efforts, guerrilla warfare and active social and consumer movements. India and Guatemala represent two ways in which impoverished people have managed to change the politics of hunger in their own

setting. In Rwanda, the politics of hunger deteriorated into genocide and humanitarian disaster. In each case people in the industrial countries have also been involved, more or less directly, more or less decisively. This chapter asks how the politics of hunger were changed, and how citizens, NGOs and international aid agencies might be more influentially and successfully involved in empowering poor people in future struggles.

India: amid chronic hunger, famine and starvation are politically unacceptable

India has a remarkably effective record in preventing and responding to potential famine situations. Since independence it has maintained an effective distribution system that relies on employment creation and emergency food supplies to prevent famine. Agricultural technologies and a well-organized administration are sometimes credited, but research by Amartya Sen has pointed to an unexpected explanation: "Open journalism and adversarial politics" in India have made it extremely hard for local or national governments to:

> get away with neglecting prompt and extensive anti-famine measures at the first sign of a famine…. India's relatively free media and newspapers, and the active and investigative role that journalists as well as opposition politicians can and do play in this field…yields a rapid triggering mechanism and encourages preparedness for entitlement protection.[11]

Public knowledge and public action require governments to prevent and respond. The accomplishment is remarkable given the frequent dips in food supply and occasional drought that could easily trigger famine in

USE THE POWER OF THE MASS MEDIA AGAINST HUNGER

another situation. Promoting the development of participatory and accountable democratic institutions at all levels of society can help prevent hunger.

But there are limits to what public reporting and party politics can accomplish in reducing hunger. Inequality and chronic deprivation remain widespread in India, especially among women and lower caste individuals and families. There, as elsewhere, chronic suffering is not "newsworthy." Famine may be politically unacceptable, but the Indian government can spend

vast amounts on nuclear tests and technological development, knowing it faces relatively little pressure for economic and social policies that would rapidly expand opportunities for the poorest citizens. Democracy enables poor people to organize and act, but it does not assure that the majority will support policies that serve their interests.

Guatemala: amid extreme inequality and repression, some shifts

The poor majority in Guatemala is beset by landlessness, civil war, mass repression of indigenous peoples and a history of harsh autocracies backed by the military. But in the last two decades the politics of land, political participation and employment have begun to change. An active peasant movement led by Father Andrés Girón, a Roman Catholic priest from the country's steamy Pacific coast, pressed for land reform during the 1980s, at the same time that USAID began to support a Guatemalan foundation's program for market-based land distribution, purchasing land on the market and settling previously landless people on farms to grow crops for food and market. The peasant movement helped make the government receptive, and USAID funding gave legitimacy to the land reform demands.[12]

Guatemala's social welfare, health and education spending was bolstered somewhat in the 1980s by governments of the Christian Democrat party, which articulated the concept of a "social debt," won election and domestic support and gained financial support from aid agencies as well as from European Christian Democrat parties. But more important was the negotiated end of the civil war, thanks largely to the efforts of regional leaders in Central America, notably former Costa Rican President Oscar Arias Sánchez. Political peace is tenuous, as the April 1998 murder of the head of the country's human rights commission demonstrated.

Increased trade and integration in the Western Hemisphere confront Guatemala and most of Central America with new issues and challenges. Labor organizing has long been a volatile issue in Guatemala and the region, with

Some important changes in the politics of hunger have occurred at the sub-national level, in states, provinces and localities where a social movement, election or other key initiative changes the balance of power over resources. The cases below underscore why it is important to support the empowerment of poor people and to build participatory democratic institutions at all levels of society.

In 1973, several women initiated the now-famous "Chipko" movement in India's Himalayan province of Uttar Pradesh. Chipko changed the politics of hunger and deforestation, using

గ్రామీణ మరియు ప్రాంతీయ స్థాయిలో దాగియున్న సంబంధిత నూతన విజ్ఞానాన్ని వెలుగులోకి తెచ్చి, ఉపయోగించు.

Convention to Combat Desertification (CCD) Youth for Action RIOD – India.

"Bring Out Traditional Wisdom, Use Local People's Knowledge."

high-stakes tree-hugging (the name means embrace) to stop state-licensed logging in stands of trees that were central to their villages' subsistence economies. Chipko's local expression of India's tradition of non-violent resistance became politically influential, provoking new legislation and 15-year bans on logging in the province.

The department (municipality) of Cajamarca, Peru, faces the formidable social and environmental problems of most poor Andean communities. Ninety percent of the rural population and 40 percent in urban areas are poor. But a local tradition of *rondas campesinas* (peasant circles) became the basis for a new local political structure when long-time trade union and nongovernmental organization (NGO) activist

Luis Guerrero Figueroa was elected mayor in 1992. Now broader consensus-building round-tables involve NGOs, community organizations, local government and business in forging development plans that are noted for their ecological soundness and broad support. The roundtables have initiated programs aimed at child nutrition, neighborhood electrification, potable water, seed banks, irrigation and rotating credit funds, built on consensus support from the communities' key actors. Guerrero was elected president of the Peruvian Mayors' Association in 1996, inspiring hope that Cajamarca's experiment with open political decision-making could be replicated elsewhere.[1]

The Mexican state of Oaxaca, like neighboring Chiapas, is among the country's poorest. Unlike Chiapas, where unresponsive government and the extreme poverty of the indigenous population have contributed to ongoing conflict since 1994, Oaxaca has a tradition of participatory local decision-making practices. Local authorities, for example, tend to be chosen by local election, rather than appointed by mayors or state officials, as in Chiapas. A 1995 study of social funds designed for municipal programs in Oaxaca highlights the effectiveness of decentralized decision-making where democratic institutions exist and operate at the municipal level.[2]

---

[1] Jaime Joseph, "The Roundtable for Consensus Building in Cajamarca, Peru," *Grassroots Development* vol. 21(1), 1997, 40-45.

[2] Jonathan Fox and Josefina Aranda, "Decentralization and Rural Poverty in Mexico: 'Municipal Solidarity Funds' and Community Participation in Oaxaca," Paper presented at the Latin American Studies Association, Washington, DC, September 28-30, 1995. See also World Bank, *World Development Report 1997,* Oxford: Oxford University Press, 1997, 122.

Rwandan refugees arrive in Tanzania, fleeing the genocide of 1994.

organizing often violently suppressed on fruit plantations and in the country's few foreign-owned factories since the 1950s.[13] Current struggles over the right to organize are centered in the textile industry, where international clothing manufacturers contract with locally managed factories to produce finished apparel. International support from unions and the public have helped win some victories in wages, working conditions and job security for factory workers.[14]

Rwanda: a politics of maldevelopment and chronic structural violence

The world was shocked in 1994 by the enormity and apparent suddenness of genocide in Rwanda. Hundreds of thousands of people were killed, and more died of illness and starvation as they fled or hid from the violence. Refugee camps stocked with international agencies' food and medicine became bases for guerrilla terror.

Governments and international organizations have been roundly criticized for failing to intervene promptly and decisively to stop the genocide, when warning signs were plentiful.

Rwanda's politics of hunger were deliberately transformed into the politics of terror and genocide, and the calamity was rooted in a pattern of maldevelopment visible in much of sub-Saharan Africa. Official agencies and the Rwandan government have long portrayed the country's economy as a development success. But national policies encouraged extreme inequalities for a generation before the genocide, and international aid was complicit in maintaining them.

> Rwanda's genocide was the extreme outcome of the failure of a development model that was based on ethnic, regional, and social exclusion; that increased deprivation, humiliation, and vulnerability of the poor; that allowed state-instigated racism and discrimination…; that was top-down and authoritarian; and that left the masses uninformed, uneducated, and unable to resist orders and slogans.[15]

Official statistics portrayed inequalities in Rwanda as comparatively small, but recent studies show that half the population was desperately poor, 40 percent poor, and perhaps 10 percent, landowners and civil servants, relatively wealthy. Ethnic Hutu people were excluded economically, culturally, socially, and anti-Tutsi racism was both a tool of elites, who focused attention on ethnic rather than economic and structural inequalities, and the reaction of ordinary downtrodden people.

After 1990, government authorities and the media encouraged what has been called "state-supplied racism."[16] As the government was threatened by external invasion, internal discontent and pressure from aid agencies newly interested in democratization, racial hatred was radicalized in a grisly chain of murders and hate propaganda leading up to the 1994 explosion of genocidal violence.

In Rwanda as elsewhere, the structural violence of poverty and indignity, propped up by the politics of hunger, is clearly linked to the

BY CRAIG COHEN

Hunger makes you selfish to the point of letting your own child perish, a Rwandan proverb.

Jean Mureramanzi walks along a dirt road, the sun and his field at his back, the darkening hills ahead. His feet are dragging – perhaps tired, hesitant – and the dust forms a soft orange cloud in the dimming light. Mureramanzi is making his way toward his home in Butare, in Rwanda's south.

Up ahead in his small mud-brick house, a boy and girl, 6 and 9 years old, roll a ball made from plastic bags back and forth over a dirt floor. Mureramanzi pauses before entering his house, knowing that tonight there is not enough food for the entire family to eat. Normally he can find a day's work, but today his search has proved as fruitless as his field. Mureramanzi's hands are empty and his mind is full. Tonight, he must determine to which edge of desire to cling – hunger or love.

Mureramanzi is 20 years old, and he is not the father of the two young children who stop playing when he opens the door to the fading light. He is their brother. The family of children have lived alone since their parents were killed during Rwanda's genocide in 1994. At that time, Mureramanzi had not been prepared to lead a family. He had dropped out of primary school in 1991, because, he says with a smile, "I am not intelligent." Now, on his way to prepare dinner, he walks by his sister, kicks her the ball, thinks of his friends who are finishing their nightly game of football. He thinks of the decision he must make tonight, the decision that no parent should have to make. Is the stomach preferred to the child?

It is a difficult question to answer without first asking, who is the child? Mureramanzi says: "I am not an adult, and I am not a child. In the middle. I can do the work of men, but I never discuss things with them. The only adult I speak with is my grandmother, but she is worn down. I am not an adult," he says, "but I am a father. I provide for my family. I know I have a family because a family is a group of people who are in some way united."

Tonight, as a father, Mureramanzi sacrifices hunger for love and passes his portion of beans on to his brother and sister. When he lies down to sleep later that night, the taste of dust from the road is still in his mouth. He is smiling. Lying in bed, there are certain things he tries not to think

20 year-old Jean Mureramanzi must now provide for his younger siblings.

of. Other things take no effort – they are never thought about. "I never think about getting married," he says, "because even if I had to feed only myself, life would not be easier." These are things of which he does not think, and he is smiling. "I am happiest like tonight," he says, "when my brother and sister have what they need."

It is late now and his siblings are sleeping, and the dark and quiet create a feeling of emptiness. "It is rare," he says, "that I feel lonely," and he turns away from the bars of the window that keep out the night.

* Excerpted from "No Home Without Foundation: A Portrait of Child-headed Households in Rwanda," New York: Women's Commission for Refugee Women and Children, December 1997, 5.

outbursts of violence and starvation that draw the world's attention (see "The Stomach Is Preferred to the Child," p. 29). Some 300 aid agencies managing 1,000 projects – national aid agencies, international organizations and NGOs – did little to challenge an ingrained politics of hunger, and much of the aid provided helped to strengthen and sustain the inequalities.

Can aid change the politics of hunger?

Can aid help those who are trying to change the politics of hunger? Clearly poverty-focused aid can improve poor people's material conditions, at least in the short run, by providing health care, creating jobs or educating children. But can it help address the *politics* of hunger, the relations of power that keep poor people poor? There are skeptics, and with good reason, given the record. Official aid programs have supported corrupt and self-serving governments in Zaire under Mobutu, the Philippines under Marcos, Kenya under Moi, as well as highly inefficient quasi-socialist governments in much of Africa until the 1980s.

Aid can support political change by supporting peasant or women's organizations, broad-based labor movements, community and church organizations, but the aid agencies that will support such politicized partners tend to be small and non-governmental. Aid can be deployed, as a promise or a threat, to win some concessions from an unwilling government in policy areas such as health and education spending or human rights.

Such external pressure sometimes helps create political space for poor people's organizations, but aid can help through another route: well-planned, participatory programs of any kind, including social services, can help poor people, especially women, gain decision-making rights that change the politics of hunger in their everyday lives.

Take for example the Tanzania Child Survival and Development Program, begun by the government in the early 1980s with support from the World Health Organization (WHO), UNICEF and the Italian government.[17] Beginning in five districts in Iringa province,

the program now covers half of the population. With no new technologies and a minimal role for outside expertise, local practitioners used monthly growth monitoring meetings, in community settings, to provide advice, support and build greater understanding of nutritional and health needs and resources for pregnant women and mothers with young children.

Even during severe economic decline in the 1980s, the government remained committed to policies that made community initiative and participation the centerpiece of the program. The result, after a trend of increasing mortality and malnutrition among children in the 1980s, is a virtual disappearance of severe malnutrition and reduced malnutrition in milder forms. The program has had ups and downs, but UNICEF describes "durable progress" built on active village participation in which women win decision-making power in the community and in their households.[18]

Similar UNICEF support for the Roman Catholic Church's Child Pastorate in Brazil has strengthened its role as a service provider and a voice of conscience for children in Brazil. UNICEF's programs have received growing international support, including from the U.S. government, in a period of financial crisis for the United Nations (U.N.) and many of its agencies, thanks in part to the advocacy of the U.S. Committee for UNICEF, Bread for the World and RESULTS. A 1986 article that examined UNICEF and other child survival funding during a period of reduced funding for most aid programs concluded that "direct, focused and organized constituent pressure was almost certainly what turned congressional indifference into broad-based support."[19]

Aid programs can make a positive difference, and citizen action for responsive, sustainable aid can both save lives and help change the politics of hunger. Aid agencies, like anti-hunger activists, must begin by supporting the people who can change the politics of hunger – poor people themselves – and focus their aid in countries where governments will permit changes that matter.

Self-help projects can serve as tools for community organizing. Here women in Mexico participate in a workshop on nutritious foods.

Beyond the Aid Agenda: Coming to Terms with the New Politics of Hunger

When we think of anti-hunger action and politics we tend to think of advocacy for national legislation on food, welfare and development policy in the United States. But the cases of this chapter show that the politics of hunger are broad and multi-faceted, and that the movement against hunger is – and must be – broader than we sometimes think.

The movement against hunger is broader than we think

Relief and development aid have played a part in the changing politics of hunger. Aid programs and policies have been a major focus of many of the public and private anti-hunger efforts in the last generation – Bread for the World, RESULTS, World Hunger Year, Food for the Hungry and World Food Day.

But political movements that go by other names – human rights, environment, labor, women's rights – may have had as much impact on the conditions and opportunities of hungry and poor people as have the efforts of anti-hunger advocates. Increasing women's educational opportunities and their legal and economic rights can change the well-being of half the population and of the next generation, male and female (see "Women and Children Last," pp. 6-7). U.N. studies show that when nutrition does not improve with economic growth, discrimination against women is usually present.[20]

The labor movement in some underdeveloped countries has been stifled as governments seek to attract foreign investment. Advocates in the United States have helped to mobilize public opinion and U.S. union action to support the right to organize and bargain collectively in Guatemala, where the spotlight of public attention and the threat of consumer boycotts have helped impoverished seamstresses and other textile workers to negotiate for living wages.

Environmental activism on international issues focuses as much on protecting poor communities' control of their lands and their human rights as on conservation. Organizations such as the Environmental Defense Fund, International Rivers Network and Friends of the Earth have been in the forefront of pressing for environmen-

"Building Our Identity" – a workshop on gender issues, El Salvador.

tal reform. Their work to reshape energy development policy and to resist major hydroelectric dam projects supports and strengthens local organizations of indigenous peoples, communities that would be displaced by the flooding the dams create, and advocates of locally controlled, sustainable development strategies.

The politics of hunger are multi-faceted[21]

Political change at many levels affects the political opportunities for poor and hungry people. Electoral politics are fundamentally important. In the United States, the Reagan-Bush years had devastating effects on efforts to alleviate hunger and inequality in the poor countries. Aid spending tilted toward military aid at the expense of development; trade promotion and liberalization dominated foreign economic policy; human rights took a back seat. Congressional elections in 1994 ended the prospect for fundamental reform of U.S. aid programs, much hoped for in the early years of the first Clinton administration.

But elections, of course, are only the beginning of the story. Effective democratic participation requires that concerned citizens become better informed about how policies and aid can best serve poor and hungry people. Policy

decisions on aid, trade and development policy happen quietly in most cases, and have generally not been election issues. A deliberate effort is required to make them public issues and draw congressional attention to them at all. Even more detailed attention and advocacy are required to ensure that good policy is in fact implemented, a priority at present, for example, in advocacy for participatory strategies in USAID and World Bank projects.

And the politics of hunger – like environmental politics – increasingly happen outside of government and the formal political arena altogether. Governments are sometimes brought into negotiations of labor and environmental codes for firms, including multinational corporations, but often it is direct advocacy by shareholders and consumers that raises the question. Labor rights, child labor, infant formula marketing and dumping of toxic wastes in poor countries – all of these are issues in the last decade where political action has been primarily in corporate boardrooms rather than Congress or parliaments. And all of them are critical issues for the quality of life of hungry and poor people.

The new politics of hunger

The politics of hunger are changing. Poor people have more opportunity to vote and express their views in many countries than in recent memory, and local and national organizations are more densely linked to international networks that support them. Their governments, however, may have less control over their economies than they did a generation ago. Where the increasing influence of the global economy is shifting control away from national

SUPPORT THE EMPOWERMENT EFFORTS OF POOR PEOPLE

governments and toward international organizations and corporations, new arenas are emerging in which some campaigns for justice will be carried out.

The increasing prominence of international political arenas is both an opportunity and a danger. International advocates can, and have, added political leverage that was not available to local communities in environmental, human rights, trade union and other campaigns. But campaigns will need to be mindful of the politics they are creating and shaping, careful even as they lobby at international levels that part of the goal should always be to move decision-making power and open participation as close to the local level as possible.

Of course, opportunity for democratic voice, even at the local level, does not translate into the ability to control governments' or companies' policies. Open political processes in the industrial countries have surely not guaranteed widespread support for policies that create opportunity and assure adequate nutrition. But solidarity and consistent efforts to open political processes at all levels to poor peoples' input at least creates the opportunity for the beginnings of influence and accountability. As anti-hunger advocates find new ways to apply this principle to policies in trade, labor, aid, foreign policy and corporate investment, they will continue to transform the politics of hunger toward a politics of opportunity and equity. In the process they will be enriched as they are drawn closer to their partners and heroes among those who tackle, and change, the politics of hunger.

PAUL NELSON is an assistant professor with the Graduate School of Public and International Affairs at the University of Pittsburgh.
E-mail: pjnelson@pitt.edu

PROMOTE PARTICIPATION IN FAIR, DEMOCRATIC, PARTICIPATORY STRUCTURES AT **ALL LEVELS** OF PRIVATE AND PUBLIC LIFE

BY ANTHONY EDWIN KOOMSON

Civil conflict profoundly affects all aspects of development from planning through implementation and evaluation. The status of conflict can change rapidly, forcing development practitioners into conflict management for which they have little training or experience.

The intensity of conflicts ranges from friction between beneficiaries on the placement of a development project to protracted civil wars as in Sudan. My field experience has exposed me to tribal wars in northern Ghana; to Liberia as part of an advance team to assess food and relief needs in a civil war that ended with elections; and to Sudan where I saw what the intermittent 42-year war has done to an impoverished land with great potential for self-sufficiency. While this article focuses on Sudan as an example, it is broadly applicable to many poor countries enduring civil conflicts.

Forced Conscription and Displacement of Social Spending

When countries go to war, social spending takes a back seat. This includes human as well as economic resources. In Sudan, the government rounds up young men and women daily for recruitment into the *Mujahedeen* or holy soldiers, and universities are periodically closed enabling forced conscription of students. This disrupts the supply of qualified graduates who could aid the economic and social development of the country. The average length of time required to complete an undergraduate degree in Sudan is now 10 years, and will be as long as the war continues.

In wartime, social programs are put on hold for varied reasons. First, because national governments refuse to invest in programs that rebels will either destroy or take over for their own benefit. Second, already-scarce fiscal resources are further drained by military expenditures. Third, what social infrastructure exists is redirected to support the war effort.

The Timing of War Intensity

Seasons affect the timing of war intensity and therefore food production. The arrival of the rainy season brings a halt to most activity, including the war. The regular period of intensive war activity is the dry season just before the rains. This disrupts planting, which must also take place before the rains, and so the cycle of poverty continues. Those people who do manage to plant then risk having

their crops looted during the harvest season when intense fighting erupts again.

The civil war exacerbates existing structural causes of hunger. The average farm size in rural southern Sudan is under a tenth of an acre, clearly not enough to feed a family.

Effects on Infrastructure

Civil conflict takes an obvious toll on an already sparse infrastructure. Roads are destroyed by both government troops and the rebels as each attempts to keep the other from crossing into its territory. Water sources also suffer greatly, leading to frustrating reversals in hard-won health gains. Of the thousand hand-dug wells reportedly put in place by development agencies in the war areas, only about 10 percent functioned as of June 1997. According to UNICEF and CARE officials, the only factor preventing their repair is the continuing insecurity. Unsanitary water has resulted in a jump in guinea worm cases, which were nearly controlled by these agencies during a lull in hostilities in 1991.

Even countries that have achieved peace suffer from war's after-effects in the way of land mines, which not only constitute a direct threat but contribute to hunger by making areas of potentially arable land unusable because they are too risky to walk on.

Despite flaws, food assistance continues to reach hungry people. This child is waiting for food at a UNICEF relief station in Uganda.

Effects on Human Rights, Especially Women's Rights

Human rights are a dramatic casualty in wartime. Slavery persists in Sudan, with young people forcibly taken from their homes and sold as farm hands in the north. Observers fear government complicity in the slave raids. Women's human rights are affected as well. In traditional societies that tightly circumscribe the role of women, the situation of widows is especially precarious because it is difficult to remarry. Large populations of women in Khartoum and in the north have lost their husbands to the war and are left to care for their children with no assistance from the financially strapped government. Other young women are forced into prostitution to survive.

Disabled veterans are another vulnerable group. I personally saw one hold a group of soldiers hostage with their own AK-47, enraged at being abandoned by the government.

Relief, Dependency and Coping Mechanisms

With the unpredictability of war making planning impossible, international agencies are not undertaking any major development activity. Development activities simply cannot be sustained in a country as insecure as Sudan; donors fear development aid will be diverted to the war, especially by the government.

Instead, relief projects create dependency for innocent civilians who are forced to adopt dangerous coping mechanisms so they can keep receiving aid. Some persons have manipulated the criteria for receiving food rations. One such criterion is the nutritional status of children under 5; the children's registration at immunization centers is another. In some instances, the same child was registered by two families so they could increase their food rations. Worse, in one case I witnessed, we learned that a family had the same child immunized more than once to increase the food rations she received. We prayed the child would not die from an overdose, and felt powerless to sanction the parents, who had no other means of survival.

What Relief Workers Can Do

The myriad obstacles thrown up by a civil conflict dramatically increase the need for innovation in solving the daily problems of development work.

It is sometimes possible to provide relief in a way that contributes to rehabilitation. For example, the program I worked with tied food donations to school attendance – the school site being anything from a thatch-roofed building to a baobab tree stump. Red Crescent clinics were also tied to the feeding program, with children fed according to a nurse's advice. Thus, emergency food contributed to improved education and health care.

What Governments Can Do

There is only so much that development agencies can do. In Sudan as in so many other warring places, peace is a prerequisite to reducing hunger. In 1989, the international community negotiated the humanitarian access agreement, Operation Lifeline Sudan, which established peaceful corridors for the delivery of relief. Many lives were saved through the islands of peace and relief operations made possible by international negotiation. Operation Lifeline was later compromised, as the Sudanese government began to manipulate the flow of supplies and punish some parts of the country by withholding food.[1]

International pressures finally convinced the government and rebels to begin a three-month cease-fire in July of 1998. The cease-fire came too late for food to be transported by land until the next dry season. Even so, it offered a potential window of opportunity, prompting Sudanese statesman Francis Deng to assert: "The international community must therefore seize this opportunity to pressure the parties into serious negotiations for a just and lasting peace."[2]

In August, the U.S. government bombed a Sudanese chemical factory that was reportedly connected with terrorism. The United States devoted high-level attention, military force, and a significant publicity effort to this operation. Apparently, fighting terrorism is a higher priority for the U.S. government than fighting hunger.

What Outside Individuals Can Do

Despite the flaws, food assistance continues to get through to hungry people.

Charitable contributions and U.S. government food aid save lives. Citizens must also support "the collective imagination of the international community" by urging their governments to give priority to the search for peace.[3]

ANTHONY EDWIN KOOMSON is concluding graduate work in Social Development Policy at American University, and has worked in Sudan, Haiti and Ghana.

[1] J. Brian Atwood, "Saving Sudan's People..." *Washington Post*, August 2, 1998.

[2] Francis Deng, "...And Ending Its Cruel War," *Washington Post*, August 2, 1998.

[3] Atwood, op. cit.

CHAPTER 2

NORTH-SOUTH POLITICS IN THE GLOBAL ECONOMY

BY PATTI L. PETESCH

Hunger in a Global Economy: Hunger 1998 concluded that "the market-oriented global economy creates great wealth for a few, provides benefits and reduces hunger for many, while increasing hunger, misery and insecurity for many others."[1] When looked at in aggregate terms, infant mortality is lower, people live longer and are better educated than they were 25 years ago.

While economic indicators have risen overall, the share of wealth accruing to the world's poorest countries and poorest people is small and decreasing, whether measured in world trade, private investment or aid dollars. The growing duality between rich and poor people translates into massive losses in human potential and poses long-term threats for international stability and for democracy (see "Campaign Finance Reform," p. 66).

People in the industrial countries remember the Great Depression of the 1930s as a time of immense hardship and suffering. Yet today, over 100 developing and transition countries suffer "disastrous failures in growth and deeper and more prolonged cuts in living standards," according to the United Nations Development Programme (UNDP).[2] Strategies to reverse this staggering trend abound; various world bodies have each produced plans to reduce poverty, all remarkable for their similarities.

The problem is not that there are no workable and affordable strategies for improving the welfare of the 1.3 billion men, women and children who survive on less than a dollar a day. Rather, the politics of hunger need to be changed. It is urgent that social, economic and political institutions be mobilized and held accountable to the common good, and especially the well-being of hungry and poor people.

This chapter surveys the politics behind key international development initiatives – all, one way or another, related to the growth of the global market economy – important for reducing hunger and poverty worldwide. It examines North-South decision-making in trade, finance and aid and explores the power dynamics of international policy-making. Specifically, it probes policy initiatives to remove protections in food trade, reduce debt and reorient aid programs toward overcoming hunger. It also seeks lessons for advocacy and strategies for more inclusive and equitable development.

New Economics, Changing Politics

Ten years ago, private investment from rich into poor countries totaled $34 billion. By 1997, the total had multiplied over sevenfold to $256 billion.[3] This leap in financial flows results from an unprecedented convergence in economic policies worldwide. Almost all nations have prioritized private sector development by opening domestic markets to international competition. The strategy emphasizes limiting state intervention in the economy; the sale of state-owned companies; prices unsubsidized by the state; free trade; and keeping the national currency cheap enough to boost exports. When poor countries in economic crisis turn to the International Monetary Fund (IMF) and the World Bank for help, these policies are leading conditions for receiving assistance.

Objections grew during the mid-1980s that this policy package gives short shrift to social development, environmental protection and democratic governance. The World Bank responded with safety nets, which have not been adequate. Nonetheless, the principle of directing resources to vulnerable groups harmed by shocks from the global economy or domestic economic reforms has been established.[4]

According to the U.N. Conference on Trade and Development (UNCTAD), the big story since the 1980s is rising inequality and slow growth in the world's economy:

In Africa, where the gap has been widening over the last three decades, average per capita income is now only 7 percent of that of the industrial countries. In Latin America, the change has been more abrupt: average per capita incomes have fallen from over one third of the northern level in the late 1970s to one quarter today…. The middle strata of developing countries, with incomes between 40 percent and 80 percent of the average in advanced countries, are thinner today than in the 1970s.[5]

UNCTAD also reports rising inequality within countries as well as among them.

For the most part, the quality of relations between the world's rich- and poor-country diplomats has been low. Power politics, inadequate representation of dissenting interests and long-standing policy discords still shape many international policy dialogues important to the developing world. The economic and political influence of international businesses is rapidly rising – transforming trade, financial and aid policy-making worldwide. It is against this unstable political backdrop that we understand the limited intergovernmental response to the challenges of economic globalization.

The Malaysian Ambassador and previous President of the U.N. General Assembly describes the continued tensions in North-South political relations which reach well beyond environmental politics:

Since Rio [the 1992 Earth Summit], we have seen a further continuation of North-South trench politics. Governments and NGOs [nongovernmental organizations] from the developed world vigorously promote environmental protection, without shouldering the greater burden of adjustment on consumption and production patterns. Nor do they emphasize with equal balance the importance of fulfilling global responsibilities with national ones. Meanwhile, many developing countries continue to emphasize their rights to development, without placing sufficient stress on social equity and transparent, participatory decision-making. Neither approach bodes well for the future.[6]

The policies of individual nations still have more impact than international agreements. But in an increasingly globalized economy, it becomes ever more important that collaborative political alliances be forged at all political levels to effect changes that benefit hungry people.

The Power Politics of Trade Diplomacy

Trade diplomacy belonged, and largely still belongs, to the rich countries – a winding story of tough negotiations that, bit by bit, have yielded increased access to each other's markets. While a more liberalized trading system brings broad benefits to the international community, multilateral trade negotiations have not adequately addressed the special needs and interests of the poorest . developing countries. Instead, the industrial countries grant special market access terms for poorer countries mostly on a country-by-country and product-by-product basis. The latest Clinton administration initiative to provide special trade privileges for Africa follows this approach.

The rich countries' initiatives to help developing nations expand trade have fallen far short of promoting adequate development. On the one hand, developing-country exporters contend with a patchwork of constantly changing trade rules set by the rich countries. On the other hand, the "special" status enjoyed by developing country exporters for a few products, especially raw materials, may have led them away from diversifying and boosting their countries' economies. The policy-making environment has been driven by security, political and commercial considerations inside the rich countries and protectionist policies inside the developing ones.

For these and other reasons, developing countries began in the late 1980s to identify multilateral and regional trade arrangements as more promising means to gain markets for their exports. The last major reworking of the global trade rules, the Uruguay Round of the Global Agreement on Tariffs and Trade (GATT), saw new levels of involvement by the newly industrializing nations. This participation produced important policy gains for developing countries. The Uruguay Round agreement phases out the Multi-Fiber Arrangement (MFA), which limits exports of developing-country textiles and apparel to the developed countries.[7] The agreement also strengthened dispute settlement provisions for the new 132-member World Trade Organization (WTO).[8] Excepting the MFA, however, the agreement did little to liberalize trade in areas where developing countries enjoy a comparative advantage.

"International Decision-making Rules and Realities" (see p. 39) explores the mechanics of trade negotiations, providing glimpses into why greatly increased participation from developing countries did not yield greater results in market access. The pressures for more successful participation by poor countries will probably increase. Today, China, India, Indonesia, Brazil and Russia account for half the world's population but less than a tenth of its gross domestic product (GDP).[9] As early as 2020, their share in world trade may grow to be half again larger than Europe's.[10]

Signs of the changing economic balance can be found in the rise of the Cairns Group, an issue-based coalition of several rich and middle-income countries (Australia, Canada, New Zealand, and countries chiefly in Southeast Asia and southern South America) that export agricultural goods.[11] The group worked collectively in the Uruguay Round for major reforms in the subsidy, tariff and other trade-distorting practices that have favored the agricultural interests of the United States and the European Union.

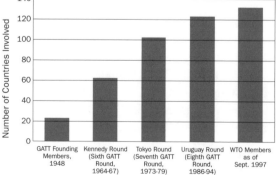

Figure 2.1 **The Number of Countries Involved in Multilateral Trade Negotiations Increased, 1948–1997**

Source: World Trade Organization. WTO data posted at <http://www.wto.org>.

BY PATTI L. PETESCH

The limited accomplishments of developing countries in multilateral trade policy may seem surprising. A developing country enjoys the same voting rights as a rich country in trade negotiations, and most of the developing countries participated in the Uruguay Round. But formal governance arrangements are only part of how decisions are made. In many cases, informal mechanisms are more important.

International governing bodies with universal memberships and equal voting rights only rarely put major proposals on the table for a vote. This is because the wealthier members can be easily out-voted and would decline to participate altogether if they could not defend their interests. Instead, decisions are most often crafted on the basis of consensus, with proposals coming forward from an array of informal and formal meetings among groups of negotiators.

Few developing countries can afford large delegations of specialists to follow the numerous and technical issue tracks in trade negotiations. "The truth is," according to the Chilean trade negotiator for the Uruguay Round, "that the number of countries deeply involved in the negotiations on most issues does not exceed two dozen."[1] The Uruguay Round, moreover, covered more than 30 issue areas. Trade delegations from rich countries often overwhelm developing-country negotiators.

Meanwhile, consensus-building processes can reduce transparency and accountability.[2] Core bargains are made in informal and unrecorded meetings. Countries not part of key informal meetings do not have the chance to get their way when formal negotiations begin and may not even know what deals have already been made.

Still, some developing country diplomats – and international nongovernmental organizations (NGOs) – have beaten these odds through skilled advocacy, expert policy analysis and strategic coalitions such as the Cairns Group.

---

[1] Ernesto Tironi, "Some Lessons from the Uruguay Round: Reflections of a Developing Country Trade Negotiator," In: *UNCTAD Review*, United Nations, 1995, 213.

[2] Ngaire Woods, Executive Summary, "Governance in International Organizations: The Case for Reform in the Bretton Woods Institutions," Prepared for the G-24, draft, (undated) 1.

According to trade and development expert Diana Tussie, the Cairns Group proved pivotal in breaking European intransigence over farm policy reform, and in gaining an unprecedented global commitment to reduce agricultural protection over time and to freeze existing levels of protection. These gains have produced only a modest liberalization in the sector to date, but the Cairns countries and other exporters anticipate benefiting over the long term as domestic and international agricultural markets open up.

Tussie identifies as key sources of the group's influence the added force of working in coalition, strong leadership and expert technical contributions from Australia, and the presence of high-level (ministerial) commitment. Still, the United States and Europe largely determined the final outcome. The Cairns Group's main contribution has been to ensure "that agriculture would remain at the forefront of negotiations," instead of being sidelined by intractable differences between the United States and the European Community.[12]

However, a much larger set of poorer countries that must import food and/or depend heavily on bilateral trade was not part of the Cairns Group and these countries may suffer from less-protected food markets as the Uruguay Round agreement is implemented (see Chapter 6, p. 83).[13] Member states worried that higher food prices and market instability could cause increased hunger in some countries; and in Marrakesh, Morocco, in 1994 an agreement was reached to provide compensation. The terms of compensation, however, were left vague and there has been little meaningful follow-up.

BY SAM NICKELS AND CINDY HUNTER

What went wrong? Where is peace in El Salvador six years after the accords were signed? Where is the prosperity for which 80,000 people died? These questions permeate life for one community 18 kilometers outside the capital, San Salvador.

Residents of *La Línea* (The Line) came here in the 1980s as internally displaced refugees. They built mud-and-bamboo houses along the railroad line owned by the government – the only landlord who wouldn't immediately evict them.

Today, six years after the joyful signing of the Peace Accords of 1992, and after six years of economic liberalization, *La Línea*'s residents still live in their mud houses, few with electricity, few with education for their children, none with running water, and all with fear for their families' safety.

Anselma lives in *La Línea*. Her husband died last year in a fire that he and other farmers ignited to clear their fields before planting. Feeding the family was hard enough before his death, and now when bean prices double and triple every year, Anselma just goes without. So do her children. When the push to privatize government functions came into vogue in the 1980s, government-held grain reserves were sold, and prices were left to market fluctuations.

Concha also lives in *La Línea*. She cares for several grandchildren during the day while her adult children work in the export factories (*maquiladoras*) of the free trade zones where corporations don't have to pay taxes. Her husband farms a small plot of beans and corn. But his income, and the combined incomes of their children, were not enough for them to get electricity.

For that they relied on a daughter working in the United States. With her help they pulled together the required $100. Now with three light bulbs and one outlet, they have access to the mixed global opportunities of helping their grandchildren with homework at night and watching violent and sexist soap operas during the day.

That was a year ago. This year Concha's electric bill increased 60 percent and is expected to climb higher. Why? The government says that to privatize the electric and other utility companies in the country, it must adjust prices to meet costs and make the companies salable. However, Concha's income did not go up 60 percent this year.

Exports are increasing! Over 30,000 Salvadorans now work manufacturing jeans, shirts and underwear that fill every department store in the United States. Many of the factories

International Financial Flows: Crucial, Skewed and Volatile

International investment has skyrocketed again in the 1990s, this time mainly through stock markets and foreign ownership of companies. Virtually all developing countries have been scrambling to attract foreign investment, but international investment remains volatile.

A dozen or so developing economies – which receive most of the private capital flows – are of growing importance to industrial economies. Yet their policy-makers have largely delayed acting to reduce the risks of increased interdependence. Gaps in international financial supervision and regulatory safeguards, and in rescue assistance loomed large in the 1994 Mexican *peso* crisis and again during the 1997 economic meltdown in Southeast Asia. The IMF has

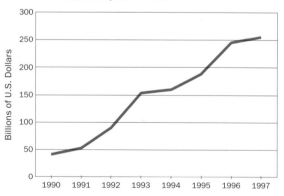

Figure 2.2 **Private Resource Flows to Developing Countries, 1990–1997**

Source: The World Bank, *Global Development Finance 1998, Analysis and Summary Tables* (Washington: World Bank, 1998).

suffered mounting criticism for failing to predict these events and, according to some analysts, exacerbating the crisis.[14]

A church in El Salvador bears a mural of martyred Archbishop Oscar Romero.

has not deterred men who came in the middle of the night to try to break in with machetes. Until she received help from a local relief organization to secure her home, Antonia could not sleep at night and suffered psychosomatic symptoms. She is better now, but the crime rate still mars her country's hopes for an end to violence. The murder rate in El Salvador is as high now as the death rate was during the 12-year civil war. The jobless rate is estimated at 3 to 13 times higher, depending on how one counts the underemployed.

The people of *La Línea* suffered through a Cold War-related civil war. Now they are buffeted by global economic changes and national economic policies far beyond their control.

Getting power into their hands – if only enough to have some control over their daily lives – is an urgent moral imperative.

SAM NICKELS AND CINDY HUNTER, former BFW interns, and their children Heather, Alex and Analidia, live in La Línea, San Salvador, El Salvador, under the sponsorship of the Mennonite Central Committee. E-mail: SamCin@vianet.com.sv

came from Guatemala, where the workers there lost their jobs to the workers in El Salvador. And the factories came from Asia before that, where the workers lost their jobs to Guatemalans. And they came from the southern United States before that, where the workers lost their jobs to the Asians. But at least exports are growing in El Salvador, and people can work double shifts and sleep on piles of clothing overnight (since buses stop running at 9 p.m.) and earn the minimum wage of 5 dollars a day.

Antonia and Carlos live in a mud house surrounded by barbed wire and fierce dogs. But that

The 1998 summit of the G-7 countries (the United States, Great Britain, Germany, France, Canada, Japan and Italy) recommended reforms for greater stability in international financial markets. These center on increasing the IMF's lending reserves and oversight functions and on greater disclosure of financial information. Measures are pending to push private lenders to refrain from fleeing when countries face economic shocks. Other industrial countries will likely join the United States in considering proposals to further strengthen the IMF's public information policies and evaluation functions. The Asian financial crisis dramatizes the vital importance of these complicated and remote decisions to millions of poor and hungry people around the world (see "Women and Children Last," p. 6, and Chapter 6, p. 87).

Foreign Aid's Dollar Diplomats

Better management of international finance, though crucial, will be inadequate to help the far larger number of developing countries that have yet to attract significant levels of private investment. For these countries, aid remains crucial.

Perhaps the biggest burden facing developing countries is their crushing foreign debt, which drains scarce resources from economic and social development. "Citizen Advocacy Reduces Debt" (see pp. 46-49) explores the IMF and World Bank's HIPC initiative, which seeks debt relief for "Heavily Indebted Poor Countries," and the newly launched Jubilee 2000 campaign of religious and other groups pressing for more sweeping debt cancellation.

Much of the official North-South policy dialogue on foreign aid has focused on how to increase aid rather than on how to improve its quality. Resources and programs are widely scattered across scores of international agencies – as well as countries – so the results tend to be scattered and diffuse.

Despite such difficulties, the politics of foreign aid is undergoing change – it is hoped, for the better. A combination of eroding aid budgets and added public scrutiny has led international aid agencies to make their programs more efficient and effective. The transition is yielding greater international effort against poverty than was the case a decade ago. To attain core poverty-reduction and other objectives, donor agencies are being urged to improve their relations with aid recipients and strengthen the contribution of civil society to development decisions and operations.

The industrial countries provided just under $50 billion in official development assistance (ODA) to developing countries in 1997 (see Figure 2.3). In real terms, this is a 16 percent drop from 1992. This trend of falling assistance seems likely to continue.[15]

As Figure 2.4 shows, the United States devotes just 0.08 percent of its gross national product[16] to foreign aid, the lowest among members of the Development Assistance Committee (DAC) of the Organization of Economic Cooperation and Development (OECD).[17] Moreover, the poverty content of the U.S. aid programs is also inadequate as around half of the budget goes to the relatively well-off countries of Egypt and Israel, mainly for security programs.

At the global level, indicators on the proportion of aid specifically oriented toward poor people are difficult to find. Despite the data gaps, development expert Howard White estimates that a generous indicator might put the percentage of poverty-oriented aid at 20 percent.

Pro-poor aid focuses directly on the needs and opportunities of poor people and is often described as "social" grants or lending, as opposed to large-scale macroeconomic policies or infrastructure investments. The World Bank is the largest source of international finance for basic education, health, nutrition and related social sector programs. In Latin America, the Inter-American Development Bank has this lead role, and several governments (e.g., the Nordic

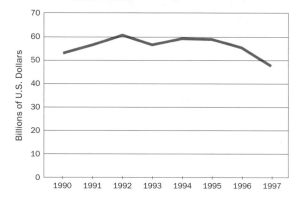

Figure 2.3 **Overseas Development Assistance (ODA) from DAC Member Countries and Multilateral Agencies to Aid Recipients, 1990–1997**

Source: Organization for Economic Cooperation and Development (OECD), data posted at <http://www.oecd.org>. Data for 1997 are provisional.

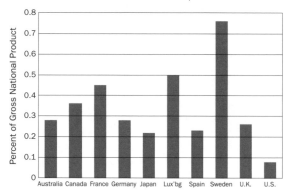

Figure 2.4 **Official Development Assistance from Selected DAC Members, 1997**

Source: OECD data posted at <http://www.oecd.org>.

countries and the United Kingdom) also give priority to basic social programs.

The World Bank reports that its social lending, just 5 percent of its portfolio in the early 1980s, grew to 25 percent between 1994 and 1996.[18] Other World Bank reforms in the early 1990s included country-level poverty assessments, stepped-up poverty monitoring, microfinance projects, social funds and related community development programs.

Meanwhile, the United Nations has undertaken important reforms to better focus its resources on poverty. All agencies have undertaken major reorganizations and the lead development agencies, the UNDP and UNICEF, have sent more staff and resources to field offices.

UNDP has launched a major new anti-poverty initiative to help poor countries develop national strategies with time-bound goals for reducing poverty. The International Fund for Agricultural Development (IFAD) was established after the World Food Conference in 1974 specifically to focus on rural development and small farmers. Significantly, the U.N. development agencies are collaborating in developing a safety net for Indonesia in the wake of the economic crisis there.

These efforts have yet to translate into greater support for the United Nations in the U.S. Congress – fueling serious political tensions for the world body. According to one former U.N. senior official, "Most developing country governments suspect that the U.S. seeks to destroy the capacity of the United Nations in areas which are not of direct U.S. interest, such as economic development activities."[19]

The painful truth is that North-South aid relations are contentious throughout the aid system. For example, the World Bank's Country Assistance Strategy (CAS) document, a three-year plan for each country outlining its economic situation and the World Bank's strategy to improve it, though highly influential, is much criticized. Civil society organizations say the CASs devote too much attention to macroeconomic reform and investments in large infrastructure projects such as dams and roads, to the detriment of social and environmental goals. They argue that too much aid is devoted to policies to accelerate globalization and too little to safety nets to mitigate globalization's harmful effects. At the same time, some developing country governments do not involve their own citizens in a meaningful dialogue about CAS goals or strategies.

The result is poor coordination and lack of effectiveness among donors. Some countries, particularly the poorest, face a massive backlog of unfinished aid projects because they lack the required budget, staffing and other inputs. Governments that give aid increasingly recognize the need for better relations with recipient governments. Rich-country officials have rarely allowed developing countries to take charge of the design and implementation of donor-sponsored projects and policies. The disappointing results reflect poor recipient ownership of, and commitment to, the donor-funded activities.

Thus, for international poverty initiatives to have broader impacts, North-South development alliances need to be strengthened, donor poverty programs need to be better coordinated and poor people as well as their governments need to be empowered.[20]

Decision-making procedures within the international financial institutions are long overdue for reform. Currently, rich countries contribute more money and consequently are allotted more votes than poor ones. A "one country, one vote" system would likely drive the rich countries to find another decision-making venue to reflect the real-world balance of power. Nonetheless, the current voting structure should be reformed to more nearly equalize power so that participation can be fair, if not exactly equal, and produce more accountability and better results for less powerful partners.[21]

The Emergence of an International Civil Society

The close of this century has witnessed a dramatic, if unevenly distributed, surge in the numbers and presence of civil society organizations and NGOs worldwide. By far the largest share of civil society organizations work locally, grappling with community problems and the failure of their governments to provide basic services such as water, health clinics and schools. International agencies and industrial countries have actively supported the explosion of NGOs in developing countries by channeling aid through them instead of through governments. This presents an opportunity not only for more effective community development, but for North-South NGO ties that can lead to more effective advocacy. It can also create tensions between NGOs and their own governments who may feel that official political and planning processes have been bypassed.

NGO issue networks bring together advocates from rich and poor countries to press for policy change in international institutions with increasing frequency and success. The Internet has made possible dramatic gains in global NGO communication and coordination of activities (see Chapter 3).

Among the most successful international NGO advocacy initiatives are the environmental campaigns directed at the World Bank. More than a decade of NGO advocacy, research and coalition-building has resulted in greater public access to information as well as improved social and environmental policies at the bank. The Development Bank Watchers' Project (BWP) of Bread for the World Institute has, with other groups, supported the efforts of NGOs in developing countries to reform the World Bank's policies and practices, to make its decision-making processes more participatory and to influence its country assistance strategies.[22] There is widespread agreement that these measures have helped to increase the bank's transparency and accountability to member governments and civil society – thereby strengthening its contribution to sustainable development.[23]

The 1992 Rio Earth Summit was a turning point on the road toward a more open international society. Working individually, through national and transnational networks, and through alliances with sympathetic government officials, northern and southern NGOs shaped the outcomes of the Earth Summit and subsequent U.N. conferences.

NGOs are also monitoring the priorities agreed to at the U.N. conferences on social development, population and women. The two biggest outcomes of the Social Summit are a call for a time-bound commitment to eradicate poverty and the 20/20 Compact among developing countries and donors to allocate 20 percent of a country's public sector *and* foreign aid budgets to core poverty programs such as basic education and health services. Some 30 countries have adopted time-bound targets; and a few developing countries such as Bolivia and Burkina Faso have taken up the 20/20 Compact. The global NGO network, Social Watch, monitors the progress achieved in meeting the goals of the Compact and the Beijing conference on women.[24]

A few NGO networks are arguably more influential than many governments. Some developed and developing country diplomats find this alarming, although the legitimacy of the NGOs'

Advocates calling for debt relief form a human chain at the G-8 summit in Birmingham, England, June 1998.

role in development decision-making is less and less a matter of controversy. Indeed, two experienced analysts suggest that developing-country diplomats, instead of resisting civil society participation, should learn about, and where interests coincide, attempt to work with NGO coalitions for policy change.[25] Such alliances could help transform today's international institutions.

The NGOs' heightened profile has been followed by increasing attention to their own accountability. This includes the attempts of some governments to regulate, or restrict, NGOs.[26]

Forces for Change

Opportunities exist to make gains against hunger and poverty in the post-Cold War era. There is greater commitment (at least rhetorically) among governments to "the goal of eradicating poverty in the world…as an ethical, social, political and economic imperative of humankind."[27] Equitable development, both within nations and among them, is now widely recognized as the foundation for peace, social cohesion and economic prosperity.

Economic globalization has deepened interdependence among nations as never before, presenting substantial additional pressures for improved international cooperation. As the trade in goods, services and investments among nations escalates, so do problems of drugs, pollution, population pressure, resource degradation, migration and pandemic diseases. These can only be managed successfully if nations work collectively and only if the underlying forces driving these trends – particularly rising poverty – can be reversed. It is in the self-interest of both rich and poor countries to focus attention on the large parts of the world where hunger and poverty continue to prevail.

A final source of optimism: International bodies and national governments alike are compelled by globalization and a more influential civil society to adopt more transparent, accountable and inclusive governance arrangements. Such democratic decision-making is increasingly vital to both the legitimacy and performance of public institutions.

There are also causes for concern. The late economist Mancur Olsen argued that, paradoxically, long periods of peace and stability make it hard to establish the necessary instruments for advancing "the common good" internationally. In the absence of conflict, self-serving interest groups gather strength and influence in politics and markets.

Nations' competition for global markets may lead them to minimize social goals and costs as they attempt to maximize economic gains. The need to attract financing from multinational businesses in lieu of rich governments can drive developing-country governments to neglect their majority poor populations. These changes are problematic because the pressures of globalization require greater social and environmental investments, not less.

Faced with these dilemmas, governments and international institutions turn to NGOs for resources, expertise and policy allies. Carnegie Endowment President Jessica Mathews argues that government cutbacks have helped push NGOs to a central role in shaping multilateral policies; and in the transition, this is likely to "weaken rather than bolster the world's capacity to solve its problems."[28] Yet a mission to reduce global poverty and hunger calls for more capable intergovernmental institutions as well as more democratic ones.

In sum, poverty campaigners in governments and out, and across countries both rich and poor, will need to join forces and greatly increase their advocacy, policy analysis and networking capacities to: (1) improve the transparency of the leading international trade, finance and aid institutions, and their accountability toward representative Southern constituencies; and

FORGE
COLLABORATIVE
POLITICAL
ALLIANCES
TO BRING EFFECTIVE
CHANGES
AT ALL LEVELS
– COMMUNITY TO INTERNATIONAL

(2) redirect these institutions to seek results on specific poverty goals. Five areas stand out for more focused poverty advocacy:

■ The debt of the world's poorest countries should be canceled and more concessional instruments created so that the cycle of rising public indebtedness is never repeated (see "Citizen Advocacy Reduces Debt," p. 46);

■ Aid decisionmaking at the country level should be transformed to promote greater ownership, participation and results on poverty objectives;

■ Better safety nets are required to protect people in Southern countries who may be adversely affected by World Bank and IMF economic reform programs and WTO decisions;

■ The governance procedures of the international financial institutions should be reformed to better reflect the economic weight and development management responsibilities of developing countries; and

■ Trade and investment policies require improved regulation, supervision and transparency to reduce risks and enhance globalization's contribution to social and environmental goals.

PATTI PETESCH is an international development consultant who specializes in poverty and environmental problems, civil society participation and aid coordination. E-mail: plpetesch@igc.apc.org

BY KATHLEEN A. SELVAGGIO

And the fiftieth year shall be a holy time to proclaim liberty throughout the land to all enslaved debtors and a time for the cancellation of all public and private debt.... it shall be a Jubilee year for you...

—LEVITICUS 25:9-12

In May 1995, a World Bank vice president insisted to a group of development agency representatives that "debt was not a problem" for the poorest African countries. A year later, the same official declared debt was a critical issue demanding urgent attention from the World Bank and the international community.

Nongovernmental organizations (NGOs) played an important role in bringing on this about-face. Although the debt crisis had disappeared from policy-makers' radar screen after solutions to Latin American debt were found in the late 1980s, NGOs have protested that the crisis is hardly over, especially for the poorest African countries. Through lobbying and pressure campaigns, NGO activists have helped to put debt back on the agenda and to shape policy responses.[1]

Bread for the World was one NGO that positively influenced U.S. government policy on poor-country debt relief over the past decade. Through staff and grassroots lobbying, Bread for the World helped persuade the U.S. Congress to adopt legislation in 1989 and 1990 authorizing the forgiveness of debt accumulated through U.S. development and food aid lending programs. Approximately $2.7 billion was written off in 1990-1991.

More recently, a global network of development, environment and religious groups has drawn policy-makers' attention to "multilateral" debt – debt owed to international financial institutions like the World Bank and the International Monetary Fund (IMF). In 1993, NGOs, mainly based in Europe, began lobbying Western governments through the annual G-7 economic summits, and lobbying World Bank and IMF officials during their annual meetings. Their persistent efforts yielded results: In September 1996, the World Bank and IMF boards adopted the Heavily Indebted Poor Countries (HIPC) debt initiative.

Although HIPC is increasingly viewed as too little, too late, for too few countries, it is groundbreaking for at least two reasons. For the first time, multilateral institutions are reducing their share of poor countries' debt, not just rescheduling or lending new money to cover old debts. Also, while decisions to grant debt relief had previously been ad hoc and uncoordinated, HIPC coordinates the action taken by all creditors – international lending institutions, foreign governments and private banks.

Oxfam International: Leading the charge on HIPC

NGOs deserve considerable credit for bringing about the historic HIPC initiative and for pressing for its fullest implementation, although new leadership at the World Bank was also a significant factor. A senior World Bank official told *The Christian Century* magazine, "I don't want to say it was NGOs that forced us to change, but NGOs played a major role." He especially acknowledged some NGOs' mastery of details and ability to make forceful arguments.[2]

Oxfam International, representing 11 regional Oxfam development and relief agencies around the world, has played the leading role among NGOs in campaigning for multilateral debt relief. Several major strategies account for Oxfam's success:

■ Sound technical analysis and information dissemination. Oxfam produces a steady stream of policy papers widely used by advocates and the media. Electronic communication allows them to be broadly distributed.

■ Overseas programs and partnerships. Oxfam has drawn on its network of staff and partners in debtor countries for testimonial and statistical information documenting debt's social impact.

■ Relationships with policy-makers and debtor government officials. Oxfam lobbyists have cultivated official contacts and engaged in high-level dialogue. Sometimes, allies within these institutions are willing to share data, information or arguments to strengthen Oxfam's advocacy with key decision-makers.

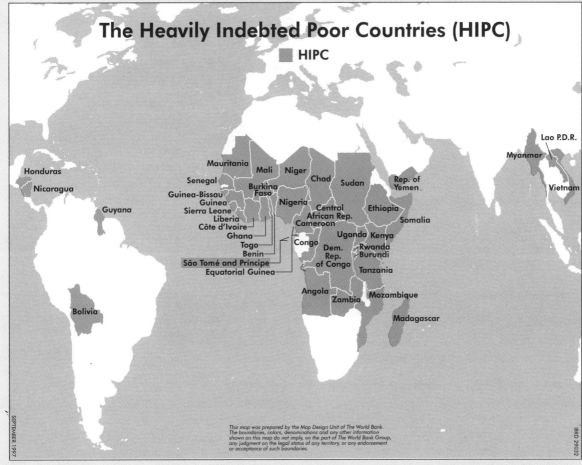

The Heavily Indebted Poor Countries (HIPC)

■ HIPC

Lao P.D.R.
Myanmar
Vietnam
Honduras
Nicaragua
Guyana
Bolivia
Mauritania
Mali
Niger
Chad
Sudan
Rep. of Yemen
Senegal
Burkina Faso
Guinea-Bissau
Guinea
Nigeria
Ethiopia
Sierra Leone
Central African Rep.
Somalia
Liberia
Cameroon
Côte d'Ivoire
Ghana
Uganda
Kenya
Togo
Congo
Benin
Dem. Rep. of Congo
Rwanda
Burundi
São Tomé and Príncipe
Equatorial Guinea
Tanzania
Angola
Mozambique
Zambia
Madagascar

This map was prepared by the Map Design Unit of The World Bank. The boundaries, colors, denominations and any other information shown on this map do not imply, on the part of The World Bank Group, any judgment on the legal status of any territory, or any endorsement or acceptance of such boundaries.

SEPTEMBER 1997

IBRD 29032

Source: The World Bank and International Monetary Fund. Data posted at <http://worldbank.org>. Used with permission.

■ In a few cases, Oxfam has forged partnerships with debtor-country governments to push for the most generous debt relief under HIPC. In fact, Ugandan Finance Minister Mayanja Nkangi noted Oxfam's "significant role in sparking off and informing the public debate [on debt relief for Uganda] just before the critical IMF and World Bank Board meetings" and thanked them for their "valued and timely intervention."[3]

■ Media campaigns. Oxfam cultivated relationships with journalists, resulting in attention at key moments during the campaign. For example, when HIPC debt relief for Mozambique was under negotiation in January 1998, NGOs were concerned that creditor governments were trying to minimize the amount granted. Oxfam launched an intensive media effort, resulting in coverage by the *Washington Post, Financial Times, Wall Street Journal, The Guardian* and several wire services. In fact, a press spokesperson for the Paris Club, the group of creditor governments, complained of the extraordinary press attention. The effort may have paid off, since the final debt relief package for Mozambique was not as inadequate as had been feared.

Under Oxfam's leadership, HIPC advocacy has chiefly meant Northern NGOs lobbying decision-makers in financial capitals. However, since 1996, Oxfam agencies have actively supported debtor-country NGOs as their countries come up for consideration under HIPC. Oxfam agencies help with funding, information-sharing and strategy-planning to help the Southern NGOs with lobbying. So far, grassroots education and mobilization have not played a major role in HIPC advocacy, though efforts are underway in Asia and Latin America to bring a wider array of groups into the discussion on debt, aid and development.

The worldwide Jubilee 2000 movement: Affiong Limene Southey speaks about solving the problem of unpayable debt.

For example, in Uganda and Mozambique, local NGOs worked with international ones to encourage their own governments' transparency in using debt relief. In Nicaragua, a network of civil society organizations advocates and educates on debt issues and seeks Nicaragua's inclusion in HIPC. In Honduras, another NGO network carries out constituent education on the debt, and plans to host the launch of Jubilee 2000's Latin America campaign.

Because members of the U.S. Congress have been largely hostile to the concept, U.S. activists have made little effort thus far to engage their support for a far-reaching debt reduction initiative. But as the Jubilee 2000 movement takes hold in the United States, citizen activists are trying to change that.

Jubilee 2000: A Moral Appeal

By contrast, the Jubilee 2000 movement has been characterized by large-scale mobilization of faith communities seeking clemency for severely indebted countries by the year 2000, the beginning of the third millennium. The campaign takes its name and inspiration from the biblical principle of Jubilee, which calls upon rulers to forgive debts, free slaves and return land to the community every fifty years in order to give disadvan-

taged people a fresh start. Pope John Paul II and Archbishop Desmond Tutu are among religious leaders calling on the world to observe the coming millennium with a Jubilee effort to resolve the debt. An official of the Evangelical Lutheran Church in Tanzania wrote Bread for the World Institute:

> We are at the moment campaigning for debt cancellation by the year 2000. Our government spends 35 percent of her revenue to pay external debts while schools have no desks and children die of malnutrition. Can [your] institute lobby for us so that the [U.S.] government can influence the IMF and World Bank to consider debt cancellation and channel the resources gained for promoting education and health?[4]

Jubilee 2000 was launched in the United Kingdom in 1996, and has since spread to a few dozen countries, including several in Africa. Enthusiasm for the campaign abounds, partly due to the perceived inadequacy of policy responses like HIPC. The campaign relies primarily on popular education, the media and mass mobilization strategies, like organizing mass demonstrations and collecting 22 million signatures to present to policy-makers. At the 1998 G-8 Summit in

Birmingham, England, 50,000 Jubilee 2000 supporters formed a "human chain" 7 miles long around the summit site, to symbolize the chains of debt strangling poor countries.

Although united under the broad banner of debt forgiveness, Jubilee 2000 campaigns in each nation develop their own platforms, policy priorities and action plans. There has been a spontaneous character to the national Jubilee 2000/USA campaign. When it was slow to get underway, Catholic parishes in Lansing, MI and Los Angeles generated their own educational materials and action strategies.

The Jubilee campaign has several strengths:

■ Moral authority. The moral authority of world religious leaders Pope John Paul II and African Anglican Archbishops Desmond Tutu and his successor, Njonhonkulu Ndungane, lends credibility to the Jubilee call for deep debt forgiveness. Addressing 735 Anglican bishops at a once-in-a-decade meeting in July 1998, the Archbishop of Canterbury, Dr. George Carey, said international debt was "a moral problem of enormous proportions." "The depths of suffering which we continue to see in many parts of that great continent (Africa) go far beyond what is tolerable in a civilized world," he said. "The churches have a key role in creating the climate for change." The World Bank's President Wolfensohn was distressed.

■ Mass membership. Jubilee 2000 campaigns are quickly amassing hundreds of thousands of organizational and individual members through churches in several dozen countries. This expanding membership base could create the political will to provide deeper debt relief.

■ Popular education. The campaign has enjoyed relative success in making a complex issue understandable to a wide audience. However, the more popular and straightforward the education and advocacy message, the more policy-makers tend to dismiss it as simplistic and unrealistic.

The global Jubilee 2000 campaign faces considerable challenges. Given its decentralized nature, coordination can be slow and weak. Despite the campaign's success so far in popularizing the debt issue, it is still difficult to make the issue compelling and intelligible to average citizens. Some citizen activists have shied away because they perceive debt as technically complex, and find it difficult to keep up with developments in dozens of indebted countries. Other potential activists worry that debt relief will not go toward social spending. The role of watchdog groups in the debtor countries becomes all the more crucial in this light. The NGO group, Uganda Debt Network, states:

> We...firmly believe that borrowed money should be spent prudently to generate more value in the economy. The extent to which this will happen depends on the capacity of civil society to hold policy planners at all levels accountable and to demand that benefits, however small, should reach the wider community rather than the minority.[5]

Finally, in the United States, the lack of support in Congress for debt forgiveness and foreign aid presents a tough obstacle to overcome. Yet despite the challenges, activism continues, as sophisticated lobbying campaigns like Oxfam's and the mass mobilizations inspired by the Jubilee vision can complement each other.

Jubilee 2000 will be Bread for the World's main campaign, its nationwide Offering of Letters, in 1999. Tens of thousands of concerned citizens and church groups will urge their members of Congress to help cancel the oppressive debt of the poorest countries and to make sure the benefits get to poor people. Jubilee 2000 may involve ordinary citizens in an international economic policy question – other than foreign aid – more than any previous NGO campaign. For information, contact Bread for the World.

KATHLEEN SELVAGGIO, former policy analyst with Bread for the World, is now debt project manager at Catholic Relief Services. E-mail: kselvaggio@catholicrelief.org

[1] This piece draws extensively from Elizabeth A. Donnelly, "Transnational Issue Networks: The Case of Third World Debt and Structural Adjustment," In: Kathryn Sikkink, James V. Riker and Sanjeev Khagram, eds., Restructuring World Politics: The Power of Transnational Agency and Norms, forthcoming.

[2] "Policy Changes for the World Bank," Christian Century, November 6, 1996.

[3] Letter from Mayanja Nkangi to Oxfam International, April 1998.

[4] Letter from Rogate Mshana to Bread for the World Institute, August 1998.

[5] Zie Gariyo, Uganda Debt Network, "Will debt relief give Ugandans a better life?," The Monitor, April 13, 1998.

CHAPTER 3

THE GLOBAL COMMUNICATIONS REVOLUTION

BY JAMES V. RIKER

The question of the day is whether global electronic connections make citizens more aware of world problems and more able to contribute to their solution.

— CLAUDE MOISY, "MYTHS OF THE GLOBAL VILLAGE," *FOREIGN POLICY*, NO. 107, SUMMER 1997, 78.

The global communications revolution poses new challenges and offers new opportunities for anti-hunger political strategies. Innovations in information technologies such as satellite broadcasting, mobile phones, computers and the Internet connect people around the planet. Yet access to the "global village" and the benefits of the information age have been limited to relatively few.

The global media, through news, advertising and entertainment programs, shape political culture. Media stories can denigrate public life, move governments to action or make it seem as though public participation is, at best, an optional footnote to "the good life." The portrayal, packaging and control of news and information is a powerful force with increasing importance to our lives.

The media have brought the moral urgency of hunger into our homes, beaming television images of starving children in Sudan, food riots in Indonesia and soup kitchens in the developed world. "Media images of human suffering have motivated people to express their concern and their solidarity with those in distant places by contributing to relief efforts and by demanding explanations and action

American Public Health Association/David Fouse

from governments."[1] At the 1996 World Food Summit in Rome, Italy, the director general of the Food and Agriculture Organization of the United Nations (FAO), Jacques Diouf, felt it was important to appear on television (including the Cable News Network – CNN) to answer viewers' questions concerning international action for alleviating hunger.[2]

Some suggest we are witnessing "the CNN-ization of the world," where instant news and analysis shape the agendas and actions of world leaders.

> By focusing daily on the starving children in Somalia, a pictorial story tailor-made for television, TV mobilized the conscience of the nation's public institutions, compelling the [U.S.] government into a policy of intervention for humanitarian reasons.[3]

Former U.N. Secretary-General Boutros Boutros-Ghali once commented that "CNN is the 16th member of the U.N. Security Council."[4] Humanitarian organizations may use the media to tell the story, and governments may produce funds, programs or new long-term policies in response.

> But it is an unequal triangle. Both the humanitarian organizations and the government count on their aid and their policy to succeed. The media have their story either way – success or failure.[5]

And it is tricky. Politicians may use media events as rationalizations for decisions that are actually motivated by political ideologies or other, unseen, goals.

It is very clear that for good and for ill, the media have a hugely powerful influence on public life and that anti-hunger activists need to utilize the power of the mass media to portray the depth of, and causes and solutions to, hunger. New technologies enable individuals and organizations to influence government policies and corporate practices affecting hungry and poor people around the world.

Global Disparities: Unequal Access

The transformative potential of the global communications revolution remains elusive to most of the world's people. Not everyone is able to participate. At this stage, information technologies are accentuating inequality worldwide.[6] Information flows overwhelmingly favor those who speak English and have access to communications technologies in the developed world, while too many people in the developing world lack access to the most basic technology and services. One strategy to help would be to provide the equipment and software needed for anti-hunger and environmental nongovernmental organizations (NGOs) so they can gather information and forge better connections with colleagues around the world.

The global disparities between the "haves" and "have nots" are striking:

■ Two billion people still lack electricity, and therefore have no access to television, computers or the Internet;[7]

■ In 1994, over 60 percent of the people in Bolivia, Eritrea, Haiti and South Africa, a total greater than the population of Germany, had no access to any postal services;[8]

Table 3.1 **Primary Language Groups Use of Internet by Percent**

Language Group	Percentage of Internet Sites Worldwide
English	70 percent
Germanic (German, Dutch and Scandinavian Languages)	11 percent
Romance (French, Italian, Portuguese and Spanish)	9 percent
Japanese	5 percent
Other Languages	5 percent

Source: UNESCO, *World Communication Report*, Paris: UNESCO Publishing, 1997, 96.

- CNN International reaches only 3 percent of the world's population, while 80 percent of the world's people do not have access to a television set;[9]

- While nearly 200 countries are now connected to the Internet, only 12 percent of the world's Internet hosts are located in the developing world, with most of these based in the Asia and Pacific region; and

- South Africa accounts for over 96 percent of the Internet hosts for the entire continent of Africa.[10]

Even within the United States, the information age contributes to widening the gap between rich and poor workers. In June 1998, President Clinton stated that: "History teaches us that even as new technologies create growth and opportunities, they can heighten economic inequalities and sharpen social divisions."[11] Some observers argue that the dynamics of the global economy have created "a Darwinian approach" where unskilled workers – those who lack technological proficiency – "are going to be left behind."[12]

Paradoxically, while the reach of global communications technologies is spreading, coverage of the world may be shrinking, and with it our understanding of world events. Since the end of the Cold War: "News is moving away from foreign affairs towards domestic concerns; away from politics towards human-interest stories; away from issues to people."[13] The post-Cold War period has seen a dramatic decrease in television coverage of international events and issues.[14]

At the same time, the number of foreign news bureaus has decreased. Moreover, leading U.S. news magazines give less coverage to international events and news than they did a decade ago.

Mortimer B. Zuckerman, chairman of *U.S. News & World Report*, argues that the public's interest has waned since the end of the Cold War: "The poorest selling covers of the year are always those on international news."[15]

The majority of the general public finds international events to be of little relevance to their lives, and given the complexity of modern life, it becomes more and more difficult to understand world events, especially hunger and poverty, which are not newsworthy until a major crisis erupts. Then the public becomes crisis-and-response oriented rather than attuned to long-term political changes – hold governments accountable, support the empowerment of poor people, promote participation – that can mitigate or prevent the crises before they erupt.

Elites tend to be more well-informed and engaged in international affairs, seeking to

Table 3.2 **Declining Coverage of Foreign News on Network Television**

	1970s	**1990-1991**	**1995**
Percent of Foreign Stories	35	41	23
Percent of Time	45	n/a	13.5
Average Length of Foreign Story (minutes)	1.7	2.2	1.2

Source: Cited by Claude Moisy, "Myths of the Global Information Village," *Foreign Policy*, No. 107, Summer 1997, 82.

Table 3.3 **Declining Coverage of International News in Leading U.S. News Magazines**

News Magazine	Percentage of Coverage Devoted to International News	
	1985	**1995**
Newsweek	22	12
Time	24	14
U.S. News & World Report	20	14

Source: Robin Pogrebin, "Foreign Coverage Less Prominent in News Magazines," *New York Times*, September 23, 1996, D-6.

influence foreign policy in economic and political affairs abroad.[16] But this does not guarantee the passage of policies that give priority to the needs of hungry and poor people.

In the United States, shrinking coverage of statehouse politics is also occurring: "Twenty-seven state capitals have fewer reporters covering that beat than in the early 1990s."[17] This may limit coverage of how state welfare debates and programs are proceeding in this crucial period when the federal welfare reform act of 1996 is being tested by what happens at state and local levels (see Chapter 5, pp. 74-79).

The number of people who watch network television news is declining. The percentage of people who watch only evening network news programs has fallen in the United States from 30 percent in 1993 to 15 percent in 1998.[18] People increasingly are looking to other sources: "In 1995, 4 percent of Americans used a [news] Web site; this year 20 percent did."[19] Internet use is growing exponentially, becoming an important source of information about political events and analysis worldwide, and in turn an important vehicle for mobilizing advocacy efforts through information sharing and action alerts.

Voter turnout in the United States remains very low. Millions of campaign dollars are spent on the media to get voters, mainly middle-class and wealthy people, to support candidates and act on specific legislation and referenda. Yet tens of millions of low-income voters, especially in urban areas, are politically disengaged from politics and no longer vote. Suburban voters outnumbered urban voters for the first time in the 1992 presidential election.

With a decreasing presence and influence at the polls, hungry and poor people had a greatly diminished political voice at a time when the stakes were highest in 1994.

> Perhaps no other election in the past 60 years has carried greater significance for poor people. Yet even as Republicans announced an attack on entitlement programs in the Contract with America, low-income people stayed away from the polls in huge numbers.[20]

Only one in five low-income voters – those making $10,000 per year or less – went to the polls, while three out of five upper middle-class voters participated in the 1994 elections.[21] Middle-class voters are also better informed, as one in 10 voters used the Internet for news about candidates and election information in the 1996 presidential election.[22] The need to empower hungry and poor people so they can engage in the political process is urgent. Otherwise their concerns will not be adequately addressed.

Figure 3.1 **Growth in Internet Use Worldwide, 1990-1998**

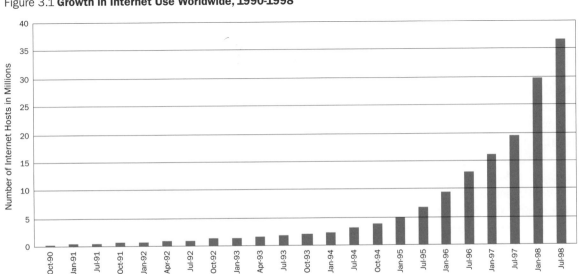

Source: Network Wizards, accessible at: <http://www.nw.com>.

Distorting Effects

The global media transmits consumerist values that shape individuals' choices. The media messages of Madison Avenue, sitcoms, movies and late night shows can powerfully shape tastes and expectations about the world. At times the media simplifies the viewpoint presented to the public in a sound bite: Do those who have the most toys really "win?" Does government "waste your money?"

Moreover, the topics chosen for in-depth news reporting reflect editorial policies often influenced by powerful advertisers and business interests. Together, these forces color the accuracy and breadth of coverage and conceal important information. "Apprehension about the concentration in media ownership is linked to worries that this sector's power to shape the agenda of political action may not be matched by a sense of responsibility."[23] The global consolidation of media conglomerates raises important concerns about the type and quality of news coverage around the world.

A further problem is declining belief in the media. News organizations' drive to get a "breakthrough story" without verifying all of the facts has too often undercut media credibility even among the mainstream press. On June 7, 1998, CNN and *Time* magazine published a shocking report that the U.S. military had used deadly sarin nerve gas against American military defectors in Laos in 1970. When challenged to prove the claims behind this news story, both news organizations issued full retractions "on the air, in print, and on-line."[24] Ted Turner, CNN's founder, chagrined by this event, suggested that intense pressures for media ratings and profits in the global media had contributed to the fiasco.[25] While half of the U.S. public believe that news organizations will play a positive role in improving the quality of life in the United States, 39 percent think that the media constitute "a major threat to the country's future."[26]

Despite heightened consumer interest in food, health and safety issues, media stories on the corporate practices and products of the agricultural and food industry rarely hit the front page or the TV screen. Corporations have sought to stifle investigative news stories or have filed

Celia Escudero-Espadas

lawsuits where their interests have been threatened. "On June 28, *The Cincinnati Enquirer* published a front-page and on-line apology – and paid a $10 million settlement – because of controversial investigative stories on the Chiquita Banana Company."[27] The high-profile yet unsuccessful lawsuit against Oprah Winfrey filed by Texas beef producers focused national attention on the right to free speech and the potential health risks of eating beef.

The Potential and Peril of Cyber-Advocacy

How influential are the global media, and whom do they serve? The global media have diffused democratic and human rights values worldwide (see Chapter 1). Some analysts argue that the global media have also become "the new missionaries of corporate capitalism" and agents for Western cultural imperialism.[28] The media have, on the one hand, provided quick sources of worldwide information never before available, and on the other, advanced the goal of corporations and investors seeking access to growing global markets, by releasing either highly critical or positive reports of government policies depending upon the business strategy needed to get established in those markets.[29] Clearly the media are not monolithic.

The global media have contributed to the changing political discourse on North-South relations over the past 25 years, from critiquing the New International Economic Order (NIEO) proposed by the Group of 77 in the 1970s, to supporting free-market policies and structural adjustment programs in the 1980s, to trumpeting the triumph of the global economy in the 1990s and questioning the somewhat hollow triumph in Asia today.

The global media have shaped political discourse about the proper role of governments. States' commitments to social welfare policies are changing with the move toward privatization and free-market policies worldwide.

Freedom of expression has become an issue, especially in countries where sensitivities over political issues (and domestic as well as foreign advocacy efforts) are of concern to leaders. In Singapore, the international press have been careful to self-censor any reports that would be critical of the government, given numerous instances of previous government action to fine or ban leading international newspapers and news magazines.[30] Some governments, such as China, Malaysia and Singapore, have sought to monitor and/or regulate access to and the content of the Internet.[31]

Internet politics have taken many new forms, from cyber-nationalism, where groups halfway around the globe advocate for self-determination and freedom for their brothers and sisters, to cyber-democracy where various forms of direct representation of peoples' interests can occur.[32] By strategically using the Internet to target international lobbying efforts, a growing network of private citizens, researchers and activists affiliated with the Food First Information and Action Network (FIAN) and other anti-hunger groups engage in cyber-advocacy to protect people's right to food. International agencies and NGOs have established computer networks in Africa and elsewhere in the developing world to monitor the extent of hunger and to share strategies for its alleviation.[33] New cyberspace communities are emerging linking people and NGOs engaged in effective issue advocacy such as the

USE THE POWER OF THE MEDIA TO PORTRAY THE DEPTH OF, AND CAUSES AND SOLUTIONS TO, HUNGER

successful International Campaign to Ban Landmines (see Introduction, p. 9).

Media Advocacy Strategies for Influencing Policy

New media strategies have emerged and are needed to influence policies and political leaders at multiple levels. Transnational advocacy campaigns have effectively used the media and the Internet to dramatize human rights and labor practices around the world, the Nestlé infant formula boycott and demands for accountable international institutions such as the World Bank and IMF.[34]

Modern communications have a significant impact in shaping public consciousness on hunger issues. As information consumers, we each make choices about the type and quality of news that informs our perspective of the world. We need to take an active role in deciding what sort of programming we want, and seek out and support alternative voices in the media that provide us with the necessary information to inform us about political and social realities of hunger and poverty in our communities and around the globe.

Chapter 7 suggests specific ways to use the power of the media to portray the depth of, and causes and solutions to, hunger; one of the most important steps that could be taken to end hunger worldwide.

Kathleen S. Daugherty

DR. JAMES V. RIKER is senior researcher with Bread for the World Institute. E-mail: jriker@bread.org

CHAPTER 4

THE POLITICS OF HUNGER IN THE UNITED STATES

BY LEON HOWELL

Over the last 25 years fundamental changes have reshaped the politics of hunger in the United States. In the 1960s and 1970s various organizations and coalitions flowing out of grassroots concerns pushed the federal government to establish a vast array of effective federal nutrition and anti-poverty programs. Repeatedly in the 1980s and 1990s those programs were targeted for dismantling. Repeatedly advocates for hungry and poor people blunted the harshest attacks, but many food and anti-poverty programs were eroded in the process. Today the U.S. government's social contract with its people has shifted toward self-reliance, privatization and free market policies and away from maintaining a social safety net for all people.

In the mid-1990s the global economy increased economic growth in the United States, but the benefits of this growth have been unequally and inadequately distributed. In the midst of this economic prosperity, how do we understand the changing politics affecting hungry and poor people?

Hunger in 1997

Hunger remains a pervasive reality for millions of people in the United States. A U.S. Department of Agriculture (USDA) study reports that 11.2 million people live in hungry households that cannot afford enough food for all in the household. Thirty-four million people live in households that are food insecure, or at risk of hunger.[1]

By many indicators, hunger increased in 1997. Requests for emergency food grew by 16 percent in 1997, with 19 percent of the requests estimated to have gone unmet.[2] Almost 1 million legal immigrants, most of them taxpayers, lost their food stamps in 1997 as a result of the 1996 welfare reform law (see Chapter 5), though an advocacy campaign led Congress to restore food stamps for an estimated 250,000 immigrants beginning in November 1998. Physicians for Human Rights found 79 percent of 682 Latino and Asian legal immigrant households they surveyed in March 1998 to be "food insecure," a rate nearly seven times greater than the general population.[3] Second Harvest, whose network of food pantries and kitchens fed 26 million people (many multiple times) in 1997, determined that 45 percent of the people they serve are employed. They make too little money to feed themselves without assistance.

The need is clear. The need is great. The turn of the century provides an excellent time to empower poor people and, with them, mobilize the political will for a new assault on hunger.

Helping Hungry People Find Food

The modern story of the federal politics of hunger begins in 1967. The civil rights movement exposed hunger in the South. The Field Foundation sent a team of pediatricians from Harvard to examine thousands of rural children. They reported that the children were "hungry, weak, apathetic. Their lives are being shortened."[4] Senator Robert Kennedy and his aide Peter Edelman visited a number of places in Mississippi on an itinerary arranged by Marian Wright, a young civil rights attorney, who later founded the Children's Defense Fund (CDF). Newspaper headlines and television sets carried the shocking news across the nation. Hunger was so bad that some children had diseases normally associated with very poor countries. The media outcry had an effect.

The Senate established the Select Committee on Nutrition and Human Needs in 1967 to address this national problem. The media helped galvanize public attention about the extent of hunger nationwide. CBS-Television produced a documentary, *Hungry in America,* that stirred the nation. The Citizen's Board of Inquiry into Hunger and Malnutrition in the United States released *Hunger U.S.A.* with an introduction by Kennedy two months before his assassination. Nick Kotz received a Pulitzer Prize for his 1969 book, *Let Them Eat Promises: The Politics of Hunger in America*, a still fascinating account of how presidents and the power-

FORGE COLLABORATIVE POLITICAL ALLIANCES TO BRING EFFECTIVE CHANGES AT ALL LEVELS

ful barons of the Agriculture Committees were reluctantly forced to acknowledge and respond to the problem of hunger.[5]

In the first year of his presidency – 1969 – Richard Nixon hosted a White House Conference on Food, Nutrition and Health, boldly stating "the moment is at hand to put an end to hunger in America." But Nixon told his secretary of agriculture, in lines surely paraphrased by many politicians to follow, to "use all the rhetoric so long as it doesn't cost money."[6]

Federal attention and much grassroots activity led to a burst of anti-hunger legislation in the 1970s, always bucking strong opposition. The agriculture committees in both houses of Congress preferred the commodity programs, the direct distribution of surplus food to poor people. Farmers supported that strongly. The ground work was done to start or enhance what are now 12 USDA food and nutrition programs that reach one in six Americans. USDA spent $36.4 billion for that purpose in fiscal year (FY) 1997.

Federal Nutrition Programs

Food stamps, by far the largest of the government's food assistance programs, offer a useful window into the federal politics of hunger. Food stamps were used in a small way during the Depression. Each year from 1945 to 1960, legislation was introduced in Congress to reinstate food stamps. Each year the agriculture committees sidetracked it. President John Kennedy – who had confronted hunger while campaigning

Table 4.1 **USDA Food and Nutrition Programs for FY 1997**

Program	Description	1997 Actual (Dollars in Millions)
Food Stamp Program	Coupons for low-income people to purchase food in retail stores	$21,767
Nutrition Assistance for Puerto Rico	Cash and coupons for low-income people to purchase food in retail stores	1,174
Total, Food Stamp Program		22,941
Child Nutrition Programs	Increases low-income children's understanding of nutrition and improves their diet through programs such as School Lunch, School Breakfast, and Summer Food Service	8,965
Special Supp. Nutrition Program (WIC)	Coupons for high-nutrition food, health screening, and nutrition education for low-income, nutritionally vulnerable pregnant and nursing mothers, infants, and children up to age 5	4,039
Commodity Assistance Program: *Commodity Supp. Food Program (CSFP)*	Distributes commodities to people in need; Commodities for low-income elderly and women, infants, and children; WIC participants may not also participate in CSFP	93
Nutrition Program for the Elderly	Cash and commodities for senior citizens; served in senior centers or provided by meals-on-wheels programs	146
Soup Kitchens, Food Banks and The Emergency Food Assistance Program (TEFAP)	Commodities distributed to needy families	172
Gleaning Initiative	Food for needy households	0
WIC Farmers' Market Nutrition Program	Provides WIC participants access to fresh fruits and vegetables and expands the awareness and use of the farmers' markets	7
Total, Commodity Assistance Program		418
Total, Food and Nutrition Programs		**$36,363**

Source: United States Department of Agriculture (USDA), 1999 Budget Summary, 50, 51, 53

for the presidency, especially in West Virginia – started a pilot food stamp program through the Department of Agriculture.

The Food Stamp Program became permanent in 1964. Urban legislators voted for farm subsidies in exchange for farm state support for food stamps, most important in urban areas. That often fractious coalition has been an important ingredient in food politics ever since.

The 1964 legislation was a milestone, but many states did not participate. Participants had to have cash to buy stamps; the government help was a "bonus" added on top after the recipient's

financial outlay. This "purchase requirement" prevented many of the poorest people from participating. By 1970, 4.3 million people received food stamps at a cost of $577 million. It was a start. But fewer than one-fifth of people living in poverty received food stamps or commodities.[7]

Given the national concern about hunger and after careful political groundwork, a Democratic Congress and a Republican president, Richard Nixon, agreed in 1974 to national eligibility and benefit standards and required all states to make the stamps available. The money was federal. The administration was local.

The program exploded in size. By 1975 it served 17 million people, by 1980, 21 million. Large numbers of people gained basic nutritional support from what came to be called the "safety net under the safety net." Peak usage was almost 28 million in March 1994, and, according to the USDA, 22.9 million in FY 1997, costing $26.3 billion.

During the Carter administration a concerted effort to *E*liminate *P*urchase *R*equirements – lobbyists wore buttons saying EPR – came to fruition in 1977, making it much easier for those without cash to secure the food stamp benefits. But, this victory was part of a compromise. A cap was put on the amount of money that could be spent on food stamps in any year. It took until 1980 to get rid of the cap.

Other federal initiatives benefited hungry people in the 1970s. The School Lunch Program, which was begun in 1946, was strengthened (it served 300,000 children in 1968, 3 million in 1978) and given federal standards. So too was the School Breakfast Program.

The WIC – Special Supplemental Nutrition Program for Women, Infants and Children – Program got under way in 1972. It gained steam later in the decade. WIC provides high-nutrition food, medical attention and nutrition education to at-risk pregnant and nursing mothers, infants and children up to age 5. A much-quoted study found that every dollar spent on WIC for pregnant women saves up to $3.50 in Medicaid costs.

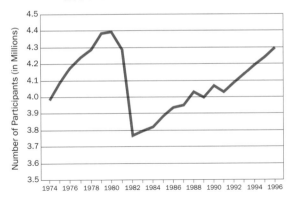

Figure 4.2 **School Lunch Program Participation, 1974–1996**

Source: USDA, Food and Nutrition Service, Oct. 1998

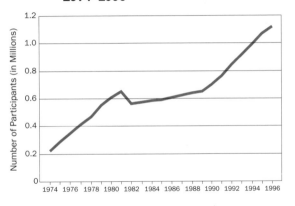

Figure 4.3 **School Breakfast Program Participation, 1974–1996**

Source: USDA, Food and Nutrition Service, Oct. 1998

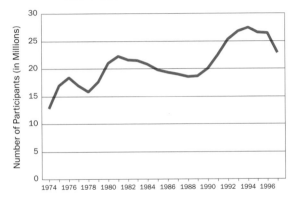

Figure 4.1 **Food Stamp Participants, 1974–1997**

Source: USDA, Food and Nutrition Service, Sept. 1998

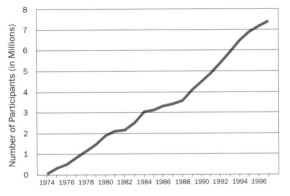

Figure 4.4 **Special Supplemental Nutrition Program (WIC) Average Monthly Participation, 1974–1997**

Source: USDA, Food and Nutrition Service, Sept. 1998

In 1977, 10 years after the Field Foundation funded the riveting 1967 report on hunger, it sent six teams of doctors to investigate conditions again. Their visit found "far fewer grossly malnourished people…than ten years ago." And the doctors added that "food stamps help more people today than any other social program except Social Security."[8]

In the early 1980s, the Reagan administration enacted severe cuts in all programs for poor people. One-third of the reductions in federal spending in 1981-1983 occurred in low-income programs that comprised 10 percent of the total budget. The harsh recession of 1981-1983 hit at the same time. Many people were poorly prepared to weather it. The result led to a dramatic growth in homelessness and voluntary feeding programs. The Food and Hunger Hotline in New York City knew of 30 emergency food providers in the city in 1980. They grew to 487 by 1987 and 730 by 1991.[9]

Approximately 150,000 soup kitchens, food banks and other private agencies provided an estimated $4 billion worth of groceries to hungry people nationwide each year. Through it all some members of Congress, often working in a bipartisan way, including Senators Patrick Leahy (D-VT), then chair of the Senate Agriculture Committee and Robert Dole (R-KS), then ranking minority member, joined to blunt some of the most egregious proposals to slash or end important social programs. School lunches were cut; business lunch tax deductions were not.

By mid-1983 the worst had ended. Political reaction to the ripped safety net was increasingly negative. The economy began a recovery. Congress refused to devolve block grants for food programs to the states. Food stamps had been cut by billions. But they still were a program administered by the states, paid for by the federal government, which maintained a national set of standards. Piece by piece some elements were restored, especially in the 1985 farm bill. Once more urban and rural representatives cooperated.

Federal initiatives strengthened the safety net from 1985 through 1994. The percentage of poor children covered by Medicaid went up from 15 percent to 23 percent. Supplemental Security Insurance (SSI – offering special help to disabled people) was made available to 800,000 more children. The expansion of the Earned Income Tax Credit (EITC, begun in the Reagan administration, reduces or eliminates taxes for many low-income working people and, in some cases of very low incomes, provides funds) helped lift several million children out of poverty. When the recession of 1990-1993 hit, low-income people weathered it much better than a decade earlier.[10]

To pull that off during the end of the Reagan administration and the beginning of Bush's took focus, determination and hard work by many people. President Bush's first budget called for a $21 billion cut in domestic programs, including WIC and other food programs. Using the slogan, "Keep WIC Lit," Bread for the World, the Center on Budget and Policy Priorities (CBPP), the Food Research and Action Center (FRAC) and other nonprofits initiated a national campaign. Citizens sent tens of thousands of candles to congressional offices. WIC got its biggest funding increase in five years, reaching 200,000 more people. Timely action can sometimes effect significant changes.

In late 1994, the Republican Party took control of both the House and the Senate for the first time in 40 years. Many of the newly elected members of Congress were eager to dismantle the welfare system as dysfunctional and counterproductive, and defund many programs serving poor people. "The 1994 elections led to a broad philosophical challenge to federal food programs," recalls Rob Fersh, director of FRAC for more than a decade.[11]

Once again Congress sought to make sharp cuts in federal food programs. Once again these programs were to be administered through block grants, removing federal standards. Once again coalitions formed around the country to protest the changes. Once again the largest changes were beaten back.

A story illustrates the battle. U.S. Rep. William Goodling (R-PA) had been a moderate supporter of food programs until he became the new chair of the Education and Workforce Committee in the Republican House. His committee targeted the school lunch and breakfast programs for cuts. Food providers from schools around the country – many brought together by the American School Food Service Association – organized to protest. They overwhelmed Goodling, those on the committee who agreed with him and their allies. That battle gained a name: "They were school lunched."

Then something happened that would have been unimaginable in the past half century. A Republican Congress and Democratic president passed the Personal Responsibility and Work Opportunity Reconciliation Act (PRWORA) in August 1996, which did indeed end welfare as we know it. The full implications of this change for welfare programs are discussed in Chapter 5.

Peter Edelman, who went to Mississippi with Robert Kennedy 30 years earlier, resigned from his position in the administration and wrote a cover story for the *Atlantic Monthly* called "The Worst Thing Bill Clinton Has Done." Edelman points out that PRWORA not only eliminated food stamps for 935,000 legal immigrants but also cut another $24 billion in food stamp expenditures over six years. Edelman argues: "Neither the cuts for immigrants nor the food-stamp cuts have anything to do with welfare."[12] The media, on the other hand, featured welfare-mom-turned-wage-earner stories and whatever the merits and demerits of the change, were winning the publicity war.

Boom for Whom?

The back-and-forth struggle over nutrition and anti-poverty programs has been waged against the backdrop of two decades of declining real wages for low-income workers. Economic growth is a necessary, but not sufficient, condition for reducing poverty, as prosperous times demonstrate.

As this is written, it is boom time in the United States. "The current economic performance…is as impressive as any I have witnessed in my near half-century of daily observations of the American economy," Alan Greenspan, chair of the Federal Reserve, declared in June 1998.[13]

"In the first quarter, unemployment was the lowest in 28 years," President Clinton said in April 1998, "inflation the lowest in 30 years, consumer confidence at its highest in 30

The distribution of gains and losses from the globalizing economy has political dimensions.

Massachusetts AFL-CIO

years…. We are living in an American economic renaissance in which opportunity is abundant, communities are getting stronger, families are more secure and more prosperous."

More than 16 million jobs were created during the five-plus years of the current administration (compared to 2.6 million in the previous four years). More people than ever – 66 percent of families – own their homes. Violent crime declined for the sixth straight year, the FBI announced in May 1998. The long-running game of budget chicken came to an end with the proposal for a balanced budget for FY 1999. Garnished with a hint of – could it be? – surpluses. They are apparently real, more than a $1.5 trillion in the next decade by some estimates. They are almost all part of the Social Security funds. Fiscal politics will remain vigorous – tax cuts or Social Security? – but perhaps less venomous.

Complex and difficult international problems persist, not least the Asian fiscal crisis and the expanding trade deficit. But the country confronts nothing like the Cold War or Vietnam or double-digit inflation. Instead, the United States must come to grips with a global economy that contributes to both increased economic growth and inequality for its people.[14] How do we understand this reality and the political challenge it poses?

Opportunity and Inequality in the Global Economy

The rising tide that Presidents Kennedy and Reagan often said would raise all boats was succeeding in the 1960s and part of the 1970s. More recently, it has hit our economic shore – lifting too few boats and leaving the American dream beyond the reach of many people. While our focus is on hunger, people who are poor are those most vulnerable to hunger. Since hunger data for the United States has, until recently, been piecemeal, the anti-hunger community has sometimes used poverty data as a surrogate for hunger numbers.

Poverty has not declined significantly. About 36.6 million people lived below the poverty line in 1996 (comprising 13.7 percent of the U.S. population, compared to 13.1 percent in 1989 and 11.7 percent in 1979).[15] Many families fall below the poverty line, which in 1997 was $12,515 for a family of three, $16,036 for a family of four. Those who rise above it by, say, $2,000 are hardly living in luxury.

Children are the hardest hit. In 1996 in the South and the West, 22.9 percent of children lived in poverty, "although most states in the regions have robust economies," said a 1998 CDF study.[16] The national average for children below the poverty line in 1996 was 20.5 percent. (It was 14 percent in 1969). That is 14.5 million children, almost three times the total population of Israel. Almost 25 percent of children under the age of 6 live in families below the poverty line, contrasted with France where the equivalent figure is 6 percent.[17]

Unlike previous U.S. economic expansions, poverty has not diminished significantly in recent years in spite of the strong growth of the late 1980s and mid-1990s. Economist Rebecca Blank worked as a senior staff person for the White House Council of Economic Advisers in 1989 and returned as a member of the council in 1998. She found that the Census Bureau figures for 1988, a year of solid growth, did not demonstrate any decline in poverty rates. Her boss told her to explain why in a report to President Bush.

> I dutifully went back to my desk, sat down at my computer, stared at it a while, and

realized I had no explanation to offer.... The apparent problem has become worse over the years.... [It is] one of the most discouraging facts for American social policy: an expanding economy no longer guarantees a decline in poverty.[18]

Wages have drifted downward for workers low on the totem pole in part because of technological changes in the workplace (consider ATMs and self-service gas stations), the increasing internationalization of the U.S. economy and weakened labor unions.

CAN'T WE BEGIN TO SEE THROUGH EYES OF A POOR CHILD?*

BY JIM SHIELDS

A few years ago, my child came home from school with an assignment to find pictures of tall buildings, cut them out and put them in a report.

We subscribe to the *Houston Chronicle*, *The New York Times* and several magazines, so my young student was excited about her homework. She knew she would do well. We have paper and scissors, glue and tape, all close at hand. My wife and I each have a car to go to the store to fill any unmet needs.

In my daughter's class was a student who came from a one-parent household. There were no newspapers or magazines in her house, or no school supplies. Her mother didn't have the disposable income (or even the time, for that matter) to help her child with the assignment. Moreover, there were more pressing needs, like where dinner was going to come from. On weekends, the child sold newspapers at a shopping center to supplement the family income. She was not excited about her homework assignment.

The next day in class, one student was praised for exceeding the requirements of the assignment and one student received yet another blow to her self-esteem for failing to complete such a simple task.

This trivial example, repeated in thousands of variations, day after day, takes a toll on children living in poverty.

JIM SHIELDS is a BFW activist in Houston, and a member of the Bread for the World Institute board.

* Reprinted from the *Houston Chronicle*, May 27, 1997.

The meaning of higher employment. In a stunning development, unemployment had dropped to 4.3 percent in April 1998, the lowest in 30 years. "Almost every demographic group had an easier time finding work," wrote *The New York Times*. That included teen-agers and high school dropouts. Good news indeed. And a hint that wages even for the lowest-paying jobs might be easing upward slightly. If so, that could finally mean a leveling, and perhaps a decrease, in poverty figures.

Low unemployment, real wage gains – up 4 percent for those in the lowest one-fifth of the male work force, 2.7 percent for women, from 1996 through March 1998 – and increased minimum wages led to an encouraging upward income trend for the poorest workers. At the same time cuts in health care and other benefits took a negative toll on workers' ability to cope.

Income inequality grows. Rich people in America are richer than at any time since World War II. Poor people are poorer. The United States, according to *Forbes*, had 13 billionaires in 1982; at last count it had 170. The wealthiest 1 percent of U.S. citizens in 1996 had more wealth than the bottom 90 percent combined, according to the Internal Revenue Service. The share of national income accruing to the top 5 percent of households rose to 21.4 percent in 1996, the highest level in the 50 years the Census Bureau has recorded this figure.[19]

AFL-CIO President John Sweeney and American Federation of Teachers President Sandra Feldman join workers at a rally for a livable wage.

Figure 4.5 **U.S. Income Distribution, 1997**

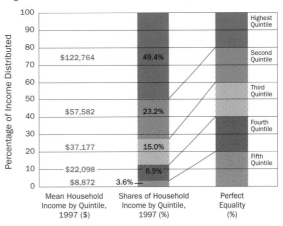

Source: U.S. Bureau of Census, March 1998, Current Population Survey.

The lowest 20 percent received 3.7 percent of national income in 1996. Put it another way: since the mid-1970s the income of the richest fifth of U.S. citizens has grown by 30 percent; the income level of the poorest fifth has fallen by 21 percent.

In fact, the share of income received by the bottom 80 percent was close to an all-time low. And for the bottom 60 percent it has declined steadily since 1974. One dramatic illustration of the change: The average chief executive officer of a major corporation received 34 times the earnings of the average worker in 1965. Today it is about 212 times as much.[20] Which probably does not include Disney's Michael Eisner, whose total 1996 compensation was $565 million, almost 13,500 times the $43,300 earned by an average family in 1996.[21] Income inequality in the United States is wider than in any of 14 western industrial countries.[22] The British magazine, *The Economist*, comments: "The gap between rich and poor, skilled and unskilled, [in the United States] remains far wider than a civilized country should accept."[23]

Microsoft's Bill Gates' stake in his company's stock reached $47.8 billion early in 1998 (which equals the net financial worth of the lowest 40 percent of Americans).[24] The typical middle-class family had no more than $20,000 in stocks and mutual funds in 1995.[25] Even if the bull market doubled that amount, the gap between the rich and the typical family remains the same. And, it is not hard to trace the connection between wealth and political influence.

Give me shelter. More than 5 million poor families live in grossly substandard housing, or spend more than half their income on shelter. They represent 12.5 million people – 4.5 million children, 1.4 million elderly and as many as 1.4 million adults with disabilities.

Joyce Scott, a mother of three living in Baltimore, has been on a list to secure federally funded housing for 15 years. Scott's rent is $386 a month (low for an urban area). She is employed full-time and earns $6 an hour. Scott makes above minimum wage and her total of $11,000 a year (if she works all 52 weeks) falls $5,000 below the poverty line. Imagine raising three children on $210 a week and paying $4,632 a year in rent. "I am just trying to make ends meet," she says.[26]

Conservative estimates suggest that at least 750,000 people are homeless on a given night. Some estimates – they vary widely – put in the millions the number of those homeless at some time during the year. For people in these circumstances, the political and policy crisis is right now.

Health coverage is uneven. In 1996 about 41.3 million citizens under 65 (those older are eligible for Medicare) had no medical insurance, up from 33 million in 1989.[27] The number of children covered by Medicaid fell by 1 million – from 16.3 million to 15.3 million – from 1995 to 1996. Several million of those without health coverage are workers who cannot afford the premiums on the insurance their employers do make available.[28]

Millions Lifted Above the Poverty Line by Federal Programs

Last year's hunger report, *Hunger in a Global Economy*, outlined feasible changes to make the global economy work better for hungry people. These include the attachment of a labor rights provision to international trade agreements, for example, and increased effort to make sure that every child gets a good education. Federal nutrition and anti-poverty programs also help, contradicting much propaganda to the contrary.

Government "should see to it that no one is without food, clothing and shelter," said 72 percent of those polled in 1998 by the Pew

Table 4.2 **Number of People Living Below the Poverty Line, 1997 (in thousands)**

People	Number	Percent
White	24,396	11.0
White, not Hispanic	16,491	8.6
Black	9,116	26.5
Asian and Pacific Islander	1,468	14.0
Hispanic origin	8,308	27.1
Total	**35,574**	**13.3**
Region		
Northeast	6,474	12.6
Midwest	6,493	10.4
South	13,748	14.6
West	8,858	14.6

Source: U.S. Bureau of Census, March 1998, Current Population Survey

Research Center for the People and the Press, the same figure as in the 1960s. Most people just do not think the government is effective in delivering its social programs. Sixty-four percent expressed "frustration" (those "angry" were a much lower percentage) with the government's performance, finding it "inefficient and wasteful."[29]

Big public bureaucracies are often cumbersome, and government programs have their downsides. Some people who could work do not. But government programs do, in fact, reduce poverty. Twenty-seven million people were lifted above the poverty line in 1996 by federal safety net programs. That cut the number of those still below the line almost in half, leaving 30.5 million people.[30]

Social Security alone reduced the proportion of elderly people living below the line from 50 percent to about 12 percent in 1996. One in three children that would have fallen below the line was removed from poverty by the programs, especially the Earned Income Tax Credit (EITC). If crossing the poverty line is a modest enough achievement, some hopeful developments emerge. In the years between 1989 and 1997, the increased minimum wage and the EITC raised the income of working single mothers with two children from $9,850 to $13,950 a year, a dramatic 42 percent jump.[31]

The federal programs have kept the worst from happening in the lives of many people. Federal, state and local governments, as well as the private sector, could produce more ways to help the best to happen – jobs that pay a living wage, education that educates, health care that promotes well-being, safe housing that does not bankrupt.

The Politics of Anxiety

Much of the domestic politics of the past 25 years has been built around the understandable anxieties of large numbers of Americans and the exploitation of those fears by political and economic forces. The problems outlined above are only a sampling of things that produce fertile soil for agitation or resignation.

Politicians at all levels used the "issues of race and taxes [to foster] the creation of a middle-class, anti-government, property holding, conservative identification among key white voters," political observers Thomas and Mary Edsall have written. Ironically, many of the people swept up into this new political reality did not profit from "tax cuts skewed in favor of those at the top of the income distribution – from the $749 billion 1981 tax cut to continuing efforts to do away with the capital gains tax."[32]

The political process has been distorted deeply by the hundreds of millions of dollars that flow into political campaigns. A lot of that buys television time that shapes public perceptions (see Chapter 3). Most legislation favors vested interests. Money also creates access that the poor do not have. "You can't buy my senator and you can't buy me," a chief aide to a top senator once said in my presence.

> But when the Senate is in session, I often get 100 phone calls to return in a day. I can't do that physically. If you are a campaign donor, I will get back to you. I'll try to get back to Bread for the World or Children's Defense Fund. I will get back to a donor.

For too long now civil disagreement over ideas has not been part of the political coin. One participant said in a 1993 political seminar in Washington:

> The comments that are most successful today are those that are pointed, that are

sharp, that are memorable, and that might make your opponent something of a laughing stock…. Logical arguments don't very often win the day.[33]

In the late 1960s and the early 1970s, conservative activists and intellectuals decided to create a set of institutions to champion their ideas in the public arena and combat think tanks like the Brookings Institution. It was led by people such as Paul Weyrich – who named the Moral Majority, founded the Heritage Foundation and then created the Free Congress Foundation, which started the National Empowerment Television cable network – and Irving Kristol, former leftist intellectual now known as the "godfather of neoconservatives." Corporate and conservative foundation money was merged with think tanks to provide the ammunition for the war of ideas.[34]

From places like the Heritage Foundation (a major player in dismantling welfare), the Free Congress Foundation (a major player in turning the courts to the right) and the Rutherford Foundation (the law group behind Paula Jones' legal work) have come a stream of concepts aimed at changing the terms and rhetoric of U.S. political debate.

Part of the static from the war of ideas has been to make people think that big government is now the monster that lurks in the darkness. An election night poll in 1994 showed that those canvassed thought either welfare or foreign aid was the biggest item in the federal budget. In fact together they are just about 3 percent, far behind such items as defense (18 percent) and interest on the debt (15 percent).[35] These inaccurate public perceptions, fueled by the dramatic shift in political discourse, have fundamentally reshaped debate about federal anti-poverty and social programs.

The New Realities of Federal Hunger Politics

Modest expenditures on federal safety-net programs have helped millions to move above the poverty line. Those who made it possible – the people, the activists, the politicians, the public policy groups, the community organizations,

BY REBEKAH JORDAN

In 1974, the average cost of a U.S. Senate campaign was estimated at $450,000. Today it has increased tenfold to $4.5 million! Many people warn that money's influence in our electoral process is distorting government policies. Senator Wendell Ford (D-KY) announced his retirement in 1997 after 23 years of public service, stating that he did not want to have to "raise $100,000 a week starting today for the next year."[1]

The source of money also concerns many people. Reform groups find that corporations and wealthy individuals give tens of millions of dollars to political parties each election cycle.[2] A recent study found that individuals who contributed $200 or more to congressional candidates were an overwhelmingly homogeneous and affluent group:

> Ninety-five percent of the contributors were white. Eighty percent were men. Eighty percent were over the age of 45, and nearly half were over 60...81 percent had annual family incomes higher than $100,000... 20 percent...had annual incomes higher than $500,000.[3]

Poor and hungry people lack not only economic resources but the political power to represent their interests. How can they influence policy to meet their urgent needs when they can only offer their voices compared to the millions of dollars others are using?

Officials who accept contributions yet do not want to grant donor favors inevitably feel pressure to do so. Some officials have found it harder to get re-elected when they have supported legislation on its merits, rather than acceding to donor wishes. Elected officials who rely on large donors will prioritize meeting with them over anyone else, including their own constituents (see Chapter 4, p. 65). Before the 1996 presidential race, experts estimated that a viable candidate for office needed to raise at least $20 million, or $54,794 a day for a full year before the election. Is our political system equitable if a candidate must raise more money a day than most Americans earn in a year? Pouring torrents of money into election campaigns is no way to build democracy.

It may be no coincidence that, in the words of the watchdog group, Common Cause, "The most costly campaign in history – $2 billion for federal races [in 1996] alone – produced the lowest voter turnout since the 1920s."[4]

The current trend in excessive contributions has roots in the 1970s. According to another watchdog group, Public Citizen:

> The Federal Election Commission made a series of rulings that allowed the parties to collect *unlimited* contributions from corporations, labor unions, and wealthy individuals.[5]

While the intent was to permit contributions for "party-building activities" such as voter registration and get-out-the-vote drives, these "soft money" contributions have been used to promote candidates for election.

During 1995-1996, soft money contributions came to $260 million, more than triple the total raised in 1992.[6] "Of that amount, $214 million was from corporations and wealthy individuals."[7]

The increase in soft money has been accompanied by yet another loophole, the so-called "phony issue ads," which "are exempt from the financing limitations and disclosure provisions of federal

PROMOTE PARTICIPATION IN FAIR, DEMOCRATIC, PARTICIPATORY STRUCTURES AT ALL LEVELS: THE RIGHT TO VOTE, THE RIGHT TO ORGANIZE, FAIR FINANCING OF ELECTIONS

election law."[8] Instead of focusing on issues as required, such ads are barely concealed messages in support of or opposition to specific candidates. About $75 million was spent on phony issue ads by business, labor, environmental and other groups in the 1996 election cycle.[9]

Many advocates say that for real reform to be effective it must both tackle soft money and close the loophole on issue ads, because closing only the soft money loophole will simply result in more money going toward the phony issue ads.[10]

Common Cause and other groups across the United States advocate for campaign finance reform in a nonpartisan manner. They encourage citizens to press elected officials because without pressure from the electorate, those favored by the system have no incentive to reform it. As Rep. Sue Collins (R-ME) said when the House of Representatives did not consider the Shays-Meehan campaign finance reform bill in March of 1998, "There is not enough grassroots anger about this issue."[11]

REBEKAH JORDAN, former research assistant with Bread for the World, is currently a student at Central College, Pella, IA.

[1] *Congressional Quarterly*, March 15, 1997, 660.

[2] "Party Favors," Common Cause, 1998.

[3] Study by the Joyce Foundation of Chicago, cited by Bob Herbert, "The Donor Class," *New York Times*, July 19, 1998.

[4] Common Cause, "Campaign Finance Reform," undated.

[5] "Soft Money = Special Access," by Public Citizen's Congress Watch, undated.

[6] Common Cause, "The Shays-Meehan Bill," undated.

[7] "Soft Money = Special Access," by Public Citizen's Congress Watch, undated.

[8] Ibid.

[9] Annenberg Public Policy Center, cited by Common Cause in "The Shays-Meehan Bill," undated.

[10] Steve Weissman, Legislative Representative for Public Citizen, personal communication, August 17, 1998.

[11] Helen Dewar, "Petition Drive May be Last Hope for Campaign Reform," *Washington Post*, April 1, 1998.

the religious congregations, the labor unions, the shifting political coalitions – should be gratified. Yet those most deeply engaged – in a small town, in an urban ghetto, in a Washington advocacy office – know viscerally how inadequate it all is. Each of the programs – food, housing, Medicaid, fuel subsidies, others – could be much improved, and reach many more people who deserve help.

The diverse community working to address these issues would like much more, of course. They dream of a nation that values the common good sufficiently to construct a society that provides nearly all people with the tools, the work and the income to make such programs unnecessary. They dream of a social safety net for those who – because of disability, for example, or age – are really unable to work for a living. That is the broader political vision for which most strive.

Many of those involved in this political constituency recognize their limited ability to influence public debate on hunger issues. Janet Poppendieck, a Hunter College professor, in *Sweet Charity? Emergency Food and the End of Entitlement*, describes with admiration the efforts of tens of thousands of people that provide food for those who need it. But she worries about the implications of that effort. "My argument, in short, is that this massive charitable endeavor serves to relieve pressure for more fundamental solutions." Then she turns to the broader society:

> The problem is there is not a powerful social movement for justice and equality, for efforts to eliminate poverty in this society and seriously reduce inequality, and without such a movement, what advocates can accomplish…is severely limited. In fact, as we have seen, the contemporary "hunger lobby" was not only not powerful enough to forestall a punitive and damaging welfare reform, it was not even powerful enough to preserve intact the Food Stamp Program.[36]

These painful political realities have compelled a number of organizations to explore effective alliances for political advocacy. That is why key national anti-hunger organizations –

The anti-hunger movement seeks new approaches. In the nation's capital, DC Central Kitchen, a private organization, trains formerly homeless persons for careers in the food service industry.

These anti-hunger organizations rallied support for the Hunger Has A Cure bill, which called for increased funding of WIC, food stamps for those with high shelter costs and more support for summer meals programs. It also called for restoring food stamps to the legal immigrants who lost them in 1996. The coalition helped win restorations to the nutrition programs of about $3 billion in 1997 and 1998.

"The most remarkable achievement of organized anti-hunger advocacy in the United States is its persistence since 1970 despite the fickleness of public interest," argues Pat Kutzner, longtime director of the World Hunger Education Service.[37]

The anti-hunger lobby has won some and lost some. Because of their efforts, far fewer people are hungry than would be otherwise. That is not a revolution. But it helps. That proximate goal takes tenacity, energy, patience and courage. And it nudges the society toward greater justice for all.

For the future, the challenge is to redirect middle-class anxieties from attacks on poor and minority groups toward insistence on a more broadly shared prosperity.

One element in this process must be intellectual, just as one element in the attack on anti-poverty programs has been the work of intellectuals and think tanks. We need fresh policy initiatives to overcome hunger and poverty and new ways of making the case for them.

including Bread for the World, the Center on Budget and Policy Priorities, the Food Research and Action Center, RESULTS, Second Harvest, Tufts University's Center on Hunger, Poverty, and Nutrition Policy and World Hunger Year – and several state and regional anti-hunger groups – joined in 1990 to form the Medford Group. This group re-energized public leadership against hunger by issuing *The Medford Declaration to End Hunger in the U.S.* (see Chapter 7, p. 91), which argued that an expansion of the national nutrition programs could quickly end virtually all domestic hunger. The Medford Declaration also called for more far-reaching changes to improve the job prospects for low-income people.

A wide array of anti-hunger organizations now coordinate their advocacy efforts. In 1997, the Medford Group and many other organizations joined together for the "Hunger Has A Cure" campaign. They supported federal legislation to restore crucial funding for the national nutrition programs. They also coordinated efforts to strengthen advocacy on welfare reform issues at the state-government level, expand private charities' capacities to assist people in need and explore policies to improve the job market for low-income workers.

Senator Patrick Leahy (D-VT)

"Hunger is a moral issue," Vermont's Senator Leahy (and former Bread for the World board member) says in most of his public appearances. The great Christian ethicist Reinhold Niebuhr emphasized that the fate of those in need could not be held hostage to the whims of the rich. The Bible, he said, demands that political structures produce justice. The time is now. The need is great.

LEON HOWELL, former editor of *Christianity and Crisis* magazine, is a freelance writer and editor.

BY SHOHREH KERMANI PETERSON

In 1998, Tampa Bay anti-hunger leaders convinced county commissioners to appoint and fund a blue-ribbon task force on hunger, including low-income people. This first-ever task force was formed because the activists prepared and published a booklet on hunger in Tampa Bay, complete with children's drawings and local hunger data.

In Portland, ME, anti-hunger leaders, working with the Maine Coalition Against Hunger, organized Portland's first Food Festival to educate the community about hunger, nutrition and the impact of public policy; and they formed a food co-op to educate and engage people in public policy and advocacy.

High school students in Phoenix drew up a bill to end hunger and gained support for it from their state legislators. The H.R. 2004 Resolution, the

SUPPORT THE
EMPOWERMENT
EFFORTS OF
POOR PEOPLE,
ESPECIALLY
WOMEN

first of its kind, was passed unanimously by the Arizona House of Representatives in 1996, and the Governor appointed one of the students from this low-income community to the state's hunger committee.

The Hunger Task Force of Milwaukee is pulling together the first statewide Transforming Hunger coalition. The Task Force created 15 grassroots networks to fight hunger locally and statewide. Groups in Montana and Kansas are drawing on the Wisconsin model.

New Orleans' anti-hunger leaders worked closely with Loyola University to develop the first comprehensive study on the impact of hunger in their city. The study was widely disseminated among academic, public and private sectors.

All these people are part of Bread for the World Institute's Transforming Anti-Hunger Leadership (TAHL) program. Leadership training helps people move beyond being "doers" to

become "leaders" – that is, people who mobilize others to make a difference in their communities. The TAHL program has made diversity, local autonomy and coalition-building hallmarks of its strategy.

Local autonomy is a key grassroots capacity-building strategy. It helps empower participants and ensures local ownership and sustainability of projects.

Building on Diversity

The TAHL program has had considerable success in cultivating race and income diversity among anti-hunger leaders. Creating and maintaining diverse teams takes effort – lots of effort. Groups that have not worked together in the past learn to accept differences and find new ways to build on the strengths that different points of view and life experiences bring to the table.

Successful leadership teams emphasize "relationship-based associations" – to relate as colleagues and friends, not as helpers and recipients – and attempt to level the playing field by rotating meeting places and providing support (e.g., child care, transportation) for low-income participants.

Once established, TAHL leadership teams identify the most critical food security needs in their communities and develop a response. They develop training strategies to build skills – such as advocacy, working with the media and fundraising – necessary to carry out their strategies.

In 1995-1996 TAHL projects tended to be city-wide and their advocacy efforts mostly local and national in scope. With the passage of the welfare law of 1996 and the ensuing devolution, most TAHL teams have shifted their strategies to state-level coalition building. TAHL teams frequently seek to strengthen and link together direct service and anti-hunger advocacy at the local, state, regional and national levels. In the process, the TAHL program is developing an evolving and dynamic capacity-building model that helps bolster anti-hunger initiatives by low-income people across the United States.

SHOHREH KERMANI PETERSON is a program coordinator, along with Niloufer De Silva, of the TAHL program with Bread for the World Institute. E-mail: TAHL@bread.org

BY ELENA MCCOLLIM

The United States reaffirms the right of every person in this country and throughout the world to food and a nutritionally adequate diet.

– THE RIGHT-TO-FOOD RESOLUTION, ADOPTED IN THE U.S. CONGRESS, SEPTEMBER, 1976.

Bread for the World was launched 25 years ago in the wake of the early 1970s famines and the 1974 World Food Conference in Rome, itself a response to the world food crisis. Arthur Simon, a Lutheran pastor working in New York's Lower East Side, gathered a group of Protestant and Roman Catholic clergy and laity to mobilize a national movement against hunger.

Two years and a quarter-million letters from constituents later, the U.S. Congress had passed the Right-to-Food Resolution. A year after that, in response to Bread's second letter-writing campaign, Congress created the Farmer Owned Grain Reserve.

In 1979, Bread's third campaign was instrumental in President Carter's decision to establish a Presidential Commission on World Hunger. Its findings led three years later to reforms targeting U.S. and multilateral aid to the poorest people in developing countries.

The Offering of Letters, as Bread for the World's main letter campaign each year is called, is the spine of the organization's work. Groups of people, usually a religious congregation, offer letters to their congressional representatives as part of their Christian witness. Through the offering Bread mobilizes people to lobby for the interests of hungry and poor people. Bread for the World's campaigns result sometimes in complete, sometimes partial victories; sometimes in policy statements; more often in tangible, quantifiable gains in funding and programs that benefit hungry and poor people in the United States and abroad. In a typical year, Bread members organize from 800 to 1,000 letter-writing events and generate an estimated 90,000 to 100,000 letters.

Some Bread for the World members participate in telephone trees, called Quicklines. Bread also uses Action Alerts, directed to all members within a key district. In 1998, Senate leadership was blocking an agricultural research bill from reaching the floor for a vote. The reason? The bill included approximately $818 million for restoring food stamps to 250,000 legal immigrants – children, elderly and disabled people. Bread activists and others organized Quicklines and propelled the bill to a vote. The measure won overwhelmingly and was signed into law in June of that year.

The experience also illustrates the importance of Bread for the World's collaboration with coalitions. Bread worked not only with its usual coalition partners – other anti-hunger and religious organizations – but also with farmers' groups.

From its inception, Bread for the World based its action on analysis of the systems that cause hunger. In the mid- and late 1970s, the first oil shock of 1973 had catapulted the Organization of Petroleum Exporting Countries (OPEC) to prominence (or notoriety), dragging the developing countries with it. At the fourth U.N. Conference on Trade and Development (UNCTAD) meeting in 1974, the developing countries called for a New International Economic Order (NIEO), based on an understanding that underdevelopment is chiefly caused by declining terms of trade – that is, the gap between the money earned from exporting raw materials and the cost of importing finished goods from the North.

Bread focused on the NIEO, without endorsing it, and criticized foreign aid for its potential to induce dependency and to advance the military goals of the Cold War. Bread advocated aid to promote self-reliance, and was an early supporter of the International Fund for Agricultural Development (IFAD), a U.N. agency founded in 1978 (as an outgrowth of the 1974 World Food Conference) that focuses on small farmers and rural development.

The changed political context of the early 1980s, nationally and internationally, forced Bread to devote much energy to reactive strategies. Domestically, its 1982 offering, *Preventing Hunger at Home*, opposed funding cuts in nutrition programs. As Leon Howell chronicles (see Chapter 4), many battles to prevent cuts or restore funding had to be fought again and again in those years.

In 1982-1983, Bread's work was pivotal in establishing the Child Survival Fund (providing funding for child immunization and other health programs) as part of the 1984 foreign aid package. Although the fund initially received $25 million – half the original request – lobbying by Bread and others eventually raised the funding to $100 million. Beyond the Child Survival Fund, Bread's 1983-1984 offering won increases to basic health, water and education programs.

Bread also turned its attention to specific regional priorities: in the context of the Central American wars, it advocated land reform in El Salvador, and introduced into the Caribbean Basin Initiative (an effort to foster a free trade zone in the Caribbean and Central America) safeguards to keep export production of beef and sugar from taking land away from local consumption.

The devastating African famine of the mid-1980s propelled Bread into heightened activity. With other organizations, Bread played a key role in bringing the famine before public attention. In the late 1980s, Bread was seminal in ensuring IFAD's survival. Domestically, Bread had long been a supporter of WIC, the Special Supplemental Nutrition Program for Women, Infants and Children. In 1987-1988, a time of severe budget-cutting, the efforts of Bread and others won a $133 million increase for WIC (see Chapter 4, p. 60).

As the Cold War ended, Bread was an early proponent of a peace dividend. Its 1990 offering urged military spending cuts, with half the savings directed to reduce the federal deficit and half to help overcome hunger and poverty. Despite a 3 percent annual reduction in U.S. military spending, Bread continued to press for deeper cuts. The *Horn of Africa Recovery and Food Security Act*, signed into law in 1992, highlighted the connections between the Cold War and famine in Africa. The law has made it illegal for the United States to give aid to dictators in Ethiopia, Sudan and Somalia. At the same time, it has allowed vital aid to grassroots organizations despite unpaid debts from prior regimes.

In 1992 and 1993, Bread for the World helped win substantial funding increases for WIC, Head Start, Job Corps and the Earned Income Tax Credit (EITC). But as Congress changed dramatically in 1994, Bread shifted back to a defensive posture – trying to keep people from losing WIC or food stamp benefits, and minimizing cuts in aid to Africa.

Bread sought to break away from the old patterns of Cold War foreign aid and build a coalition of religious, development and environmental groups in support of aid for sustainable development.

With the arrival of David Beckmann as president, in 1991 Bread expanded its work to build the

Kathleen S. Daugherty

BFW President David Beckmann addresses rally on the occasion of the 1997 welfare reform's enactment.

overall constituency for efforts to reduce hunger and poverty. Bread for the World especially encouraged assistance agencies, both domestic and international, to expand their involvement in advocacy. One result was the Transforming Anti-Hunger Leadership program (TAHL, see "Anti-Hunger Leaders Make A Difference," p. 69), which has nurtured coalitions of local anti-hunger activists and organizations making the connections between service provision and public policy advocacy.

The 1990s also saw the emergence of the Development Bank Watchers' Project (see Chapter 2, p. 44), which monitors the World Bank and lobbies bank and U.S. administration officials, as well as congressional representatives serving on banking-related committees. The project monitors implementation of policy reforms to ensure that well-intentioned legislation does not remain a dead letter. Bank Watchers and TAHL alike promote the goal of increasing the participation of ordinary citizens – both North and South – in policy decisions affecting them.

As Arthur Simon points out (see p. 15), Bread has not been immune to errors in judgment or lack of foresight. Bread for the World has often had to accept "half a loaf," even while arguing for a whole one.

Recurring touchstone themes have remained central to Bread's thinking and doing. These include: self-help and jobs; political empowerment of hungry people; reducing discrimination against women and people of color; curtailing military spending and redirecting development towards basic needs. Most of all, Bread has consistently respected the creativity and determination of poor people, and the power of grassroots citizens to help overcome hunger.

ELENA MCCOLLIM is a policy analyst with Bread for the World Institute. E-mail: emccollim@bread.org

CHAPTER 5

THE CHANGING POLITICS OF U.S. WELFARE POLICY

BY LYNETTE ENGELHARDT

The political tilt toward smaller government and individual self-reliance described in Chapter 4 has had a profound impact on the United States' approach to social welfare. Legacies of Franklin Roosevelt's administration have made way for new approaches whose effectiveness is still being tested. This chapter examines the history of the federal welfare program, Aid to Families with Dependent Children (AFDC) and its replacement by the Temporary Assistance for Needy Families (TANF) program. The chapter also looks at the changeover's early effects.

Supporters and critics alike acknowledge that the previous welfare system needed reform. They differed – and still do – on the shape reform should take. Whether the new system works remains an open question.

Welfare Policy, 1932 and 1992

The presidential elections of 1932 and 1992 and the congressional elections of 1994 helped usher in radically new welfare policies in the United States. Franklin Delano Roosevelt's landslide victory in 1932 was rooted in voters' anger at President Hoover's seeming lack of response to the Great Depression. Citizens saw what Roosevelt had accomplished as governor of New York and wanted him to do the same for the nation.

In 1935, under Roosevelt's leadership, Congress passed the Social Security Act, establishing the federal government's commitment to provide a safety net for elderly and unemployed people. A landmark cash assistance program, Aid to Dependent Children, was also created for needy children.[1]

Sixty years later, in 1992, another governor who campaigned to reform welfare policy – Bill Clinton – was elected president of the United States.

In 1996, President Clinton signed into law watershed legislation abolishing the federal cash assistance program – Aid to Families with Dependent Children (AFDC) – and replacing it with the Temporary Assistance for Needy Families (TANF) block grant to the states.

Public Opinion, Campaign Promises and Electoral Politics

A principal goal of Aid to Dependent Children was to allow widows and other single mothers to stay at home and care for their children. But in the late 1960s and 1970s, as economic shifts pushed more mothers into the workplace, public attitudes changed. The Work Incentive Program (WIN) of 1967 required parents on welfare to work. But WIN was never adequately funded and failed in moving many welfare recipients into employment.

Congress again attempted to move welfare recipients into work with the Family Support Act (FSA) of 1988. This legislation required mothers with children over age 3 to participate in a program of education, employment and training. But Congress did not adequately fund the program and this attempt failed as well.[2]

The Federal government's lack of political will to provide adequate funding for employment and training did not change. What changed was Congress's willingness to balance the budget largely at the expense of poor people. The rhetoric of the preceding two decades had become rife with attacks on low-income people. Growing income inequality and declining middle- and low-income wages helped create an audience receptive to scapegoating, e.g., the characterization of poor people as lazy "welfare queens" (see Chapter 4, pp. 60-61).[3] And many people of varying political persuasions increasingly doubted the effectiveness of government programs, especially welfare. Some welfare recipients themselves were dissatisfied with AFDC (see "Recollections of Child on Welfare," p. 80) and called for changes.

Campaigning in New Hampshire in the fall of 1991, presidential hopeful Bill Clinton hit a popular chord when he promised to "end welfare as we know it." Clinton and his campaign advisers recognized that many voters felt welfare had failed at what they believed should be its main goal – moving low-income people into jobs.

The White House drafted a welfare bill in the summer of 1994. Clinton's proposal invested more than previously in education and training for welfare recipients and required people to work within two years of enrolling in order to continue receiving benefits. Under the Clinton proposal, recipients unable to find employment after two years would be given an opportunity for a subsidized job.

However, the mid-term congressional elections of 1994 brought Republicans into the majority in both houses of Congress. The Clinton administration's welfare bill was supplanted by new Republican proposals.

Determined to balance the budget via spending cuts, over the next year and a half Congress sent two welfare bills to the president. Calling the measures punitive and harmful to children, he vetoed both. By the summer of 1996, with the presidential election just months away, a third and similar bill – the Personal Responsibility and Work Opportunity Reconciliation Act (PRWORA) – was sent to the president.

This proposal abolished AFDC and ended the federal guarantee of income assistance. In its place, TANF provided a lump-sum block grant to the states. The proposal also cut other anti-poverty programs, including nutrition programs, by $54 billion over six years. The bill imposed a five-year lifetime limit on receipt of federal welfare benefits – but allowed states to set an even stricter time limit – and required recipients to start work in two years or lose benefits.

Clinton's political advisers worried the president would suffer at the polls if he did not sign a welfare reform bill.[4] Top welfare policy advisers anticipated devastating effects on low-income people, particularly children, if he did sign. Secretary of Health and Human Services (HHS) Donna Shalala told the president an HHS analysis of the bill predicted more than 1 million children would be pushed into poverty and 8 million families with children would lose income if it was enacted.

A broad coalition of low-income people, advocates, social service organizations and religious groups (including Bread for the World) opposed

BY PEGGY THOMAS

I was homeless for four years, but I never identified with being homeless. I was living in a camp trailer in the woods, and I did volunteer work at a local shelter. Then someone referred to me as homeless – and it came as a real shock to me to realize that I actually was homeless. No one wants to think of themselves as homeless, because homeless people are not an acceptable part of society. So for a week I walked around mad at everyone because I finally realized why people treat me so badly. At that point, the issue became really personal, really fast.

Most low-income people feel excluded from society, and a lot of them have no trust that anything will be accomplished by government processes.

But they should become active as citizens. Do it, because your effort really does count for something. You are an important part of the community, and you can make a difference in it. When you get tired of being a rug, get up.

What social service providers often end up doing is controlling persons, not helping them. They are into teaching us how to cook, clean and budget, as if nothing we do is good enough. If they taught members of Congress how to budget, our country would not be in the mess we are in.

PEGGY THOMAS, a low-income woman in Eugene, Oregon who serves on several county boards that deal with human needs, participates in Bread for the World Institute's Transforming Anti-Hunger Leaders (TAHL) Program.

the welfare bill. Tens of thousands of letters and telephone calls flooded Congress and the White House condemning the proposal.

But on August 22, 1996, in a Rose Garden ceremony, President Bill Clinton signed the bill into law. He promised to seek restorations of those parts that denied most federal benefits to legal immigrants and that cut the Food Stamp Program.

Bread for the World and other advocates focused on those restorations and secured some important changes. In 1997, Medicaid benefits and Supplemental Security Income (SSI provides support to aged, blind and disabled persons in need) were restored for some legal immigrants.[5] States were given additional money to help TANF recipients find jobs. In the summer of 1998 Congress restored food stamp benefits to 250,000 of the 935,000 legal immigrants who lost the benefits under the 1996 welfare law (see "Bread for the World: Twenty-Five Years," p. 70). Immigrants' access to the food stamps benefits became effective in November 1998.

A New Politics of Devolution

The welfare law of 1996 mirrored a global trend toward decentralization of government. People throughout the world are demanding greater local control over the programs and policies that concern them. In the United States, many felt welfare programs would be more effective if states and local governments had greater control.

Between 1992 and 1996, the Bush and Clinton administrations had granted waivers to 43 states so they could experiment with running welfare programs.[6] During the welfare reform debates of the early 1990s, some governors argued they could run the programs better than the federal government. They pushed for devolution – a transfer of policy responsibilities from the federal government to state and local governments.

The Personal Responsibility Act gave the governors increased flexibility in determining eligibility and work requirements in exchange for a block grant with capped federal funding. The fixed funding level also gave states an incentive to cut costs by removing people from their caseloads as quickly as possible.

Today, a second-level devolution of welfare is occurring in many states, with responsibility being passed to the county and city levels. A few states are contracting out selected welfare services to the private sector.

State Advocacy: Alabama Arise

The new welfare law requires advocates for low-income people to focus much more attention at the state level. The already overstrained forces of the anti-hunger movement now must lobby for constructive policies in Washington and 50 state capitals. The degree and level of advocacy in the states vary widely. Advocates in a few states have found it difficult to push for positive state legislation because their state legislatures do not even meet every year.

Advocates in Alabama made some positive changes to their state's welfare plan. A key reason was that they had already built an effective state-level advocacy organization called Alabama Arise. When it seemed likely that Congress would pass a welfare reform bill in 1996, Alabama Arise – a coalition of 115 religious and community groups fighting poverty – began mobilizing a grassroots campaign.

The coalition hosted listening sessions around the state, asking welfare recipients what they needed to move from welfare to work. From these sessions a position paper was written. Alabama Arise produced fact sheets and studies analyzing the need for affordable, quality child care, transportation and adequate benefit levels.[7]

Kimble Forrister, Alabama Arise's state coordinator, was appointed to the governor's commission on welfare reform and advocated policies to help people move into work.[8] When the Alabama Department of Human Resources (DHR) held public hearings across the state, Alabama Arise was always invited to participate.

Alabama Arise worked to ensure that low-income people attended each DHR public forum. At one hearing in Huntsville, a teenage mother told state officials that she had complied with DHR's rules and moved back in with her mother after delivering her baby. But when the state assessed her case, officials counted her mother's income and cut off her welfare benefits. Unable to afford child care, the young woman was forced to drop out of high school. DHR later passed regulations to provide child care benefits to teenage mothers in order to enable them to finish school.

Alabama Arise lobbied intensely during the three-month Alabama 1997 legislative session. At one point the Alabama benefit level was increased from the second lowest in the country to the average for the southeastern region – a $51 increase per month. Also a family cap – denying benefits to children born while a mother was receiving assistance – was proposed.

Ultimately, the state legislature was unable to agree on a bill. By default, the Department of Human Resources was given the responsibility for drafting the state's TANF plan.

Today, Alabama Arise members and staff remain divided on whether low-income people are better off with the DHR plan or if the legislative package would have been better. The DHR plan does not increase Alabama's benefit level, but the family cap was eliminated.

Alabama Arise played a key role in the plan's

SUPPORT THE EMPOWERMENT EFFORTS OF POOR PEOPLE, ESPECIALLY WOMEN

formation. This can be attributed to the credibility the coalition has built over the last decade in three areas: performing quality policy analysis, organizing the grassroots, and enabling low-income people to speak for themselves to policymakers. During the entire process, advocates in Alabama also continued to urge the U.S. Congress to make restorations in the federal law.

Welfare Rolls Plunge

In 1997, the number of people on welfare dropped below 10 million for the first time since 1970. Newspapers are filled with reports of former welfare recipients who have found new self-esteem in helping support themselves. At the same time, not enough is known about how former recipients are faring. While some find employment, others are becoming casualties of the reforms. The approaching cutoff date for receiving benefits adds urgency to the search for information and analysis of welfare reform's effects.

The General Accounting Office (GAO) reports that the number of people receiving welfare

COALITIONS CATALYZE CHANGE
ADAPTED FROM *WHY A COALITION?* BY THE HUNGER TASK FORCE OF MILWAUKEE

Coalitions are effective catalysts for community change because they:

- allow individual organizations to become involved in new and broader issues without having sole responsibility;

- maximize the power of individuals and groups through joint action;

- increase critical mass by helping organizations mobilize talent, resources and solutions to a problem;

- achieve objectives;

- minimize duplication of efforts and services; and

- facilitate trust and communication among competing groups.

First Steps in Organizing a Coalition:

1. Identify your organization (or individual) self-interest – what is your bottom line?

2. Identify possible constituencies to include.

3. Enlist representatives from as many segments of society as possible, especially those most affected by an issue.

4. Identify other organizations' self-interests – what will it cost to involve them?

5. Hold an organizing meeting with all potential coalition members.

Successful coalitions: set clear goals, identify outcomes and payoffs, fund and develop leaders, build on commitment, promote good communication, recognize turf boundaries, and emphasize diversity in terms of gender, race and ethnicity.

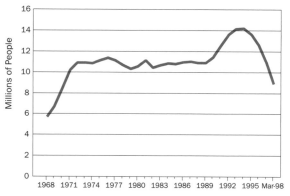

Figure 5.1 **Number of People on Welfare Rolls, 1968–1998**

Source: Department of Health and Human Services, The Administration for Children and Families, May 1998, accessible at: <http://www.acf.dhhs.gov>

470,000 adult welfare recipients needing employment.[10] The lack of jobs is an obstacle for helping people leave welfare and become self-supporting.

Tens of thousands of welfare recipients lose benefits not because they find employment, but because they fail to meet myriad eligibility requirements, ranging from missing an interview to arriving late to a training session.[11] According to the Department of Health and Human Services, nationally, 38 percent of the recipients who left welfare from October 1996 to June 1997 did so because of state sanctions for noncompliance.[12]

Some states are finding creative ways to help low-income people get jobs. The unexpected windfall received when the welfare bill was passed has helped.[13] Texas, for example, is using some of its TANF surplus to help recipients buy cars, thus removing a key barrier to employment.[14] The law's child-support enforcement provisions also play an important role in providing support for some low-income families.

Is the New System Working?

It is still too early to know the law's full impact. The law established a lifetime limit of five years on benefits, and that limit has not yet gone into effect. With the increased state flexibility, some states will find innovative ways to help people move from welfare to work. Other states may not.

benefits nationwide had dropped 37 percent from 14.1 million in January 1993 to 8.9 million in March 1998.[9]

The 1996 welfare law certainly has contributed to this caseload reduction, but the nation's long economic boom, and the low unemployment it has produced, have likewise been factors.

Job availability remains an important issue. A study of New York City estimated that it will take that city's economy 21 years to absorb the

Figure 5.2 **Change in Welfare Caseloads by State since Enactment of the New Welfare Law, 1996–1998**

State	August 96	March 98	Percent	State	August 96	March 98	Percent
Alabama	100,510	58,964	-41%	Nebraska	38,510	38,523	0%
Alaska	35,540	32,665	-8%	Nevada	33,920	27,374	-19%
Arizona	169,440	107,860	-36%	New Hampshire	22,940	15,513	-32%
Arkansas	56,230	34,901	-38%	New Jersey	275,700	207,678	-25%
California	2,578,450	2,102,704	-18%	New Mexico	99,660	69,275	-30%
Colorado	95,790	53,682	-44%	New York	1,143,960	922,675	-19%
Connecticut	159,060	132,437	-17%	North Carolina	266,470	184,382	-31%
Delaware	23,650	17,810	-25%	North Dakota	13,130	8,733	-33%
Dist. of Columbia	69,290	53,850	-22%	Ohio	549,310	372,241	-32%
Florida	533,800	290,977	-45%	Oklahoma	96,010	66,451	-31%
Georgia	329,160	209,613	-36%	Oregon	78,420	48,663	-38%
Hawaii	66,480	75,368	13%	Pennsylvania	530,520	382,901	-28%
Idaho	21,800	4,460	-80%	Rhode Island	56,460	54,425	-4%
Illinois	640,870	531,623	-17%	South Carolina	113,430	71,382	-37%
Indiana	141,850	92,551	-35%	South Dakota	15,840	10,187	-36%
Iowa	85,940	67,189	-22%	Tennessee	238,890	154,428	-35%
Kansas	63,780	35,659	-44%	Texas	647,790	408,776	-37%
Kentucky	170,890	129,770	-24%	Utah	39,060	29,698	-24%
Louisiana	228,120	124,031	-46%	Vermont	24,270	20,178	-15%
Maine	53,790	41,860	-22%	Virginia	152,680	104,338	-32%
Maryland	194,130	125,337	-35%	Washington	268,930	221,274	-18%
Massachusetts	219,580	176,412	-20%	West Virginia	89,039	45,255	-49%
Michigan	501,440	370,715	-26%	Wisconsin	148,890	47,444	-68%
Minnesota	169,740	146,257	-14%	Wyoming	11,400	2,974	-74%
Mississippi	122,750	61,045	-50%	Guam	8,314	7,461	-10%
Missouri	222,820	158,492	-29%	Puerto Rico	151,023	127,144	-16%
Montana	28,240	19,913	-29%	Virgin Islands	4,898	4,057	-17%

Source: Department of Health and Human Services, The Administration for Children and Families, March 1998, accessible at: <http://www.acf.dhhs.gov>

Some indirect indicators are emerging. Charities and religious congregations struggled to meet emergency needs even before the new law, and the need, especially for food, has increased since the welfare bill was signed. As states implement time limits and people are cut from assistance or move into jobs that fail to meet basic needs, many charities may see larger increases in the number of those seeking assistance (see Chapter 4, p. 56).

In February 1998, Tufts University's Center on Hunger, Poverty and Nutrition Policy released *Are States Improving the Lives of the Poor?* that examines 34 decisions made by the states, mea-suring whether they have adopted policies which will increase or decrease family economic security. The study says: "The majority of states have created welfare programs that ultimately will worsen the economic circumstances of the poor." [15] Fewer than one-third have implemented policies that are likely to improve the conditions of low-income families. The Tufts study did find, however, that all states except Wyoming have improved their child care policies.

A 1998 *New York Times* study indicates that although members of all racial/ethnic groups are leaving welfare at unprecedentedly high rates, African Americans and Hispanics are leaving at

Jobs must provide good wages and benefits to sustain workers over time.

a lower rate than White recipients. The scapegoating and racial stereotyping that long marred the welfare debate make this particularly disturbing news. Theories advanced to explain the different rates included possible discrimination by employers or landlords and differing levels of education. But the most significant factor seemed to be the scarcity of jobs in central cities where welfare recipients of color tended to reside.[16]

Concern is growing over whether former welfare recipients who find jobs are earning enough. In Los Angeles County, which has a higher number of recipients than 48 of the 50 states, 43 percent of poor families required to participate in the city's new welfare reform program got jobs, as compared with 32 percent of a control group not so required.[17] However, many who left welfare for jobs did not earn enough to move off public assistance. "The typical welfare recipient who was working was earning $6.45 an hour.... Recipients need to earn $7.82 an hour before they make enough to stop receiving assistance."[18]

A study by NETWORK, a Catholic social justice lobby, illustrates the dangers of withdrawing

public assistance before welfare recipients find an adequate job. The study surveyed people using soup kitchens and other forms of emergency assistance and concluded:

> The acquisition of a job at a hardly sustainable average wage of $13,312 a year does not compensate for a loss of government assistance.... Despite the acquisition of a job, this population is experiencing worse vital life indicators than those on government assistance.[19]

Food availability was the vital indicator most affected – 48 percent of the sample "reported having had to eat less per meal or fewer meals over the past six months because of cost."[20]

Research shows that many welfare recipients have serious barriers to obtaining full-time, uninterrupted employment, such as low skills, medical problems, depression, and chemical dependency. The most employable welfare recipients have likely already found jobs on their own. The marginally employable may or may not find – and keep – employment, depending on the support available to them. There are those who, before welfare reform, cycled on and off the system:

> Because they couldn't care properly for themselves and their children [on] a job that paid between $5 and $7 an hour with no benefits, they returned to welfare.... There is no reason to believe that the kinds of jobs that the GAO reports welfare recipients are getting today are any different from the ones they have already had. The difference is there no longer will be any welfare to return to.[21]

As increasing work requirements go into effect, states must find creative ways to help the most hard-to-employ recipients find – and keep – jobs. Ultimately, some very low-skilled people will be unable to find private-sector jobs, and publicly-funded job programs will be necessary.

The Next Debate

Much is still unknown about one of the largest social policy experiments in U.S. history. Its success rests primarily on jobs at decent wages and on job-related supports like transportation, child care, health care, education and training.

Most states currently have surplus funds to run their welfare programs. But the block grant's funding level is frozen through 2002. What will happen when the economy begins to slow and unemployment increases?

Welfare reform remains an ongoing process. Vigilance in monitoring its impact is critical. As experience accumulates and political shifts take place, further reforms will occur. Much can be learned from the changing politics of U.S. welfare policy.

First of all, elections matter.

Second, making the welfare law succeed will require the herculean efforts of federal, state and local government; non-profit groups; businesses; welfare recipients themselves; and coalitions of these groups.

Third, elected officials and the public must ensure that all who can work have access to jobs with decent wages and benefits; and that those who cannot work have a guarantee of public assistance.

Fourth, local groups must monitor welfare reform's effects in their communities, must articulate their assessment of those effects and must raise their voices regarding necessary restorations and changes in the welfare reform law.

Fifth, the anti-hunger movement needs to strengthen its advocacy, particularly at state and local levels. Within that movement, low-income people need to represent their own interests. And their allies need to support those efforts.

LYNETTE ENGELHARDT is a domestic policy analyst with Bread for the World. E-mail: engelhardt@bread.org

Affordable, quality child care is indispensable for single working parents. The Childcare Union Project seeks to provide employees with a voice in child care policy decisions.

BY JANICE A. CARDARO

We were a typical Italian-American family moving from the ethnic enclaves of Brooklyn, New York to the suburbs of Long Island in pursuit of the American dream. My father was a delivery truck driver, my mother a homemaker, and my one brother was five years my senior. My early childhood was as carefree as those of other kids raised in middle-class suburbia. As children, our days were spent riding bicycles or selling lemonade to our neighbors. Family life was strong. Relatives would migrate from "the city" to converge in our backyard for weekend barbecues, complete with a candy cane-striped swing set, an above-ground swimming pool, a doghouse for our collie, and a small family of ducks.

My mother, Anna, was the epitome of the 1950s "happy homemaker." Not only was our house immaculately clean, but our garden abundant with tomatoes, zucchini and basil. My brother routinely brought home the neighborhood kids for after-school snacks before trading *Marvel* comic books. Life was as it should be for a child growing up. Although we didn't have a lot, as children we were not aware that anything was missing.

I was barely four years old when my father deserted us without warning, presumably because of a business deal gone sour. Only later did my mother learn that he was living in Florida with another woman, a relationship that would haunt her for years to come.

It took only a few months for our world to completely fall apart, as our lives suffered one loss after another. First to go was my mother's mint green 1958 Chevy. Then the utilities were turned off one by one and the bank put the house on the market. Before we knew it, complete strangers began walking through our home, deciding where to place their sofa.

Penniless, homeless and without any source of income, my mother immediately began looking for work. She soon discovered that employment opportunities were nearly non-existent for women with a 10th-grade education and no job history. Utilizing her skills as a homemaker, my mother began working off the books as a maid for some of the wealthier families in the area. She quickly realized that we simply could not survive on her meager wages. Forced to accept that she was a single mother in need of an apartment of her own, my mother began the dehumanizing process of becoming a welfare recipient.

My earliest memories as a "welfare kid" are of a seemingly endless stream of buses taken through the suburbs of Long Island to get to the administrative offices of various municipal buildings; sitting in noisy, smelly, poorly ventilated waiting rooms for ten hours a day (with no access to food); taking naps on my mother's lap, waiting for our names to be called, only to be shuffled from one desk to another, one office to another, one case worker to another. We would do this every day for weeks at a time, first to register as new recipients or later, to drop off a single piece of paper, and inevitably to renew our status as welfare recipients. It seemed that there was always some reason for us to be there. Once processed and officially on welfare, we were entitled to receive approximately $180 per month (1965) for one adult and two children. We were also eligible for rent-controlled apartments (complete with mice and roaches), food stamps and rationed food items (such as huge bricks of hard American cheese, boxes of stale white crackers and tubs of unspreadable peanut butter). Church-affiliated charities brought us used clothing and, if we were lucky, toys at Christmas.

It was not long before my mother was indoctrinated into the culture of the welfare system; the terminology, the language (or what *not* to say to her case worker), the ritual of providing forms, bills or receipts as documentation for social services. I can only imagine my mother's disappointment when told that social services would not allow her to go back to school, as pursuing a nursing program was not "cost-effective." Abandoning her dreams, my mother returned to cleaning houses, in essence defrauding the welfare system just to keep our heads above water.

From the beginning my mother refined techniques for hiding our poverty not only from my brother and me, but from others as well. She always managed to purchase one new set of clothing for the first day of school when people seemed most likely to take notice. Her most clever method for hiding our welfare status was to send my brother and me into the candy store when it came time to pay for groceries with food stamps, hoping to prevent people from making the connection between us and her. I recall one evening in particular when my mother was forced to steal two cans of tuna fish for dinner, but could not bring herself to eat, her appetite diminished by moral disgust.

The older I became the more I realized that there was no hiding our poverty. It was particularly embarrassing when I would discover that my mother was hired to clean one of my friends' homes. Later on as a teenager, I'd decline a date rather than have a boy pick me up at our decrepit doorway that led to our run-down apartment over the local deli.

More painful than reliving the physical hardships of growing up in poverty is the emotional and spiritual decay that accompanies a life wracked by desperation and powerlessness. Worse than a welfare check arriving late is the knowledge that you are entirely dependent upon it for existence. Shame looms over every aspect of daily life. Mundane decisions are made under a cloud of guilt, as if one is undeserving of even the simplest of life's pleasures. In time, one learns to avoid feeling too happy about anything, knowing that at any moment the other shoe will drop.

Even more difficult is witnessing what poverty does to individuals and relationships. Through the years I watched my mother's metamorphosis from a happy, warm and attractive woman to someone who was virtually unrecognizable. Her constant preoccupation with our survival left her aged, exhausted, irritable and eventually, unapproachable. I sadly learned that nearly any request, no matter how small, could upset her terribly. This is the cruelest manifestation of poverty that goes undocumented, unanalyzed and untold: The fact that no one escapes unscathed from the shame, guilt and degradation of being poor.

JANICE A. CARDARO, Bread for the World Institute staff member, conducted research in Hungary and Romania for her M.A. from the University of California at Los Angeles. E-mail: jcardaro@bread.org

BFW File Photo

Poverty erodes human dignity, forcing poor and hungry people to make choices that no one should be asked to make.

CHAPTER 6

UPDATE ON THE STATE OF WORLD HUNGER

BY *KRISTY MANULIAK AND ELENA MCCOLLIM*

Every man, woman and child has the right to be free from hunger.
– WORLD FOOD CONFERENCE, 1974

Food Deficits and their Causes

Globally, there is no food shortage. If food were distributed equally, "every man, woman and child" would receive 2,500 calories a day, 150 more than the minimum needed for basic survival.[1] But some individuals and countries cannot grow or buy enough food to meet this level. Currently 87 countries are considered low-income food deficit countries (LIFDCs).[2] LIFDCs do not produce enough food for their people and lack resources to fill the gap through imports. They are distributed as follows:

41 in Sub-Saharan Africa

21 in South and East Asia

9 in Latin America and the Caribbean

6 in North Africa and the Middle East

10 in Eastern Europe and the Newly Independent States of the former Soviet Union.[3]

The International Food Policy Research Institute (IFPRI) predicts that by 2020, the difference between developing world production and demand is likely to grow from 94 million tons of cereal (as of 1993) to 228 million tons.[4] This food gap will retard overall progress against malnutrition. The number of children who are either malnourished or underweight is projected to fall

Margie Woodson Nea

from 185 million in 1993 (33 percent of the world's children), to 150 million (25 percent) by the year 2020. However, Sub-Saharan Africa is the only region where the percentage of malnourished children will not decrease; instead, it is projected to increase by 45 percent by 2020.[5]

A number of factors shaped the world food situation in 1998. Countries suffered extreme weather patterns: first the droughts and floods caused by El Niño, then the opposite system that followed it, La Niña. Civil strife in parts of Sub-Saharan Africa and in Serbia's Kosovo province, and the embargo on Iraq, disrupted food supply (see "Effects of Civil Conflict on Development, p. 34). Food aid declined from peak levels in 1993.

Not only food supply, but also food prices were volatile. Trade liberalization was one factor causing fluctuating prices. In the United States, depressed commodity prices (exacerbated by drought in some areas, by bumper crops in others) prompted calls for reform of the 1996 farm bill. Famine persisted in North Korea (see "The Politics of Famine in North Korea," p. 24) and in Indonesia severe drought coupled with financial crisis undermined that nation's food security.[6]

The changing politics of hunger shape these factors. The link between politics and hunger in places like Sudan, Kosovo and Iraq is fairly obvious. The path from politics to hunger via the Asian crisis, food market liberalization and

James V. Riker

declines in food aid may be less obvious. But as Chapter 2 shows (see pp. 36-45), the globalizing economy – which itself has political dimensions – is manifested in each of these three phenomena. And even weather is not entirely isolated from economics and politics. The El Niño and La Niña phenomena are only part of a greater overall trend in erratic global weather patterns going back to the early 1970s. These increased year-to-year fluctuations may be linked to global warming.

Trade and Aid

One aspect of the globalizing economy, trade liberalization, has culminated in the Uruguay Round of the General Agreement on Tariffs and Trade (GATT – see Chapter 2, p. 38). The Uruguay Round's greater reliance on markets may lead to increased price volatility, which in turn may increase food aid needs. When the Uruguay Round was negotiated, the richer nations of the world resolved, under the Marrakesh Agreement (see Chapter 2, p. 39), to help the very poor nations that would be hurt. But they have yet to do so.

Instead, food aid flows in 1997 continued their decline from previous years. Donor governments focused limited food aid on the countries that most need it, the LIFDCs. Food aid deliveries to LIFDCs in 1997 were 5.7 million tons, only a 2 percent drop from the 1996 level. Food aid to LIFDCs had dropped 26 percent in 1996 and 21 percent in 1995.[7]

Figure 6.1: **Changes in Food Production Per Capita Since 1980**

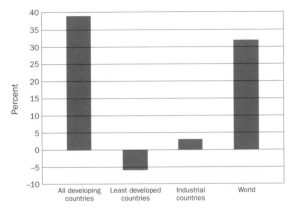

Source: United Nations Development Programme, *Human Development Report 1998* (New York: Oxford University Press, 1998), 161.

Industrial Countries

United States of America

The worst agricultural crisis in decades took its toll on farm country in the United States, with grain prices falling steeply due to a wide range of factors including bumper crops; weakened demand due to the Asian financial crisis; a strong U.S. dollar (making exports more expensive); and increased competition from Europe, Canada and Australia. Congress responded to the crisis with proposals (not yet passed into law at this writing) centered on restoring some of the subsidies removed in the 1996 Freedom to Farm Act. The Freedom to Farm Act had ended farm subsidies and defunded the Farmer-Owned Grain Reserve established in 1977 (see "Bread for the World: Twenty-Five Years," p. 70).[8]

While farmers in the Midwest struggled with falling commodity prices, low-income people used a variety of strategies to cope with food insecurity caused by poverty. Poverty persists in the United States, despite the long economic boom that started in the early 1990s. In 1997, the U.S. poverty rate was 13.3 percent, or 35.6 million people.[9] For children under age 18 the poverty rate was 19.9 percent. The poverty rate was 31.6 percent for female-headed households.[10]

The United States also suffers from deep income inequality (see Chapter 4, p. 63). In 1996, the top 20 percent of income earners earned 49 percent of all income, while the bottom 20 percent earned only 3.7 percent – a ratio of over 13 to 1, as contrasted with the European Union's ratio of 5.5.[11] This poses problems for democracy (see "Campaign Finance Reform," p. 66).

According to the 1995 Household Food Security Survey, 12 percent of all households, comprising 34.7 million people, experience some level of food insecurity.[12] Food insecurity ranges from worrying about having enough food, and reducing food quality, to reducing the amount of food served to adults and even children.

Social safety net programs provide food or food purchasing power to people in the United States (see Chapter 4, p. 58). Every tenth person relies on food stamps. Yet food stamps are often inadequate to meet families' needs. In 1996, monthly benefits averaged $73 per person and approximately $183 per household, or about $0.81 per meal.[13] It thus is no surprise that according to a survey by the Second Harvest food banks, 79 percent of food stamp recipients ran out of stamps before the end of the month. Forty-six percent of all households using emergency food services included one employed member.

Often people turn to charities to supplement their diet when food stamps run out. More than 26 million people in the United States use the donated groceries provided by the Second Harvest network of food banks.[14]

Canada

Canada is a breadbasket of the world, yet poverty persists and hunger has increased in Canada, primarily due to increasing social safety net cuts.

For example in 1995, a single parent with one child received $995 a month for shelter and food. In 1997, the same family only received $773 a month.[15] Canada has no officially recognized poverty line, using instead a series of Low Income Cut-Off (LICO) lines to determine poverty levels based on family size, residence location and amount of money spent on necessities.

The number of people receiving emergency food assistance in Canada has more than doubled, from 329,000 in 1989 to 669,887 people in 1997.[16] These people rely on the many privately run food banks across the nation. In 1991, there were more food banks in Canada than McDonalds'.

According to 1997 figures, 45 percent of the adults using food banks go without food at least once a week,[17] 30.5 percent report going without food at least twice a week, and 25 percent of their children are forced to miss meals at least twice a week.[18]

European Union

Because few systematic studies look at food insecurity in the fifteen countries of the European Union (EU), this report uses poverty and inequality as proxies for hunger. Poverty and inequality in the EU are much less marked than in the United States. A new study by

THE POLITICS OF HUNGER IN CANADA

BY KRISTY MANULIAK

In the early 1970s many Canadians first recognized the growing hunger problem and responded with food banks. Today they find that direct feeding programs alone are inadequate. Food drives arose out of national pride. They were an immediate and expedient response to hunger, never meant to become permanent features of Canadian society. Longer-term solutions require political action.

Canadians now realize hunger is symptomatic of other problems and cannot be eradicated if root causes are ignored. While Canada is often held up as a successful welfare state, the current political environment has led to massive program cuts, leaving over 5 million Canadians – 17.8 percent of the population – struggling below the poverty line. Nonetheless, the Canadian system of safety nets is more comprehensive and effective than that of the United States.

For a long time, income disparities were tempered by government subsidies. Canadians could count on old age security, child benefits and tax policies to make up for inadequate wages, and did not need charitable programs. But recent cuts in welfare programs – 21.6 percent in 1997 alone – devolution and the 1996 abolition of welfare standards have severely affected low-income Canadians. Canadian organizations tend to work on hunger through other related issues such as poverty, children, labor, welfare and housing. They do not want to lobby for food stamps or government food programs. Instead they seek a return to national welfare standards and job creation policies.

Canada's political system differs from that of the United States, and thus requires different lobbying techniques.* Because it is a parliamentary system, Canadians do not work to influence the conscience vote of individual legislators. In order to create change, they must target an entire political party. It is the party's power, rather than that of individual members of Parliament, that is key to introducing and passing legislation.

Citizens for Public Justice is, like Bread for the World in the United States, a national, nonpartisan, ecumenical organization that works for economic and social justice through research, public education and advocacy. It promotes constituent visits to members of Parliament and uses the media to inform and empower citizens.

Another organization, Choices, annually presents an alternative budget alongside the government's to show that people's needs can indeed be met. Choices' campaign has recently received much media attention.

Realizing that an informed citizenry is necessary to bring about change, major food banks like Toronto Daily Bread focus on public education. Media campaigns have also been crucial. By publicizing personal stories, organizations such as RESULTS Canada and Citizens for Public Justice have made hunger seem immediate and urgent. Even using media to embarrass political leaders into action has been successful.

Canadian advocacy is changing with the political climate. With the deficit gone, hunger advocates have the political space to promote restoration of program funding, instead of having to fight a defensive strategy to prevent cuts. These advocates urge Canadian society to allocate money, through the government, back into social welfare before lowering taxes. It is a time of much soul-searching as Canadians try to finally eradicate hunger and the need for charity.

KRISTY MANULIAK was a project associate with Bread for the World Institute, sponsored by the United Nations Association in Canada and the Canadian Department of Foreign Affairs and International Trade.

* Canada has a multi-party system in which the government is formed by the party that wins a plurality of seats (with the leader of that party assuming the post of prime minister). The party that wins the next most votes makes up the opposition party. Voting in the lower chamber is on an individual basis, but is more constrained by party loyalty than the U.S. system. Thus, lobbying means trying to ensure that a party supports legislation rather than trying to sign on as many supporters as possible regardless of party.

Eurostat – the Statistical Office of the European Communities in Luxembourg – examines thirteen of those fifteen countries and finds that the bottom 10 percent of the population receive 2.6 percent of total income, while the top 10 percent receive 24 percent (see Fig. 6.2).[19]

The EU countries are experiencing a gradual yet increasingly prevalent dismantling of their social protection networks and a restructuring of their public services. These phenomena too are part of the changing politics of hunger, because in order to start using the new currency, the

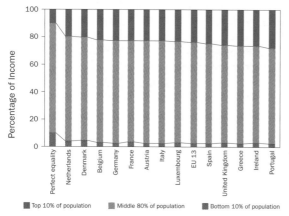

Figure 6.2: **Income Distribution in the European Union**

Percentage of Income

■ Top 10% of population   ■ Middle 80% of population   ■ Bottom 10% of population

Source: Eurostat Survey of 13 Member States. <http://europa.eu.int/compres/en/8898/6308898a.htm>.

euro, in January 1999, countries must achieve certain targets on a number of economic indicators. The move toward a shared currency may require governments to reduce traditionally generous European social safety nets.[20]

Developing Countries

Sub-Saharan Africa

Over the past 25 years, the number of people in Sub-Saharan Africa with inadequate access to food has doubled to 215 million people. The FAO projects that if current trends continue, that number will increase by 50 million in the next 12 years.

Even in the short run, food crises remain a threat.

As African economies continue to grow and the status of African agriculture improves, the need for food aid will decrease. Countries import food to fill the gap between what they need and what they produce. When they are unable to import enough to fill the gap, as in Sub-Saharan Africa, they require food aid as a supplement. Figure 6.5 illustrates that although food aid is still required, food imports supply the bulk of needs beyond what Sub-Saharan Africa produces.

The food production picture in mid-1998 was mixed, with countries in eastern Africa – Kenya, Ethiopia, Tanzania, and Uganda – experiencing favorable harvest prospects, and some countries of the Great Lakes region starting to recover

from the crisis of the mid-1990s caused by the 1994 genocide in Rwanda (see Chapter 1, p. 28).[21] However, civil strife in Sudan, Somalia, and some western African countries caused food supply difficulties. The FAO projects that "on balance, sub-Saharan Africa's cereal import and food aid requirements in 1998 are expected to be significantly higher than in 1997."[22]

The situation in Sudan illustrates the difference between the national panorama and regional conditions. The FAO reports that the 1998 wheat crop is above average, and that "a reduction of 17 percent in the area planted was partially compensated by higher yields due to adequate water supplies and favourable temperatures."[23] Yet while the food supply overall was satisfactory, in southern Sudan hundreds of thousands of people faced the threat of famine. Intensified civil war since January 1998, population displacement, regional drought, inflation and the government's restrictions on emergency aid combined to increase malnutrition and starvation.

Worst hit was the Bahr El Ghazal region in the south, where fighting in 1998 between the Sudanese government and the Sudan People's Liberation Army resulted in a malnutrition rate of 29 percent, with 9 percent of the population severely malnourished.[24] Countrywide, the U.N. estimates that 2.6 million people have been affected, with 50 percent of the children malnourished. A three-month cease-fire began in July 1998. Unfortunately, as in other years, the cease-fire came too late for food to be

WFP Photo/N. Brodeur

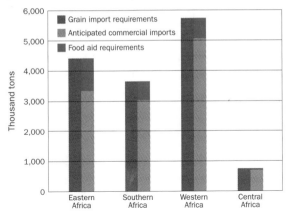

Figure 6.3: **Sub-Saharan Africa: Cereal Imports and Food Aid Requirements**

(chart legend)
- Grain import requirements
- Anticipated commercial imports
- Food aid requirements

Thousand tons (y-axis: 0 to 6,000)

x-axis categories: Eastern Africa, Southern Africa, Western Africa, Central Africa

Source: FAO/GIEWS: Africa Report No. 2, August 1998, 11.

James V. Riker

transported by land until the next dry season (see "Effects of Civil Conflict on Development," p. 34).[25] The World Food Programme delivered increasing amounts of food aid through air drops, operating under the flag of Operation Lifeline Sudan.[26]

Crops in Ethiopia, Uganda, Malawi, Angola and Zambia may be threatened by drought. But governments have tempered grim agricultural prospects by encouraging diversification, varied planting dates, and the use of drought-resistant varieties, and by distributing seed packets. Improved water conservation measures and the planting of higher-value commodity crops are further attempts to compensate for production losses.

The refugee situation increases the number of food insecure people. In the Democratic Republic of Congo 1997 and again in 1998, civil strife led to a looming food and humanitarian crisis.[27] In Rwanda, the return of over 1 million refugees and the escalating insecurity in many areas placed considerable strain on food systems.[28] Food programs had great difficulty reaching displaced people in parts of Angola, Burundi and Rwanda.

Erratic weather contributed to hunger, through drought in some areas and floods in others. Floods in Somalia, Ethiopia and northeast Kenya in late 1997 led to concerns about crop shortages, and caused livestock losses in northeast Kenya.

Asia

The Asian financial crisis has caused vast poverty and virtually wiped out the gains of the past decades. Economic growth, which had lifted so many people out of poverty, has slowed dramatically and some analyses project negative growth. The implications for food security have been severe, perhaps nowhere more than in Indonesia (see "Asian Financial Crisis Means Hunger in Indonesia," p. 88). Throughout the region, falling incomes have reintroduced food insecurity to millions of families who had moved from poverty to sufficiency over the course of a generation.

In North Korea a severe drought and typhoons followed two successive years of floods. Estimates of those who have died from famine range from 1 million to 5 million of its 29 million inhabitants (see "The Politics of Famine in North Korea," p. 24).[29]

In Southeast Asia, El Niño contributed to drought that threatened crops in Indonesia, the Philippines and Thailand.

In Bangladesh, the worst flooding in a decade affected 25 million people, leaving thousands homeless and damaging an estimated $150 million worth of crops. The government of Bangladesh estimated that its cereal stocks would meet immediate relief needs, but appealed for international aid to replenish the stocks.[30]

In China, with one-fifth of the world's population, cereal demand is predicted to rise by 43 percent between 1993 and 2020 to 490 million

Asian Financial Crisis Means Hunger in Indonesia

BY KAVITA PILLAY

Besieged by economic and political uncertainty, Indonesia faces a food insecurity problem of increasing severity. Food prices and unemployment rates have risen in tandem, thereby reducing the purchasing ability of the majority. Government measures to curtail the crisis have included fostering employment through public works projects, expanding food subsidies, raising the minimum wage and increasing its rice import target for 1998/99 (April/March) from 2.85 million tons to 3.1 million tons.*

These policies have served as a tourniquet to stanch the effects of the financial crisis. Still, resuscitating a country so wounded will be long and difficult. Before the crisis, 14 percent of Indonesia's 202 million people lived in poverty. The country's Central Bureau of Statistics projects that by the end of 1998, that figure will have skyrocketed to almost 50 percent. Forty percent of infants are malnourished, and poverty has soared in the cities and countryside alike.

The country's food distribution networks, traditionally in the hands of ethnic Chinese, were severely disrupted by the backlash of anti-Chinese riots in May 1998. It may not be possible, at least in the short run, to fill the void. Moreover, the increase in rice imports, prompted by the crisis, represents a serious setback in a country previously self-sufficient in rice.

Prospects for ensuring Indonesia's future well-being have been tied to its rich range of natural resources, a vital informal sector and the international community's support. As Indonesia forges ahead in rebuilding, its food security will be contingent on its economic health and that, in turn, linked to Indonesia's success in moving toward democracy.

KAVITA PILLAY, a Mickey Leland Hunger Fellow with the Congressional Hunger Center, is serving a policy placement with Bread for the World Institute.
E-mail: kpillay@bread.org

* FAO/GIEWS, Special Alert No. 284, July 7, 1998.

tons, while cereal production will only grow by 31 percent to 449 million tons.[31]

In India, per capita food availability has increased by 7 percent. Pakistan and Afghanistan, by contrast, have experienced declines in per capita food availability of 7.3 percent and 7.1 percent respectively.[32]

Latin America and the Caribbean

Latin America is land rich, but rapid urbanization and environmental hazards such as soil erosion, salinization and drainage problems threaten food security. The Caribbean faces a tight food supply due to prolonged drought. The worst drought in decades affected eastern Cuba severely and in September 1998 the World Food Programme announced that 615,000 vulnerable people in five provinces needed emergency assistance until the harvest in May 1999.[33]

The early impacts of El Niño also added five Central American nations to the Food and Agriculture Organization of the United Nations (FAO) list of countries facing food shortages. El Niño caused a need for $9.4 million in emergency operations in 1997, which were delivered and provided six months of emergency food assistance to 323,000 people in El Salvador, Guatemala, Honduras, Nicaragua and Panama.[34] In 1997 food aid was 0.6 million tons, a decrease of 20 percent from 1996 figures.[35]

In Brazil, the worst drought of the century has exacerbated long-standing extreme poverty and 9.7 million Brazilians now face starvation. Ten states in the northeast are most seriously affected. There, 4.8 million people faced critical food supply problems in the first half of 1998. The government eased the situation somewhat by delivering food baskets, but delivery has been sporadic and rations insufficient. Looting and raids on food stores have become a common coping mechanism. To prevent similar crises in the future, the Brazilian government will allocate funds to rehabilitate the area by constructing wells and dams and planting drought-resistant crops.[36]

Middle East and North Africa

Food insecurity and hunger are not as prevalent in North Africa as the rest of the continent. The U.S. Department of Agriculture (USDA) has deemed North Africa the only region in the developing world with adequate resources to meet nutritional needs.

Iraq is the dramatic exception. One million Iraqis have died of disease and hunger-related illness after seven years of sanctions since the end of the Gulf War, according to FAO estimates.

Despite some improvement following the implementation of the "oil for food" negotiation, malnutrition remains a scourge.[37]

In Afghanistan, food aid is directed to 2,100 families suffering from the harsh 1997 winter and long drawn-out conflict in the region.[38]

Countries in Transition

The transition from centrally planned economies to market-based capitalist systems has precipitated hunger, poverty and homelessness. Food aid has been sent to Armenia, Azerbaijan, Georgia and particularly Tajikistan, where over 16 percent of the population needs assistance to survive.[39] There, people continue to live in extreme poverty, and unresolved conflicts deter donor organizations from supporting long-term development programs.[40]

Throughout the former Soviet Union, food consumption had been projected to increase based on prospects for economic recovery, improved export performance and higher food productivity. Instead, the Russian financial crisis of mid-1998 threw all of these projections into question as the country struggled with a devalued currency and a collapsing banking sector.

In Serbia's Kosovo province, civil conflict between the central government and local ethnic Albanians uprooted 50,000 people from their homes. Estimates showed that an additional 12,000 people had crossed the border into Albania and another 8,000 people into Montenegro. The World Food Programme is sending food supplies to displaced persons in the region.[41] Fighting, abandoned and destroyed farms, livestock losses, difficult terrain and poor soils have all seriously affected food output. In 1996, wheat and maize output was 310,000 tons, less than half the 1991 level of 700,000. Projections for 1998/1999 are not favorable.

Conclusion

The politics of hunger reach into every region and country of the world to affect the most vulnerable – whether they represent the majority as in the countries of the South, or the minority as in the North. The Asian financial crisis demonstrated the interconnected nature of the globalizing economy as never before. Its dampening effect on demand reduced the volume of agricultural trade, and that reduction combined with a drop in cereals prices depressed the overall value of agricultural trade.[42] Civil strife in Eastern Europe, parts of the former Soviet Union, and Sub-Saharan Africa displaced people from their homes and in some cases blocked food aid from reaching them.

The changing politics of hunger may have also helped, as improved technologies made it possible to spot and predict food shortages earlier and react more quickly.[43] In some countries, liberalization of grain imports improved food access for the majority.[44] Targeting food aid to the most needy countries – the LIFDCs – was another step forward.

The hunger and destitution in Southeast Asia caused by the financial crisis are disheartening, all the more so when considering how far the region had come in pulling its people out of poverty. The gains now being reversed are a reminder that progress is possible, but not irreversible. Continued progress against hunger depends heavily on political choices.

KRISTY MANULIAK was a project associate in Bread for the World Institute sponsored by the United Nations Association in Canada and the Canadian Department of Foreign Affairs and International Trade.
E-mail: <kamanuliak@bread.org>.
ELENA MCCOLLIM is a policy analyst at Bread for the World Institute. E-mail: <emccollim@bread.org>.

Joan Paranka

CHAPTER 7

POLITICAL STRATEGIES TO END HUNGER

BY JAMES V. RIKER AND PAUL NELSON

I n 1974, world leaders came together at the World Food Conference in Rome and officially announced their commitment to ending world hunger. Specific goals and plans have proliferated over the past decade (see Table 7.1). In 1989 a group of non-governmental leaders adopted the Bellagio Declaration that called for cutting world hunger in half by the year 2000.[1] Hunger in the U.S. was targeted by the Medford Declaration in 1990. The 1996 World Food Summit set the goal of reducing hunger in half by the year 2015.

Despite official pronouncements to reduce or end hunger, these initiatives have lacked sufficient political leadership and a broad-based political constituency to accomplish their goals. If the 1.3 billion people who live on less than the equivalent of $1 a day had been an active political force, the 20th century would already have closed the door on hunger.[2] The imperative for action remains especially urgent and compelling.

The Changing Politics of Hunger argues that at this particular moment in history – when the global market economy, the communications revolution and the spread of democracy have provided the ways, all we have to do is provide the means – a good hard political push. The steps to changing the politics of hunger are clear:

1. **Recognize the timeliness, and recover the moral and religious urgency, of ending hunger.** Because significant progress against hunger has been achieved and the world has sufficient resources, ending hunger is both timely and a fundamental moral and religious obligation. The chief enemy is not lack of food, but political apathy.

In political campaigns, policy debates and corporate boardrooms, we need to lift up the moral principles that

Table 7.1: A Chronology of Major Statements for Ending Hunger

Year	Event or Forum	Main Goal & Objectives for Ending Hunger
1974	World Food Conference (Rome, Italy)	The Conference called on all governments to accept the goal that in 10 years' time, no child would go to bed hungry, no family would fear for its next day's bread, and no human being's future and capacities would be stunted by malnutrition.
1980	Report of the Presidential Commission on World Hunger[1] (Washington, DC)	The Commission recommended that the United States make the elimination of hunger the primary focus of its relationships with developing countries, beginning with the decade of the 1980s.
1989	The Bellagio Declaration: Overcoming Hunger in the 1990s[2] (Bellagio, Italy)	Calls for ending half the world's hunger before the year 2000, by: (1) Eliminating deaths from famine; (2) Ending hunger in half of the poorest households; (3) Cutting malnutrition in half for mothers and small children; and (4) Eradicating iodine and vitamin A deficiencies.
1990	The Medford Declaration to End Hunger in the United States[3] (Medford, Massachusetts)	Called for virtually eliminating domestic hunger by 1995: (1) Use existing channels (i.e., public programs and voluntary food providers) to see that food is available to the hungry on an adequate and consistent basis; and (2) Promote adequate purchasing power and economic self-reliance of American households to achieve the goal of a hunger-free United States.
1994	The Salaya Statement on Ending Hunger[4] (Salaya, Thailand)	Ending hunger is a credible and achievable goal: (1) Increased funding needs to be redirected to addressing the needs of poor people, especially rural and urban households at risk of food insecurity; and (2) Continued progress...can be achieved by improved communication, community organization and collaboration with local governments. Specific actions include empowering poor communities, education for women and providing safety nets for vulnerable populations.
1996	Rome Declaration on World Food Security, World Food Summit[5] (Rome, Italy)	The Summit set the goal of reducing the number of malnourished people to half their present level no later than 2015. Priority is given to promoting food security and poverty eradication for present and future generations.

[1] *Report of the Presidential Commission on World Hunger*, Washington, DC, 1980.

[2] See "Bellagio Declaration: Overcoming Hunger in the 1990s," In: David Beckmann and Richard Hoehn, eds., *Transforming the Politics of Hunger*, Occasional Paper No. 2, Silver Spring, MD: Bread for the World Institute, 1992, 54-58.

[3] The Medford Group, *The Medford Declaration to End Hunger in the U.S.*, Medford, MA: Tufts University.

[4] Robert W. Kates, Mid-Course Review of the Bellagio Declaration: Overcoming Hunger in the 1990s. *Food Policy*, 20(6): 599-600, December 1995.

[5] FAO, Rome Declaration on World Food Security and World Food Summit Plan of Action. Document WFS 96/3, Rome: FAO, November 1996.

are at stake in pragmatic decisions. Corporations like Nike have made visible efforts to respond to the moral outcry raised by enraged consumers.[3]

Members of faith groups can urge their larger synods, dioceses and conventions to adopt moral and religious statements that affirm the priority of programs and policies that empower hungry and poor people. Participate in church or community discussion groups that seek action on initiatives to end hunger in our communities,

nation and world. By participating in Bread for the World's Offering of Letters, individuals and churches can mobilize a grassroots letter-writing campaign in support of legislation that increases the self-reliance of poor people, especially women, such as the Africa Seeds of Hope Act of 1998 (see pp. 92-94).

Religious leaders themselves can act as a moral force for change, advocating policies that benefit hungry and poor people and challenging

BY DON REEVES

B read for the World (BFW) is built on the concept that citizenship is an essential part of Christian witness. Bread's most distinctive activity is the Offering of Letters, in which groups of people, most often a church congregation, offer individual letters to their members of Congress as an act of worship.

Each year Bread selects three to four legislative issues on which to work. Among these, one receives about half of Bread's total resources, and is referred to as our Offering of Letters issue. In 1998, the Offering of Letters focused on strengthening agriculture in sub-Saharan Africa, particularly on the smallest farms – worked mostly by women. The legislation was the *Africa: Seeds of Hope Act of 1998*.

The genesis and progress of *Africa: Seeds of Hope* illustrate some elements of a successful public-interest legislative campaign.

Choosing the Right Issue

Bread chooses issues that are likely to achieve significant change in the lives of hungry and poor people, and that are potentially winnable. Bread also polls its local and religious leaders to learn what issues might win support in their community or religious congregation. Among issues important to Bread, attention to sub-Saharan Africa ranks high, because hunger is more widespread there than in any other region and is increasing.

CEDPA

Shaping A Bill

Hammering out the details of legislation involves lengthy negotiations with long-term and potential new colleagues and coalitions, particularly with members of Congress who will introduce or cosponsor the measure and help it advance through Congress. Each person and group has their own agenda to advance, which may not be completely congruent with others'. Moreover, the bill needs to be relatively uncomplicated – straightforward enough that its key points can be explained in a few minutes from the pulpit, for example, at a Sunday service.

The anvil on which *Africa: Seeds of Hope* was hammered out was the clear intent of Congress not to create any significant new programs, nor expand budgets for existing ones – particularly foreign assistance programs. Bread asked what might be done by reshaping existing programs, or redirecting existing resources.

Bread built support for *Africa: Seeds of Hope* by working with a number of coalitions. The private agencies that administer food aid were especially active. The broadest ever agricultural coalition of leaders from farmer associations, agribusiness and academia is newly interested in raising attention to agriculture in foreign assistance programs. Broad-based development, including development based on successful agriculture, not only is good for developing countries but nearly always results in increased exports for U.S. agriculture.

This agricultural coalition calls for increased appropriations for international agricultural research. *Africa: Seeds of Hope* gained the support of many agriculture coalition members by asking the U.S. Agency for International Development (USAID) to develop a plan for expanded resources. Meanwhile, the bill directs USAID to give more attention to the needs of small-holding farmers, women farmers and environmental sustainability with whatever resources are available for agricultural research and outreach programs.

Negotiating a bill usually depends on cooperating with members of the appropriate congressional committee. In this case, Rep. Doug Bereuter (R-NE), Vice Chair of the House International Relations Committee and his aide Dan Martz spent many hours helping Bread develop our proposal. They, together with Rep. Lee Hamilton (D-IN) and his aide, Maria Pica, carefully sifted our ideas, tested proposals with their colleagues on the International Relations and other committees that would need to review portions of the bill, and ultimately decided what they would introduce. BFW staff wrote the bill's initial draft and lobbied to keep as much of it as possible. Representative Bereuter provided crucial leadership in getting the bill approved by the House International Relations Committee and negotiating its steps toward final passage by the House.

After *Africa: Seeds of Hope* was introduced in the House, Bread won the support of Senators Mike DeWine (R-OH) and Paul Sarbanes (D-MD). They introduced the bill in the Senate. Senator DeWine's staff devoted many hours to winning support from other key Republican senators. Since Republicans are now in the majority, their leadership and committee chairs decide what bills get considered.

Bread also found innovative ways to approach the media. Some BFW members across the country volunteered to contact local media. A panel featuring members of Congress, African ambassadors and BFW's president was teleconferenced to newspaper editors around the country, resulting in a spate of articles and editorials that built support for the bill.

Busy members of Congress and their staff cannot do a thorough analysis of every one of the several thousand bills that are introduced in each Congress. They rely on other members in whom they have confidence. Attracting the right mix of original cosponsors becomes critical in building support. Always, such a group needs to be bipartisan; in this instance it needed to include members of the International Relations Committee and the Agriculture Committee, which would need to approve this bill before it would be considered by the full House of Representatives. A parallel process was pursued in the Senate. Bread also won the support of the Congressional Black Caucus and the Women's Caucus.

Grassroots Power

BFW members' principal activity in 1998, and the focus of its 1998 Offering of Letters, was to urge their representatives and senators to co-sponsor *Africa: Seeds of Hope*. This strategy entailed specific organizing goals in each congressional district. On BFW's annual Lobby Day in June, BFW members and friends from across the country gathered in Washington to make the case for this bill to their representatives and senators. Such visits in Washington and in district offices add to the grassroots power of letters and phone calls from constituents. An estimated 60,000 letters were written in nearly 700 Offerings of Letters. In addition, thousands of phone calls were generated when key votes or co-sponsorship were needed.

A second part of the strategy was to gather endorsements for the bill from national and international organizations. More than 200 organizations endorsed the bill.

Organizing BFW's grassroots members meant preparing people-friendly educational materials that bring home the issues. This made it possible for BFW members to identify with the desire of ordinary African families for self-reliance. As Congress neared adjournment, BFW members were urged make a final push by writing to their representatives and enclosing a packet of seeds to remind them that their support could nourish seeds of hope for rural Africans.

BFW members showed creativity and enthusiasm, remembering to thank congressional supporters as well as lobby undecided members. When one group in Indianapolis found out that Senator Richard Lugar (R-IN) had become a cosponsor after nearly a year of grassroots pressure, they promptly went to his office bearing a large loaf of bread and a balloon covered with the words, "thank you, thank you, thank you."

BFW members from Cincinnati worked hard to win the support of Rep. Steve Chabot (R-OH). In 1995, Chabot, a newly-elected conservative member of Congress, was assigned to the Africa Subcommittee of the House International Relations Committee. The BFW members from Cincinnati saw an opportunity and began meeting with Chabot shortly after he took office. Knowing he was a fellow Catholic, Mike Gable, a pastoral associate of a Cincinnati parish, brought Catholic priests who worked in Africa to talk with Chabot.

"As soon as we learned he was going to be assigned to the Africa subcommittee, we asked him to visit Africa," said Gable. "He finally told us he would go to Africa if he won re-election. After he won the election, we went back to him and asked him, when are you going? We kept the pressure on every time we saw him."

Rep. Chabot joined a bipartisan congressional delegation to Africa in August 1997. Later, parishioners from seven churches in the Cincinnati area wrote about 200 letters asking him and other members of Congress to cosponsor *Africa: Seeds of Hope.* BFW members followed up with phone calls to Chabot's Washington office, and activists Bob Ehrsam and Sister Mary Cabrini Durkin prevailed on the *Cincinnati Enquirer* to publish an editorial endorsing the legislation.

Finally, the Cincinnati BFW group organized a picnic, invited congressional aides and asked them publicly for support. Chabot's aide announced that Chabot would cosponsor *Africa: Seeds of Hope.*

A week later the bill came up for a vote in the House International Relations Committee. Chabot spoke eloquently in support, and the committee voted unanimously for approval.

Gable, reflecting on this success, recalled a quote by Martin Luther King: "A dedicated minority can change a majority."

Conclusion: Conviction, Faith, and Hope

Africa: Seeds of Hope passed in both houses of Congress in October of 1998 and was expected to be signed into law imminently as this volume went to press. This bill represents a significant legislative victory and when implemented will translate into concrete gains for African agriculture and rural Africans. The bill also supports USAID's plan to refocus U.S. resources on agriculture and rural development.

Bread grounds itself in the conviction that public policy decisions are an essential focus for witness to Christians' experience of God's love. In this instance, our faith is joined to seeds of hope in rural sub-Saharan Africa, as families and struggling nations search in new ways for secure livelihoods.

DON REEVES *is a former economic policy analyst, and continues as a policy consultant, with Bread for the World Institute.*

A dedicated minority can change a majority.   – MARTIN LUTHER KING

governments to uphold justice. The urgency of moral voice combined with the use of media and public demonstrations for democratic reforms led to President Banda's ouster in Malawi in 1993 (see p. 95).

Under the banner of Jubilee 2000, Pope John Paul II and Archbishop Desmond Tutu have called for collective moral action on relieving the debt of poor countries by the year 2000. Over 50,000 people formed a 7-mile long, human chain demanding that the heads of state at the 1998 G-8 Summit in England cancel the unpayable debt of developing countries.[4] As 1999 rolls in, the Jubilee 2000 campaign for debt relief is gathering steam, largely because moral and religious voices are being raised to cancel unpayable debt that prevents poor nations from addressing their own basic needs (see "Citizen Advocacy Reduces Debt," pp. 46-49). This worldwide campaign has many expressions, enabling individuals to take part wherever their energies and voices can best be joined.[5]

2. Support the empowerment efforts of poor people. Hunger will not end until poor people have the power to participate meaningfully in political and economic processes.

The stories of poor people must be heard. We need to listen to their voices – again and again – while ensuring their dignity (see "Recollections of a Child on Welfare," pp. 80-81). Such dialogue

Empowerment of marginalized people – like these school children in Chiapas, Mexico – is the key to fighting hunger and poverty.

Celia Escudero-Espadas

BY LISA FERRARI

Malawi, a small landlocked country in Southeastern Africa, is the seventh poorest in the world.[1] Under its previous one-party system, dissenters were imprisoned, exiled, or murdered; prisoners were regularly held without trial, beaten, sometimes tortured. The government owned all media and forbade foreign journalists from residing in Malawi. The country's limited resources were absorbed by a small elite and ordinary people systematically deprived of adequate schools, health care and jobs.[2] It took intervention by Malawi's Catholic bishops to unseat the regime and open a way for change.

President Hastings Kamuzu Banda came to power in 1964, as Malawi gained independence from Britain. A popular leader at the time, Banda eventually consolidated more and more power for himself, while daily living conditions worsened. Former Minister of Justice Orton Chirwa and labor leader Chakufwa Chihana were exiled for criticizing the regime. By 1975, Banda had declared himself Life President.

In 1992, Malawi's Catholic bishops secretly wrote and distributed a pastoral letter to be read in churches nationwide on the first Sunday of Lent, the Christian season of atonement. After a preamble, the letter began:

> Christ began his public ministry by proclaiming: 'Repent and believe in the Gospel' (Mark 1:15). By this proclamation he states the program of his ministry; to call all humankind in and through His life, death and resurrection to conversion and witness. People in every age and culture are called to this conversion and to respond in commitment and faith.[3]

The parallel between Christ's message and the bishops' was clear. Like Christ, the bishops were calling for repentance and conversion. The rest of the letter was startling. Characterizing the situation in Malawi as one of "mistrust and fear,"[4] the bishops enumerated injustice after injustice in Malawian society, including censorship, violations of academic freedom and free speech, forced donations, unequal access to hospitals and markets, and preferential treatment for party members. They included a none-too-oblique criticism of Banda himself: "No one person can claim…a monopoly on truth and wisdom."[5] The bishops' statement marked the first open opposition to Banda since a failed coup attempt in 1967.

Catholics are a minority in Malawi, but the Banda regime had paraded its ties to Christianity. Clergy were given places on the platform at public events, and Banda himself was an elder of the Presbyterian Church. Thus, when the bishops, as Christian moral authorities, spoke out, they brought into question the Life President's moral legitimacy.

Public response was immediate and overwhelming. Students protested in the streets, demanding democracy and a multi-party system. More widespread protests ensued and the government quickly responded. Banda declared possession of the pastoral letter a criminal offense and police confiscated every copy they could locate. All the bishops were detained. Meanwhile, in the countryside, religious sisters running hospitals and schools clandestinely disseminated the letter.

Despite Banda's best efforts, the damage had been done. The bishops had opened the floodgates of resistance and the government crackdown could not quell the protests. In 1993, Banda agreed to allow a referendum on a multi-party system. That referendum led to multi-party national elections in which the people of Malawi voted Banda out of office.

The bishops cannot claim all the credit. Discontent had been brewing in Malawi for years, and leaders like Chihana and Chirwa helped give it focus. However, because of their ecclesial status the bishops were in a unique position, able to make claims about government morality and to deflect the worst reprisals. None were harmed in detention, though the only foreign bishop was deported. After release, the remaining bishops were free to resume their duties. No secular leader could make the same claim.

What has changed? Under the Banda regime, agricultural production and marketing were controlled by the government agricultural conglomerate ADMARC.[6] His ouster thus removed one layer of corruption and inefficiency in food production. Yet hunger remains a serious problem. Lingering government corruption still limits Malawians' access to maize, their major staple crop (although weather conditions seem equally important).[7] Over the past ten years, about 25 percent of Malawi's children have suffered malnutrition, and that figure has not effectively changed under the new government.[8]

Yet while poverty and government corruption persist, Malawians today enjoy a level of freedom unthinkable a decade ago. Malawi's Catholic bishops have continued to denounce injustices in their society. Furthermore, donor nations are increasingly emphasizing governance. The bishops' moral voice, calling for repentance, enabled the people to free themselves.

LISA FERRARI teaches Government at Hamilton College in Clinton, NY. E-mail: lferrari@hamilton.edu

[1] International Development Association, *IDA in Action,* Washington, DC: The World Bank, 1997, 1, 27.

[2] For a detailed account of repression under the Banda regime, see *Where Silence Rules: The Suppression of Dissent in Malawi,* New York: Africa Watch, 1990.

[3] Malawian bishops' pastoral letter, March 1992, Introduction.

[4] Ibid., par. 11.

[5] "Living Our Faith," par. 12.

[6] Agricultural Development and Marketing Corporation.

[7] *Economist Intelligence Unit Country Report: Mozambique, Malawi,* Fourth Quarter 1996.

[8] The World Bank, *Trends in Developing World Economies, 1996,* Washington, DC, 1996.

and exchange is essential if we are to enable poor and hungry people to take a genuine role in the policy decisions and programs that affect their lives.

Since poverty is unevenly distributed and the worst effects tend to fall on racial minorities, women, children and those at the bottom of a caste system, special efforts are needed to ensure that they have the means to speak for themselves. Experiences from around the world have shown that local self-help, self-empowerment, income-generation and microenterprise programs can be effectively targeted to those people who need it most when they have the freedom and capacity to act (see Chapter 1, p. 27).

3. Hold social, economic and political institutions accountable to the common good and especially to the well-being of hungry and poor people. Each institution and sector of society – private as well as public – has a unique role and function, but all should be held accountable.

Anti-hunger advocates have pressed for policy changes by international organizations such as the World Bank. Pressure from local communities and NGO advocates from around the world led the World Bank to establish a mechanism for an independent inspection panel for its projects in 1993. The inspection panel is part of a broader shift toward accountability and democratic participation.

Advocacy in favor of the International Fund for Agricultural Development (IFAD) in 1985 resulted in creating an extra fund for poverty-targeted rural development programs in Africa. IFAD has joined in a strategic partnership with the Popular Coalition to Eradicate Hunger and Poverty, a coalition of nearly 400 NGOs and civil society organizations from the developed and developing worlds, to "maximize the dynamism and potential of civil society to fight hunger and poverty."[6] Other examples of efforts to change the politics of hunger at the international level were discussed in Chapters 1 and 2.

Christian Aid, the overseas relief and development agency of many of the Protestant and Orthodox churches in the United Kingdom (UK) and Ireland, uses a model that links policy advocacy with daily life. Christian Aid's two-year campaign on fair trade helped its member-activists encourage grocers and food marketing companies to carry coffee and chocolate produced and processed under arrangements that pay small farmers and farm laborers higher than average "fair prices" and wages. Britain's largest supermarket chains now carry coffees under the "Traidfair" label, the kinds available in food cooperatives and special catalogues in the United States.[7]

Christian Aid's current policy campaign links trade and debt issues. Citizen activists are urging UK-based food producers and retailers to agree to a code of labor conduct and a set of mechanisms to monitor and enforce it.[8] At the same time, they press their government and international organizations for decisive debt relief to the poorest countries. Christian Aid contributors have responded enthusiastically to campaigns that make the link between trade, hunger, financial policy and their daily lives as consumers and citizens. This experience provides clues to advocates in other countries.

4. Promote participation in fair, democratic, participatory structures at all levels of private and public life. Participation influences outcomes, but requires an appropriate political and economic infrastructure, for example, the right to vote, the right to organize in the workplace and the broader society, and the fair financing of elections.

Elections, elections, elections. One of the recurrent themes in these chapters is that elections matter, no matter what your next door neighbor tells you. Whether one supports or opposes welfare reform as it is unfolding in the United States, it is unassailable that the change occurred because of the cumulative effect of millions of people voting for the candidate of their choice.

Vote. Run for office. Take someone to the polls. We all know the drill. We are just lackadaisical about following it.

Support organizations that mobilize political voices effectively for the common good, especially for hungry and poor people. Support the League of Women Voters, the NAACP, Bread for the World, FRAC, Food First, RESULTS and other organizations that provide information and mobilize constituencies around hunger and

Political participation in electoral processes is essential in the fight against hunger and poverty.

the other issues to which it is linked. One good place to start is to contact the organizations presented at the end of this report (p. 130). Many anti-hunger and anti-poverty organizations are actively engaged in building the capacities of poor people to reclaim their lives and "free themselves from poverty by their own efforts."[9] Build on those initiatives that are making a difference and revitalizing the lives and spirits of our communities.

5. Utilize the power of the mass media to portray the depth of, and causes and solutions to, hunger. Modern communications have a significant impact in shaping public consciousness on hunger issues.

Make your perspective and viewpoint on hunger issues known. Write letters to the editor as Jim Shields and others do (see "Can't We Begin to See," p. 62). Use communications technologies such as the Internet to create vital connections to other interested citizens and groups by sharing information, building awareness and mobilizing advocacy for joint action (see Chapter 3, p. 55). Carefully target and package credible news information about hunger for journalists and the media so that it reaches the broader public and policy-makers. Sustained media campaigns have been crucial for generating public awareness and political action on hunger issues (see "The Politics of Hunger in Canada," p. 85).

6. Forge collaborative political alliances to bring effective changes at all levels – community to international. Individuals, organizations and even governments can be more effective in their efforts to overcome hunger and poverty when they work together. Effective coalition-building and public policy advocacy can range from grassroots networking to lobbying at state, national and international levels (see "Lobbying Brings Change," p. 98). NGO lobbying significantly influenced the debates and outcomes of the 1974 World Food Conference and the 1996 World Food Summit.[10] These various efforts, if effectively linked, can constitute the initial basis for a vital global constituency for ending hunger.

Chapter 4 shows how citizens, churches, food banks and private voluntary organizations have come together in the United States to build a growing coalition that supports government food and nutritional programs that protect hungry and poor people. This coalition needs to be strengthened if the social safety net is to be maintained and expanded to meet their needs.

Chapter 5 notes that public advocacy for effective reform of U.S. welfare policy at the federal level is still very important. However, the shift of many decisions about welfare programs to lower levels also requires new public leadership and political action at the community, city, county and state-levels.

The linking of people across borders and the witness they bear together through joint political action, known as solidarity politics, has also become an important part of anti-hunger advocacy. Organizations such as Witness for Peace practice a form of direct support called "accompaniment" for returning refugees and communities in violence-prone areas of Central America, placing North American staff and long-term volunteers with the communities to make arbitrary violence and repression more difficult for military or paramilitary forces.

International trade union solidarity has been important to winning protections for poor workers in Guatemala's textile and other industries. Observation, financial support and regular reporting to North American supporters has reduced the impunity with which industry

BY MARC J. COHEN

Washington is full of lobbyists, from the office buildings of the "K Street Canyon" to converted row houses on Capitol Hill and glass-and-concrete towers along the infamous suburban beltway. Virtually every product, idea, cause, ethnic group, and government, from Bahrain to bakers to bankers to banning land mines, has a Washington office.

Powerful groups face off against one another, at great expense, trying to sway the U.S. Congress on abortion, smoking or property rights. Recent lobbying disclosure reports indicate that lobbying the U.S. Congress may be a $1 billion business overall.*

Many powerful lobbies – the National Federation of Independent Businesses, the American Association of Retired Persons, the National Rifle Association – also mobilize large grassroots memberships to contact their legislators.

The hunger debate is different. There is no "pro-hunger" lobby. Rather, there are differing approaches to how to address hunger: does aid or trade work better? The market, or government programs? Also, much energy goes into getting hunger higher on the agenda. Congress pays much more attention to taxes, school choice, Social Security, and NATO expansion, unless there is a famine.

Some of Washington's hunger lobbyists pursue an "inside the beltway" strategy, others stress the grassroots, and still others, like Bread for the World, rely on both approaches.

The premier insider anti-hunger lobby is the Center on Budget and Policy Priorities that specializes in research and analysis on public policy issues affecting low-income people in the United States. Its widely respected reports are used by policy-makers, advocacy groups and service providers throughout the country, as well as the media. The Center has no grassroots membership base.

At the other end of the spectrum is the East Timor Action Network/US (ETAN/US). With 5,000 members throughout the United States, it succeeded in 1997 in getting Congress to prohibit Indonesia from using U.S.-supplied weapons for suppressing resistance to its occupation of that territory. ETAN/US has also called attention to the need to keep food aid to drought-stricken Timor from becoming another weapon in the pacification campaign.

This organization only recently hired a Washington staffer, and relies heavily on Internet communications to mobilize timely letters, calls, and visits to congressional representatives. The success of ETAN/US shows that on an issue on which representatives do not hear much, a few well-timed constituent messages can make all the difference.

Bread for the World's professional policy analysts spend years developing credibility with key staffers on Capitol Hill. These lobbyists also work closely with Bread's organizers, who mobilize activists when important votes are about to take place. Bread can sometimes generate over 100,000 letters and phone calls.

In 1990, Bread employed an insider-outsider strategy to gain important changes in the U.S. overseas food aid program. During the Cold War, U.S. food aid served as a tool for disposing of farm surpluses and advancing short-term foreign policy concerns at least as often as it advanced humanitarian and development goals.

As Bread's food aid lobbyist, I worked closely with the staff of senior legislators on the relevant committees, such as Sen. Patrick Leahy (D-VT) and Reps. Doug Bereuter (R-NE), and Tony Hall (D-OH) to reshape food aid to promote food security in developing countries. One critical reform proposed was to cut program administration from five administering agencies to one; to give USAID sole responsibility for all humanitarian and development programs.

In addition, Bread wanted forgiveness of $12 billion in past loans tied to the purchase of U.S. food. This burden claimed scarce resources in poor countries that could instead have gone to health care, education, and rural poverty reduction.

House Agriculture Committee Chairman Kika de la Garza balked at the idea of reducing the Department of Agriculture's administrative role, and Deputy Secretary of State Lawrence Eagleburger personally weighed in against the reforms.

Dick Hoehn, BFW organizer, identified Kathy and Felipe Salinas, Bread leaders in de la Garza's district. Felipe and Kathy took the issue to an adult class at Holy Spirit Catholic Church in McAllen, Texas where neighbors and cousins of de la Garza worshipped. "Sure, we'll give cousin Kika a call," they said. Their lobbying from the grassroots, combined with inside the beltway lobbying, helped direct substantial amounts of food aid into famine relief and community-based development activities such as maternal and child health projects, school meals for poor children, and infrastructure building and rebuilding efforts where workers receive their wages partially or wholly in food.

Bread and the Salinases also helped developing countries gain millions of dollars in debt relief, freeing up resources for sustainable development.

DR. MARC J. COHEN, former editor of Bread for the World Institute's annual reports on world hunger, is now special assistant to the director general of the International Food Policy Research Institute in Washington, DC. E-mail: m.j.cohen@cgnet.com

* "Got a Few Extra Million Dollars? You Can Play King of [Capitol] Hill, Too," Insight, October 21, 1996, 32.

or government can limit union organizers' freedoms.

Environment and human rights advocates use solidarity strategies in supporting indigenous peoples who want to resist or influence plans for hydroelectric dams that would flood the river basins in which they live; roads that would affect their access to remote rainforest lands; and child labor practices in industries such as textiles and soccer ball production in Pakistan. In each of these fields accompaniment has helped decrease risks to community activists in struggles to win a living wage or protect lands and livelihoods.

Changing the politics of hunger does not always mean changing government policy. One of the best known mobilizations of concern in the industrial countries aimed to improve infant and child health care through a consumer campaign to protest the marketing of infant formula in poor countries. Marketing of infant formula has contributed to a reduction in breastfeeding of infants worldwide. Babies who are not breast-fed lose the benefits of immunities conveyed through breastmilk, and where pure water is not available or formula might be diluted to extend the supply, they risk sickness and malnutrition.

Advocacy by 100 groups in 65 countries contributed to the promulgation of the International Code of Marketing for Breastmilk Substitutes in 1980. Public health professionals and activists singled out the Swiss multinational Nestlé for failure to comply, and a consumer boycott of Nestlé products and an information campaign were coordinated in the United States by Infant Formula Action (INFACT). The International Baby Food Action Network (IBFAN) has worked with governments worldwide to facilitate implementation and enforcement of the code and to ensure that the baby food industry complies with these measures.[11]

7. Think creatively and actively learn about policies that can contribute to overcoming hunger. The global economy, the communications revolution, the spread of democracy, and other changes call for new analysis and make possible new approaches for ending hunger. Conservative think tanks have played a major role in the build-up to welfare reform and other recent policy shifts in the United States. An equally intensive intellectual effort is needed to develop fresh approaches to reducing hunger and more effective ways to communicate an anti-hunger policy agenda. The policies we think would end hunger will be the subject of *Hunger 2000*.

Acting Locally and Globally

This report is about politics and we believe that "getting politics right" is the essential first step before advocating specific policies. All the good ideas in the world do not make a difference if people do not act on them. It is like losing weight, quitting smoking or sustaining an exercise regime. Changing the politics of hunger must be fought one day at a time with a long-term vision clearly in mind that connects local action to global political change.

Around the world, people are mobilizing to change the politics of hunger. People mobilize against hunger in various and sometimes overlapping roles: as poor and hungry people; as their allies; as workers, consumers, investors and citizens. Each of us acts on what touches our hearts and what is part of our daily routines. As Nadine Gordimer, who now serves as Goodwill Ambassador for the United Nations Development Programme's "Decade for the Eradication of Poverty" and was awarded the Nobel Prize for Literature in 1991, argues: "an individual can contribute, in one way or another, to the fight against poverty in our world of paradox, where plenty and dire need exist side by side."[12] The choice is ours.

Join and support organizations that: keep you informed about both politics and policy, give you avenues to express your values and, when you cannot be there yourself, act on your behalf.

In the fight against hunger, every action – and every inaction – matters.

DR. JAMES V. RIKER, senior researcher with Bread for the World Institute, is editor of *The Changing Politics of Hunger*. E-mail: <jriker@bread.org>. DR. PAUL NELSON is assistant professor in the Graduate School of Public and International Affairs at the University of Pittsburgh. E-mail: <pjnelson@pitt.edu>.

APPENDIX

TABLE 1: Global Hunger – Life and Death Indicators

	Population Total (millions) 1997	Projected (millions) 2025	Projected growth rate (%) 1995-2000	Projected total fertility rate 1995-2000	% population below age 15 1998	% population urban 1995	Life expectancy at birth 1995-2000 Male	Female	Infant mortality rate per 1,000 live births 1996	% infants with low birth weight 1990-1994	% 1-year-old children immunized (measles) 1995-96	Under-5 mortality rate per 1,000 live births 1960	1996	Maternal mortality rate per 100,000 live births	Refugees 1996 Country of origin	Country of asylum
Developing Countries	**5086.0**	**7,113.7**	**1.7**	**3.08**	**35x**	**38**	**62.1**	**65.2**	**66**	**18**	**78**	**216**	**97**	**477**	**..**	**..**
Africa (sub-Saharan)	**638.1**	**1,242.7**	**..**	**..**	**..**	**..**	**..**	**..**	**105**	**16**	**56**	**256**	**170**	**980**	**2,811,000**	**2,767,000**
Angola	12.0	25.5	3.3	6.69	48	32	44.9	48.1	170	19	65	345	292	1,500	223,000	9,000
Benin	5.9	12.3	2.8	5.83	47	31	52.4	57.2	84	..	74	310	142	990	..	3,000
Botswana	1.6	2.6	2.2	4.45	43	28	48.9	51.7	40	8	82	170	50	250	..	..
Burkina Faso	11.4	23.5	2.8	6.57	47	27	45.1	47.0	82	21	54	318	158	930	..	2,000
Burundi	6.6	12.3	2.8	6.28	46	8	45.5	48.8	106	..	50	255	176	1,300	248,000	12,000
Cameroon	14.3	28.5	2.7	5.30	44	45	54.5	57.2	63	13	46	264	102	550	1,000	1,000
Cape Verde	0.4	0.7	..	3.56	40	54	65.5	67.5	54	11	66	164	73	..	..	..
Central African Republic	3.5	6.0	2.1	4.95	42	39	46.4	51.0	103	15	46	294	164	700	..	38,000
Chad	6.9	12.6	2.8	5.51	43	21	46.3	49.3	92	..	28	325	149	1,500	12,000	..
Comoros	0.7	1.3	..	5.51	46	31	57.0	58.0	83	8	48	248	122	..	..	..
Congo, Republic of	2.8	5.7	2.8	5.87	46	59	48.6	53.4	81	15	42	220	108	890	40,000	21,000
Côte d'Ivoire	14.6	24.4	2.0	5.10	44	44	50.0	52.2	90	14	65	300	150	810	..	202,000
Djibouti	0.7	1.1	..	5.39	40	83	48.7	52.0	112	11	47	289	157	..	5,000	22,000
Equatorial Guinea	0.4	0.8	..	5.51	43	42	48.4	51.6	111	..	61	316	173	..	..	..
Eritrea	3.5	6.5	3.7	5.34	44	17	49.1	52.1	78	13	38	294	120	1,400	323,000	3,000
Ethiopia	62.1	136.3	3.2	7.00	47	13	48.4	51.6	113	16	54	294	177	1,400	48,000	313,000
Gabon	1.2	2.1	2.8	5.40	39	50	53.8	57.2	87	..	38	287	145	500	..	1,000
Gambia	1.2	2.0	..	5.20	41	26	45.4	48.7	78	..	89	375	107	1,100	..	8,000
Ghana	18.9	36.3	2.8	5.28	44	36	56.2	59.9	70	7	53	213	110	740	12,000	20,000
Guinea	7.7	15.3	1.4	6.61	47	30	46.0	47.0	130	21	49	337	210	1,600	..	430,000
Guinea-Bissau	1.1	1.9	2.0	5.42	42	22	42.4	45.2	132	20	53	336	223	910	..	4,000
Kenya	29.0	50.2	2.2	4.85	44	28	52.3	55.7	61	16	38	202	90	650	8,000	196,000
Lesotho	2.2	4.0	2.5	4.86	41	23	57.3	59.9	96	11	82	204	139	610	..	..
Liberia	2.7	6.6	8.6	6.33	43	45	50.0	53.0	157	..	44	288	235	560	475,000	100,000
Madagascar	16.3	34.5	3.1	5.65	46	27	57.0	60.0	100	17	68	364	164	490	..	..
Malawi	10.4	20.4	2.5	6.69	47	14	40.3	41.1	137	20	89	365	217	560	..	..
Mali	11.8	24.6	3.0	6.60	47	27	46.4	49.7	134	17	35	400	220	1,200	16,000	17,000
Mauritania	2.5	4.4	2.5	5.03	42	54	51.9	55.1	124	11	53	321	183	930	55,000	5,000
Mauritius	1.2	1.5	1.1	2.28	27	41	68.3	75.0	20	13	61	84	23	120	..	..
Mozambique	18.7	35.4	2.5	6.06	45	34	45.5	48.4	133	20	67	331	214	1,500	..	..
Namibia	1.7	3.0	2.4	4.90	42	37	54.7	56.6	60	16	61	206	77	370	..	1,000
Niger	10.1	22.4	3.3	7.10	49	17	46.9	50.2	191	15	59	320	320	1,200	10,000	7,000
Nigeria	121.8	238.4	2.8	5.97	45	39	50.8	54.0	114	16	45	204	191	1,000	1,000	9,000
Rwanda	6.5	13.0	7.9	6.00	45	6	40.8	43.4	105	17	76	191	170	1,300	43,000	28,000
Senegal	9.0	16.9	2.7	5.62	44	42	50.3	52.3	74	11	60	303	127	1,200	7,000	41,000
Sierra Leone	4.6	8.2	3.0	6.06	44	36	36.0	39.1	164	11	79	385	284	1,800	297,000	15,000
Somalia	10.7	23.7	3.9	7.00	48	26	47.4	50.6	125	16	33	294	211	1,600	486,000	..
South Africa	44.3	71.6	2.2	3.81	37	51	62.3	68.3	50	..	76	126	66	230	..	28,000
Sudan	28.5	46.9	2.2	4.61	40	25	53.6	56.4	73	15	75	292	116	660	353,000	365,000
Swaziland	0.9	1.7	..	4.46	42	31	57.7	62.3	68	10	59	233	97	..	..	..
Tanzania	32.2	62.4	2.3	5.48	45	24	50.0	52.8	93	14	81	249	144	770	..	295,000
Togo	4.4	8.8	2.7	6.08	46	31	48.8	51.5	78	20	39	264	125	640	6000e	12,000
Uganda	21.3	45.0	2.6	7.10	49	13	40.4	42.3	88	..	63	218	141	1,200	10,000	185,000
Zaire (Congo-Kinshasa)	49.2	105.9	2.6	6.24	46	29	51.3	54.5	119	16	41	286	207	870	132,000	255,000
Zambia	8.7	16.2	2.5	5.49	47	43	42.2	43.7	112	13	93	220	202	940	..	118,000
Zimbabwe	11.9	19.3	2.1	4.68	44	32	47.6	49.4	49	14	77	181	73	570	..	1,000
South Asia	**1314.9**	**1,893.1**	**..**	**..**	**..**	**..**	**..**	**..**	**80**	**33**	**77**	**238**	**119**	**607**	**2,888,000**	**1695250**
Afghanistan	23.4	45.3	5.3	6.90	41	20	45.0	46.0	165	20	42	360	257	1,700	2,622,000	..
Bangladesh	124.0	180.0	1.6	3.14	38	18	58.1	58.2	83	50	59	247	112	850	40,000	40,100
Bhutan	1.9	3.6	2.8	5.89	43	6	51.6	54.9	90	..	86	324	127	1,600	113,000	..
India	975.8	1,330.2	1.6	3.07	34	27	62.1	62.7	73	33	81	236	111	570	13,000	323,500
Maldives	0.3	0.6	..	6.80	46	27	65.7	63.3	54	20	94	258	76	..	..	..

TABLE 1, continued: Global Hunger – Life and Death Indicators

| | Population | | | | | | Life expectancy at birth 1995-2000 | | Infant mortality rate per 1,000 live births 1996 | % infants with low birth weight 1990-1994 | % 1-year-old children immunized (measles) 1995-96 | Under-5 mortality rate per 1,000 live births | | Maternal mortality rate per 100,000 live births | Refugees 1996 | |
	Total (millions) 1997	Projected (millions) 2025	Projected growth rate (%) 1995-2000	Projected total fertility rate 1995-2000	% population below age 15 1998	% population urban 1995	Male	Female				1960	1996		Country of origin	Country of asylum
Nepal	23.2	40.6	2.5	4.95	43	14	57.6	57.1	82	..	45	290	116	1,500	..	116,000
Pakistan	147.8	268.9	2.7	5.02	42	35	62.9	65.1	95	25	78	221	136	340	..	1,215,650
Sri Lanka	18.5	23.9	1.0	2.10	27	22	70.9	75.4	17	25	86	130	19	140	100,000	..
East Asia and the Pacific	**1844.4**	**2,273.7**	**..**	**..**	**..**	**..**	**..**	**..**	**41**	**11**	**92**	**200**	**54**	**214**	**725,000**	**516,800**
Brunei	0.3	0.5	..	2.70	33	58	73.4	78.1	9	..	100 x	87	11	..	..	..
Burma (Myanmar)	47.6	67.6	1.8	3.30	35	26	58.5	61.8	105	16	86	237	150	580	215,000	..
Cambodia	10.8	17.0	2.2	4.50	42	21	52.6	55.4	108	..	72	217	170	900	77,000	..
China	1255.1	1,480.4	0.9	1.80	26	30	68.2	71.7	38	9	97	209	47	95	128,000	281,800
Fiji	0.8	1.2	..	2.76	32	41	70.6	74.9	20	12	94	97	24	..	..	..
Hong Kong[a]	6.3	6.5	0.8	1.32	18	95	76.1	81.8	5	8	77	52	6	7	..	..
Indonesia	206.5	275.2	1.5	2.63	32	35	63.3	67.0	47	14	92	216	71	650	10,000	100
Korea, N.	23.2	30.0	1.6	2.10	27	61	68.9	75.1	23	..	60	120	30	70	..	..
Korea, S.	46.1	52.5	0.9	1.65	22	81	68.8	76.0	6	9	92x	124	7	130	..	..
Laos	5.4	10.2	3.1	6.69	45	22	52.0	55.0	102	18	62	233	128	650	14,000	..
Malaysia	21.5	31.6	2.0	3.24	37	54	69.9	74.3	11	8	81x	105	13	80	..	5,200
Mongolia	2.6	4.1	2.1	3.27	38	61	64.3	67.3	55	6	88	185	71	65	..	..
Papua New Guinea	4.6	7.5	2.2	4.65	39	16	57.2	58.7	79	23	44	248	112	930	..	8,200
Philippines	72.2	105.2	2.0	3.62	37	54	66.6	70.2	32	15	72	102	38	280	..	100
Singapore	3.5	4.2	1.5	1.79	23	100	75.1	79.5	4	7	88	40	4	10	..	..
Solomon Islands	0.4	0.8	..	4.98	43	17	69.6	73.9	24	20	67	185	29	..	..	800
Thailand	59.6	69.1	0.8	1.74	26	20	66.3	72.3	31	13	85	146	38	200	..	205,600
Viet Nam	77.9	110.1	1.8	2.97	35	21	64.9	69.6	33	17	96	219	44	160	281,000	15,000
Latin America and the Caribbean	**493.1**	**681.8**	**1.5**	**2.65**	**..**	**74**	**66.4**	**72.9**	**35**	**10**	**78**	**159**	**43**	**190**	**61,000**	**76,050**
Argentina	36.1	47.2	1.3	2.62	28	88	69.6	76.8	22	7	100	68	25	100	..	10,700
Belize	0.2	0.4	2.5	3.66	40	47	73.4	76.1	36	10	81	104	44	..	..	4,000
Bolivia	8.0	13.1	2.3	4.36	40	61	59.8	63.2	71	12	87	252	102	650	..	300
Brazil	165.2	216.6	1.2	2.17	30	78	63.4	71.2	44	11	74	181	52	220	..	2,300
Chile	14.8	19.5	1.4	2.44	29	84	72.3	78.3	11	5	96	138	13	65	..	300
Colombia	37.7	52.7	1.7	2.69	34	73	68.2	73.7	26	9	95	132	31	100	..	200
Costa Rica	3.7	5.6	2.1	2.95	34	50	74.5	79.2	13	7	86	112	15	60	..	23,100
Cuba	11.1	11.8	0.4	1.55	22	76	74.2	78.0	10	8	94	50	10	95	..	1,500
Dominican Republic	8.2	11.2	1.7	2.80	34	65	68.9	73.1	45	11	78	152	56	110	..	600
Ecuador	12.2	17.8	2.0	3.10	35	58	67.3	72.5	31	13	79	180	40	150	..	200
El Salvador	6.1	9.2	2.2	3.09	36	45	66.5	72.5	34	11	97	210	40	300	12,000	100
Guatemala	11.6	21.7	2.8	4.90	44	41	64.7	69.8	43	15	69	205	56	200	30,000	1,300
Guyana	0.9	1.1	..	2.32	31	36	61.1	67.9	60	19	91	126	83	..	..	..
Haiti	7.5	12.5	1.9	4.60	40	32	52.8	56.0	94	15	31	260	134	1,000	..	..
Honduras	6.1	10.7	2.8	4.30	43	44	67.5	72.3	29	9	91	203	35	220	..	..
Jamaica	2.5	3.4	0.9	2.44	31	54	72.4	76.8	10	10	99	76	11	120	..	..
Mexico	95.8	130.2	1.6	2.75	34	75	69.5	75.5	27	8	75	148	32	110	..	30,000
Nicaragua	4.5	7.6	2.6	3.85	42	63	65.8	70.6	44	15	78	209	57	160	19,000	700
Panama	2.8	3.8	1.6	2.63	32	53	71.8	76.4	18	9	92	104	20	55	..	300
Paraguay	5.2	9.4	2.6	4.17	40	53	67.5	72.0	28	5	81	90	34	160	..	..
Peru	24.8	35.5	1.7	2.98	34	72	65.9	70.9	45	11	71	236	58	280	..	..
Suriname	0.4	0.6	..	2.39	33	50	69.0	74.0	25	13	78	96	31	..	..	..
Trinidad and Tobago	1.3	1.7	0.8	2.10	28	72	71.5	76.2	15	10	88	73	17	90	..	..
Uruguay	3.2	3.7	0.6	2.25	24	90	69.6	76.1	20	8	85	47	22	85	..	150
Venezuela	23.2	34.8	2.0	2.98	35	93	70.0	75.7	24	9	64	70	28	120	..	300
Middle East and North Africa	**369.3**	**605.1**	**..**	**..**	**..**	**..**	**..**	**..**	**50**	**11**	**86**	**244**	**65**	**323**	**4,401,000**	**5,890,250**
Algeria	30.2	47.3	2.3	3.81	38	56	67.5	70.3	34	9	68	243	39	160	..	104,000
Bahrain	0.6	0.9	..	2.97	30	90	71.1	75.3	18	6	95	203	22	..	..	..
Cyprus	0.8	1.0	..	2.31	25	54	75.4	79.8	9	..	90	36	10	..	..	..
Egypt	65.7	95.8	1.9	3.40	36	45	64.7	67.3	57	10	85	258	78	170	35,000	46,000
Iran	73.1	128.3	2.2	4.77	44	59	68.5	70.0	33	9	95	233	37	120	..	1,900,000
Iraq	21.8	41.6	2.8	5.25	42	75	60.9	63.9	94	15	97	171	122	310	526,000	110,000
Jordan	6.0	11.9	3.3	5.13	43	71	67.7	71.8	21	7	98	149	25	150	..	1,413,800
Kuwait	1.8	2.9	3.0	2.77	36	97	74.1	78.2	13	7	99	128	14	29	..	90,000
Lebanon	3.2	4.4	1.8	2.75	34	87	68.1	71.7	33	10	85	85	40	300	..	362,300
Libya	6.0	12.9	3.3	5.92	45	86	63.9	67.5	50	..	92	269	61	220	..	27,000

TABLE 1, continued: Global Hunger – Life and Death Indicators

	Population						Life expectancy at birth 1995-2000		Infant mortality rate per 1,000 live births 1996	% infants with low birth weight 1990-1994	% 1-year-old children immunized (measles) 1995-96	Under-5 mortality rate per 1,000 live births		Maternal mortality rate per 100,000 live births	Refugees 1996	
	Total (millions) 1997	Projected (millions) 2025	Projected growth rate (%) 1995-2000	Projected total fertility rate 1995-2000	% population below age 15 1998	% population urban 1995	Male	Female				1960	1996		Country of origin	Country of asylum
Morocco	28.0	39.9	1.8	3.10	35	48	64.8	68.5	64	9	93	215	74	610	86,000d	..
Oman	2.5	6.5	4.2	7.20	48	13	68.9	73.3	15	8	98	300	18	190	..	..
Qatar	0.6	0.8	..	3.77	27	91	70.0	75.4	17	..	86	239	21	..	..	..
Saudi Arabia	20.2	42.4	3.4	5.90	41	80	69.9	73.4	25	7	92	292	30	130	..	116,750
Syria	15.3	26.3	2.5	4.00	43	52	66.7	71.2	28	11	95	201	34	180	..	361,000
Tunisia	9.5	13.5	1.8	2.92	33	57	68.4	70.7	28	8	86	244	35	170	..	..
Turkey	63.8	85.8	1.6	2.50	29	69	66.5	71.7	41	8	84	217	47	180	11,000	5,000
United Arab Emirates	2.4	3.3	2.0	3.46	29	84	73.9	76.5	15	6	90	240	18	26	..	500
West Bank and Gazaa	0.9c	..	..	..	52c	..	..	..	..	..	..	..	..	..	3,743,000	1,289,000
Yemen	16.9	39.6	3.7	7.60	48	34	57.4	58.4	78	19	51	340	105	1,400	..	64,900
Countries in Transitionb	**415.0**	**417.3**	**..**	**..**	**..**	**..**	**..**	**..**	**29**	**..**	**89**	**..**	**36**	**88**	**3,037,050**	**1,532,000**
Albania	3.4	4.3	0.6	2.60	30	37	68.0	74.0	34	7	92	151	40	65	..	..
Armenia	3.6	4.2	0.2	1.70	26	69	67.2	74.0	25	..	89	..	30	50	188,000	219,150
Azerbaijan	7.7	9.7	0.8	2.30	31	56	66.5	74.5	34	..	99	..	44	22	218,000	244,100
Belarus	10.3	9.6	-0.1	1.40	20	71	64.4	74.8	14	..	74	..	18	37	..	33,500
Bosnia and Herzegovina	4.0	4.3	3.9	1.40	20	49	70.5	75.9	15	..	88	155	17	..	557,000	40,000
Bulgaria	8.4	7.5	-0.5	1.45	17	71	67.8	74.9	16	6	93	70	19	27	..	2,400
Croatia	4.5	4.2	-0.1	1.60	18	64	68.1	76.5	10	..	91	98	11	..	335,000	50,000
Czech Republic	10.2	9.6	-0.1	1.40	18	65	69.8	76.0	6	6	97	..	7	15	..	700
Estonia	1.4	1.3	-1.0	1.30	19	73	63.9	75.0	13	..	86	..	16	41	..	..
Georgia	5.4	5.8	-0.1	1.90	23	58	68.5	76.7	23	..	63	..	29	33	11,000	100
Hungary	9.9	8.7	-0.6	1.40	17	65	64.5	73.8	11	9	100	57	12	30	..	3,400
Kazakhstan	16.9	20.0	0.1	2.30	29	60	62.8	72.5	38	..	97	..	45	80	..	14,000
Kyrgyzstan	4.5	6.0	0.4	3.21	36	39	63.4	71.9	39	..	80	..	50	110	..	15,500
Latvia	2.4	2.1	-1.1	1.40	19	73	62.5	74.3	16	..	82	..	20	40	..	..
Lithuania	3.7	3.5	-0.3	1.50	20	72	64.9	76.0	14	..	96	..	18	36	..	100
Macedonia	2.2	2.5	0.7	1.90	23	60	70.3	74.7	26	..	90	177	30	..	..	3,500
Moldova	4.5	4.9	0.1	1.80	25	52	63.5	71.5	26	4	98	..	32	60	..	..
Poland	38.7	40.0	0.1	1.65	21	65	66.7	75.7	12	..	91	70	14	19	..	1,200
Romania	22.6	21.1	-0.2	1.40	19	55	66.0	73.2	21	11	94	82	25	130	..	2,000
Russia	147.2	131.4	-0.3	1.35	19	76	58.0	71.5	20	..	95	..	25	75	323,400	324,000
Slovakia	5.4	5.5	0.1	1.50	21	59	67.0	75.8	10	..	99	..	11	..	..	100
Slovenia	1.9	1.7	-0.1	1.30	17	64	69.2	77.8	6	..	91x	45	6	13	..	5,300
Tajikistan	6.2	9.7	1.9	3.93	41	32	64.2	70.2	56	..	80	..	76	130	32,000	3,800
Turkmenistan	4.3	6.5	1.9	3.58	38	45	61.2	68.0	57	5	66	..	78	55	..	13,000
Ukraine	51.2	46.0	-0.4	1.38	19	70	63.6	74.0	18	..	96x	..	24	50	..	4,900
Uzbekistan	24.1	36.5	1.9	3.48	39	41	64.3	70.7	46	..	81	..	60	55	46,000	1,250
Yugoslavia	10.4	10.7	0.5	1.80	21	57	69.8	75.3	19	..	81x	120	22	..	17,650	550,000
Industrial Countries	**843.8**	**907.8**	**0.3**	**1.59**	**..**	**75**	**70.6**	**78.4**	**6**	**6**	**83**	**37**	**7**	**13**	**..**	**1,088,950**
Australia	18.4	23.9	1.1	1.89	21	85	75.4	81.2	6	6	..	24	6	9	..	18,000
Austria	8.2	8.3	0.6	1.42	17	56	73.7	80.1	5	6	60	43	6	10	..	11,400
Belgium	10.2	10.3	0.3	1.62	18	97	73.9	80.6	6	6	70	35	7	10	..	14,100
Canada	30.2	36.4	0.9	1.61	20	77	76.1	81.8	6	6	98	33	7	6	..	48,800
Denmark	5.3	5.3	0.2	1.82	18	85	73.0	78.3	6	6	88x	25	6	9	..	13,000
Finland	5.2	5.3	0.3	1.83	19	63	73.0	80.1	4	4	98	28	4	11	..	1,600
France	58.7	60.4	0.3	1.63	19	73	74.6	82.9	5	5	82	34	6	15	..	16,000
Germany	82.4	80.9	0.3	1.30	16	87	73.4	79.9	5	..	75	40	6	22	..	277,000
Greece	10.6	10.1	0.3	1.38	16	65	75.5	80.6	8	6	90	64	9	10	..	2,100
Ireland	3.6	3.7	0.2	1.80	22	58	74.0	79.4	6	4	..	36	7	10	..	4,300
Israel	5.9	8.0	1.9	2.75	29	91	75.7	79.5	8	7	94	39	9	7	..	..
Italy	57.2	51.7	0.0	1.19	14	67	75.1	81.4	6	5	50	50	7	12	..	20,000
Japan	125.9	121.3	0.2	1.48	15	78	76.9	82.9	4	7	68	40	6	18	..	300
Luxembourg	0.4	0.5	..	1.76	18	89	73.1	79.7	7	..	80x	41	7	..	..	..
Netherlands	15.7	16.1	0.5	1.55	18	89	75.0	80.6	5	..	94	22	6	12	..	64,200

TABLE 1, continued: Global Hunger – Life and Death Indicators

	Population						Life expectancy at birth 1995-2000		Infant mortality rate per 1,000 live births 1996	% infants with low birth weight 1990-1994	% 1-year-old children immunized (measles) 1995-96	Under-5 mortality rate per 1,000 live births		Maternal mortality rate per 100,000 live births	Refugees 1996	
	Total (millions) 1997	Projected (millions) 2025	Projected growth rate (%) 1995-2000	Projected total fertility rate 1995-2000	% population below age 15 1998	% population urban 1995	Male	Female				1960	1996		Country of origin	Country of asylum
New Zealand	3.7	4.9	1.1	2.02	23	86	74.7	79.7	7	6	87	26	7	25	..	..
Norway	4.4	4.7	0.4	1.88	20	73	74.8	80.6	5	4	93	23	6	6	..	3,100
Portugal	9.8	9.4	-0.1	1.48	17	36	71.8	78.9	7	5	99	112	7	15	..	150
Spain	39.8	37.5	0.1	1.22	16	76	74.5	81.5	5	4	90x	57	5	7	..	3,300
Sweden	8.9	9.5	0.3	1.80	19	83	76.2	80.8	4	5	96	20	4	7	..	8,400
Switzerland	7.3	7.6	0.7	1.46	17	61	75.3	81.8	5	5	..	27	5	6	..	34,100
United Kingdom	58.2	59.5	0.1	1.72	19	89	74.5	79.8	6	7	92	27	7	9	..	58,100
United States	273.8	332.5	0.8	1.96	22	76	73.4	80.1	8	7	89	30	8	12	..	491,000
World	**5,929.8**	**8,021.5**	**1.4**	**2.79**	**..**	**45**	**63.4**	**67.7**	**60**	**17**	**79**	**191**	**88**	**428**	**13,923,050**	**13,566,000**

.. Data not available.
a Territory.
b Central and Eastern European countries and the newly independent states of the former Soviet Union.
c Gaza Strip only.
d Data for Western Sahara.
e Bread for the World Institute estimate.
f Palestinian refugees from various sources.
x Data refer to a period other than specified in the column heading.

TABLE 2: Food, Nutrition and Education

	Per capita dietary energy supply (DES) (calories/day) 1990-1992	DES annual growth rate 1969-1971 to 1990-1992	Daily per capita calorie supply (% of requirements) 1988-1990	Food production per capita (1989-1991=100) 1995	Food expenditures (% of household consumption) 1980-1985	Iodine deficiency total goiter rate 6-11 yrs. (%) 1985-94	Adult literacy rate 1995 Total	Male	Female	Primary school 1993-97 (net) Total (Gross enrollment ratio) 1995	Male	Female	Combined primary, secondary and tertiary 1994 Total	Male	Female
Developing Countries	**2,520**	**0.7**	**107**	**96.7**	**41**	**18**	**71**	**79**	**62**	**..**	**83**	**76**	**56**	**60**	**52**
Africa (sub-Saharan)	**2,040**	**-0.2**	**93**	**94.7**	**38**	**18**	**57**	**66**	**47**	**75**	**61**	**55**	**..**	**..**	**..**
Angola	1,840	-0.7	80	86.0	..	7	42x	56x	29x	88	..	..	31	..	..
Benin	2,520	0.7	104	103.5	37	24	37	49	26	64	74	43	35	48	23
Botswana	2,320	0.4	97	94.9	25	8	70	81	60	116	94	99	71	70	72
Burkina Faso	2,140	1.0	94	101.9	..	16	19	30	9	38	37	24	20	25	15
Burundi	1,950	-0.4	84	82.4	..	42	35	49	23	72	56x	48x	31	35	27
Cameroon	2,040	-0.6	95	94.2	24	26	63	75	52	87	69y	60y	46	51	42
Cape Verde	..	..	..	212.0	..	..	72	81	64	114	100	100	64	65	62
Central African Republic	1,720	-1.5	82	95.4	..	63	60	69	52	..	70y	55y	37	47	27
Chad	1,810	-0.9	73	101.3	..	15	48	62	35	59	..	..	25	35	15
Comoros	..	..	..	91.8	..	20x	57	64	50	81	58	48	39	42	35
Congo (Brazzaville)	2,210	0.3	103	91.1	37	8	75	87	68	..	71	50	56	..	..
Côte d'Ivoire	2,460	0.1	111	90.7	39	6	40	50	30	69	59y	46y	39	47	32
Djibouti	..	..	..	70.1	..	..	46	60	33	36	37	28	20	..	..
Equatorial Guinea	..	..	..	84.1	..	10x	79	90	68	..	..	..	64	70	59
Eritrea	..	..	..	..	..	..	..	..	..	47	33	30	24	..	..
Ethiopia	1,620	-0.3	73	..	49	31	36	46	25	23	28	19	18	21	14
Gabon	2,490	0.6	104	91.4	..	5	63	74	53	134x	87y	86y	60	60	60
Gambia	2,320	0.3	..	82.6	..	20x	39	53	25	76x	51y	43y	34	41	27
Ghana	2,090	-0.3	93	130.1	50	10	65	76	54	76	70y	69y	44	50	38
Guinea	2,400	0.5	97	105.9	..	55	36	50	22	44x	39y	26y	24	33	15
Guinea-Bissau	..	..	97	101.9	..	19	55	68	43	..	60x	33x	29	38	21
Kenya	1,970	-0.5	89	87.2	38	7	78	86	70	91	85y	83y	55	56	54
Lesotho	2,260	0.6	93	78.5	..	43	71	81	62	98	60	71	56	51	60
Liberia	1,780	-1.1	98	..	..	6	38	54	22	..	59y	53y	..	..	..
Madagascar	2,160	-0.6	95	89.4	59	24	46	60	32	89x	62y	61y	33	..	..
Malawi	1,910	-1.0	88	111.0	30	13	56	72	42	80	100	100	67	71	63
Mali	2,230	0.4	96	94.9	57	29	31	39	23	31	30	19	17	21	13
Mauritania	2,610	1.4	106	86.7	..	..	38	50	26	69	64	55	36	42	31
Mauritius	2,780	0.9	128	100.3	24	0	83	87	79	106	96	96	61	61	62
Mozambique	1,740	-0.5	77	97.5	..	20	40	58	23	60	45	35	25	30	21
Namibia	2,190	0.0	..	93.8	..	35	76x	78x	74x	136	..	..	84	..	..
Niger	2,190	0.5	95	99.8	..	9	14	21	7	29	34y	19y	15	19	11
Nigeria	2,100	-0.6	93	113.8	48	10	57	67	47	93	60y	58y	50	55	44
Rwanda	1,860	-0.4	82	71.6	29	49	61	70	52	50	76x	76x	37	..	..
Senegal	2,310	-0.3	98	100.4	49	12	33	43	23	56x	60	48	31	37	25
Sierra Leone	1,820	-0.8	83	77.9	56	7	31	45	18	..	..	..	28	34	22
Somalia	1,590	-0.6	81	..	..	7	24x	36x	14x	..	..	..	..	..	..
South Africa	2,810	0.0	128	76.2	34	2	82	82	82	111	95	96	81	80	82
Sudan	2,150	-0.1	87	108.6	60	20	46	58	35	50	59y	52y	31	35	28
Swaziland	2,680	0.7	..	80.4	..	..	77	78	76	120	95	96	72	74	70
Tanzania	2,110	0.9	95	85.6	64	37	68	79	57	70	47	48	34	35	33
Togo	2,290	0.0	99	87.5	..	22	52	67	37	102	98	72	50	62	37
Uganda	2,220	-0.2	93	99.3	..	7	62	74	50	91	65y	63y	34	39	30
Zaire (Congo-Kinshasa)	2,090	-0.1	96	85.7	..	9	77	87	68	55x	..	..	38	..	..
Zambia	2,020	-0.4	87	83.0	36	51x	78	86	71	104	76	75	48	51	44
Zimbabwe	2,080	-0.2	94	76.0	40	42	85	90	80	119	91y	90y	68	72	64
South Asia	**2,290**	**0.9**	**99**	**..**	**51**	**18**	**49**	**63**	**36**	**98**	**75**	**63**	**53**	**60**	**43**
Afghanistan	1,660	-1.3	72	..	..	20	32	47	15	31	36y	11y	..	..	..
Bangladesh	1,990	-0.3	88	89.2	59	50	38	49	26	111	82y	82y	39	45	34
Bhutan	..	..	128	102.0	..	25	42	56	28	70x	..	..	31x	..	..
India	2,330	0.6	101	104.3	52	9	52	66	38	105	75y	61y	56	63	47
Maldives	..	..	..	96.2	..	24	93	93	93	134	..	..	71	70	70
Nepal	2,140	0.6	100	92.4	57	44	28	41	14	107	80y	60y	55	68	42
Pakistan	2,340	0.3	99	122.0	37	32	38	50	24	65	71y	62y	38	50	25
Sri Lanka	2,230	-0.1	101	106.5	43	14	90	93	87	106	..	..	66	65	68
East Asia and the Pacific	**2,680**	**1.1**	**112**	**..**	**45**	**21**	**84**	**91**	**76**	**117**	**98**	**96**	**..**	**..**	**..**
Brunei	..	..	..	98.3	..	2x	88	93	83	107	91	91	70	..	..
Burma (Myanmar)	2,580	1.1	114	127.5	..	18	83	89	78	..	85y	85y	48	48	47
Cambodia	2,100	-0.8	96	81.3	..	15	65x	80x	53x	47x	..	..	58	..	..

TABLE 2, continued: Food, Nutrition and Education

| | Food supply | | | | | | | | | | Educational enrollment (% of relevant age group) | | | | |
| | | | | | | | | | | Primary school 1993-97 (net) | | | Combined primary, secondary and tertiary 1994 | | |
	Per capita dietary energy supply (DES) (calories/day) 1990-1992	DES annual growth rate 1969-1971 to 1990-1992	Daily per capita calorie supply (% of requirements) 1988-1990	Food production per capita (1989-1991=100) 1995	Food expenditures (% of household consumption) 1980-1985	Iodine deficiency total goiter rate 6-11 yrs. (%) 1985-94	Adult literacy rate 1995 Total	Male	Female	Total (Gross enrollment ratio) 1995	Male	Female	Total	Male	Female
China	2,710	1.4	112	113.3	61	20	82	90	73	109x	99	98	58	61	55
Fiji	..	..		96.9	..	47	92	94	89	..	99x	100x	79	80	78
Hong Kong[a]	3,150	0.8	125	57.1	12	..	..	..	..	..	..	..	72	72	73
Indonesia	2,700	1.3	121	112.0	48	28	84	90	78	114	99	95	62	65	59
Korea, N.	2,930	1.0	121	..	..	..	..	..	..	..	..	..	75	..	..
Korea, S.	3,270	0.7	120	111.2	35	..	98	99	97	101	98	99	82	86	78
Laos	2,210	0.1	111	102.4	..	25	57	69	44	107	70y	67y	50	58	42
Malaysia	2,830	0.7	120	103.2	23	20	84	89	78	93	91	92	62	61	63
Mongolia	2,100	-0.3	97	70.1	..	28	83	89	77	..	78	81	52	45	59
Papua New Guinea	2,610	0.9	114	95.2	..	30	72	81	63	74	..	..	38	41	34
Philippines	2,290	1.2	104	103.7	51	15	95	95	94	111	89y	91y	78	75	80
Singapore	..	..	136	41.0	19	0	91	96	86	107	..	..	72	73	71
Solomon Islands	..	..	..	90.8	..	0	62x	..	56x	94	..	..	47	..	..
Thailand	2,380	0.4	103	104.0	30	8	94	96	92	98	..	..	53	53	53
Vietnam	2,200	0.0	103	111.2	..	20	94	97	91	111	..	..	55	57	52
Latin America and Caribbean	**2,740**	**0.0**	**114**	**98.0**	**34**	**12**	**87**	**88**	**85**	**110**	**89**	**90**	**69**	**69**	**69**
Argentina	2,950	-0.5	131	103.8	35	8	96	96	96	107	..	..	77	76	79
Belize	..	..	..	118.2	..	0	80x	70	70	107	100	98	68	..	..
Bolivia	2,030	0.2	84	82.0	33	21	83	91	76	..	90y	89y	66	72	61
Brazil	2,790	0.6	114	106.6	35	14x	83	83	83	111	93y	94y	72	72	72
Chile	2,540	-0.2	102	114.5	29	9x	95	95	95	98	87	85	72	72	71
Colombia	2,630	1.2	106	92.5	29	7	91	91	91	119	90y	91y	70	67	72
Costa Rica	2,870	0.8	121	99.4	33	4	95	95	95	105	86x	87x	68	69	67
Cuba	3,000	0.6	135	61.5	..	10	96	96	95	104	99	99	63	61	65
Dominican Republic	2,270	0.6	102	90.8	46	5	82	82	82	97	79	83	68	67	69
Ecuador	2,540	0.8	105	94.2	30	10	90	92	88	123	91	92	72	73	71
El Salvador	2,530	1.5	102	102.1	33	25	72	74	70	79	78	80	55	55	55
Guatemala	2,280	0.4	103	89.5	36	20	56	63	49	84	61y	55y	46	50	42
Guyana	2,350	0.1	89	142.0	..	..	98	99	98	98	90	89	67	66	67
Haiti	1,740	-0.6	89	83.7	..	4x	45	48	42	..	68y	69y	29	30	28
Honduras	2,310	0.4	98	88.6	39	9	73	73	73	112	89	91	60	59	61
Jamaica	2,580	0.1	114	110.2	36	..	85	81	89	109	100x	100x	65	64	67
Mexico	3,190	0.7	131	101.5	35	3	90	92	87	112	..	..	66	67	65
Nicaragua	2,290	-0.2	99	89.0	..	4	66	65	67	103	82	85	62	61	63
Panama	2,240	-0.1	98	96.70	38	13	91	91	90	105	91x	92x	70	69	71
Paraguay	2,620	-0.1	116	105.0	30	49	92	94	91	112	89	89	62	62	62
Peru	1,880	-1.0	87	110.6	35	36	89	95	83	119	91	90	81	84	77
Suriname	2,510	0.6	..	88.6	..	0	93	95	91	..	..	..	71	..	..
Trinidad and Tobago	2,630	0.3	114	101.3	19	..	98	99	97	94	83	94	67	67	67
Uruguay	2,680	-0.5	101	105.7	31	..	97	97	98	109	95	95	75	70	80
Venezuela	2,590	0.4	99	106.7	23	11	91	92	90	96	87x	90x	68	66	69
North Africa	**2,960**	**0.3**	**123**	**..**	**39**	**20**	**59**	**70**	**47**	**97**	**85**	**76**	**..**	**..**	**..**
Algeria	2,900	2.2	123	101.7	..	9	62	74	49	103	99	91	66	70	61
Bahrain	..	..	..	98.2	..	..	85	89	79	111	99	100	85	83	87
Cyprus	..	..	..	114.3	..	..	94x	98x	91x	101	96	96	75	75	75
Egypt	3,340	1.4	132	107.4	49	5	51	64	39	97	83y	72y	69	75	63
Iran	2,760	1.4	125	117.7	37	30	69	78	59	105	99y	93y	68	..	..
Iraq	2,270	0.0	128	94.2	..	7	58	71	45	91	83x	74x	53	59	46
Jordan	2,900	0.8	110	137.0	35	..	87	93	79	94	89x	89x	66	..	..
Kuwait	2,460	-0.3	..	132.9	..	..	79	82	75	..	65	65	57	56	57
Lebanon	3,260	1.6	127	105.4	..	15	92	95	90	115	..	..	75	74	76
Libya	3,290	1.4	140	74.6	..	6	76	88	63	110	98x	96x	91	91	90
Morocco	3,000	1.0	125	70.6	38	20	44	57	31	73	81	62	46	52	39
Oman	..	..	..	74.7	..	10	59x	71x	46x	85	72	70	60	..	..
Qatar	..	..	..	110.7	..	..	79	79	80	90	81	80	73	71	74
Saudi Arabia	2,730	1.8	121	80.6	..	..	63	72	50	75	63	61	56	59	53
Syria	3,220	1.5	126	107.8	..	73	71	86	56	105	95	87	64	68	59
Tunisia	3,260	1.7	131	81.0	37	4x	67	79	55	118	98	95	67	71	64
Turkey	3,510	0.8	127	96.1	40	36	82	92	72	103	98	94	63	70	55
United Arab Emirates	3,370	0.3	..	129.8	..	0	79	79	80	110	84	82	82	80	85
West Bank and Gaza[a]	..	..	..	c	..	..	..	..	..	..	..	..	..	..	..
Yemen	2,160	0.9	..	..	..	32	33x	53x	26x	..	73y	39y	52	..	..

TABLE 2, continued: Food, Nutrition and Education

	Per capita dietary energy supply (DES) (calories/day) 1990-1992	DES annual growth rate 1969-1971 to 1990-1992	Daily per capita calorie supply (% of requirements) 1988-1990	Food production per capita (1989-1991=100) 1995	Food expenditures (% of household consumption) 1980-1985	Iodine deficiency total goiter rate 6-11 yrs. (%) 1985-94	Adult literacy rate 1995 Total	Adult literacy rate 1995 Male	Adult literacy rate 1995 Female	Primary school 1993-97 (net) Total (Gross enrollment ratio) 1995	Primary school Male	Primary school Female	Combined primary, secondary and tertiary 1994 Total	Combined Male	Combined Female
Countries in Transition[b]	**3,230**	**-0.5**	**128**	..	..	**20**	**97**	**98**	**96**	**97**	**95**	**94**	**75**	**73**	**77**
Albania	2,630	0.3	107	132.2	..	41	..	..	..	96	95	97	59	59	60
Armenia	..	..	..	..	..	10	100	100	99	90	..	..	78	74	83
Azerbaijan	..	..	..	..	..	20	100	100	99	89	..	..	72	74	71
Belarus	..	..	..	..	..	22	99	100	99	96	97	94	80	79	81
Bosnia and Herzegovina	..	..	..	..	..	..	..	..	..	..	..	..	..	..	..
Bulgaria	3,160	-0.5	148	64.5	..	20	98	99	98	92	98	96	66	64	69
Croatia	..	..	..	..	..	..	98	98	97	85	83	82	67	67	68
Czech Republic	..	..	..	..	..	..	..	..	..	103	98	98	70	69	70
Estonia	..	..	..	..	..	..	98	98	98	83	93	94	72	69	74
Georgia	..	..	..	..	..	20	99	100	99	..	81	82	69	68	69
Hungary	3,560	0.3	137	72.3	25	0	99	99	99	95	92	94	67	66	68
Kazakhstan	..	..	..	..	..	20	100	100	99	86	..	..	73	71	75
Kyrgyzstan	..	..	..	..	..	20	97	99	95	..	86y	87y	73	71	74
Latvia	..	..	..	..	..	..	100	100	100	83	86	82	67	66	69
Lithuania	..	..	..	..	..	..	99	100	99	92	..	..	70	68	72
Macedonia	..	..	..	..	..	..	..	..	..	87	86	84	60	60	61
Moldova	..	..	..	..	..	..	99	98	99	77	..	..	67	66	68
Poland	3,340	-0.2	131	83.7	29	10	..	99x	98x	98	97	96	79	79	80
Romania	3,160	0.2	116	100.8	..	10	98	99	97	95	92	92	62	62	62
Russia	..	..	..	..	..	..	99	100	99	107	100	100	78	75	82
Slovakia	..	..	..	..	..	..	..	..	..	??	..	..	72	71	73
Slovenia	..	..	..	..	..	..	99x	100x	99x	97	100	99	74	72	76
Tajikistan	..	..	..	..	..	20	100	100	100	89	..	..	69	70	67
Turkmenistan	..	..	..	..	..	20	98x	99x	97x	..	81y	80y	90	90	90
Ukraine	..	..	..	..	..	10	99	98	99	87	..	..	76	75	78
Uzbekistan	..	..	..	..	..	18	100	100	100	80	83y	83y	73	75	71
Yugoslavia	..	..	..	..	..	..	98	99	97	..	69x	70x	..	..	..
Industrial Countries	**3,410**	**0.5**	**134**	..	**14**	..	**98**	**98**	**96**	..	**98**	**98**	..	..	..
Australia	3,180	0.0	124	105.3	13	0	..	..	..	108	98	98	79	77	80
Austria	3,530	0.4	133	95.4	16	0	..	..	..	103	100	100	87	88	85
Belgium	3,670d	0.6d	149	111.2d	15	5	..	..	..	99	98	98	86	86	86
Canada	3,100	0.1	122	104.6	11	0	97x	..	..	105	96	94	100	100x	100x
Denmark	3,620	0.6	135	104.6	13	5	..	..	..	98	98	99	89	87	90
Finland	3,030	-0.2	113	91.6	16	0	..	..	..	100	99	99	97	92	100
France	3,640	0.4	143	97.0	16	5x	..	..	..	106	99	99	89	87	91
Germany	3,410	0.3	..	84.6	12	10	..	..	..	97	100	100	81	83	79
Greece	3,770	0.8	151	101.1	30	10	97	98	95	..	98x	98x	82	83	80
Ireland	3,790	0.5	157	103.8	22	..	..	..	..	103	100	100	88	87	89
Israel	3,140	0.1	125	97.3	21	..	95x	97x	93x	95	..	..	75	74	76
Italy	3,540	0.2	139	99.0	19	20	98	99	98	98	..	..	73	72	74
Japan	2,900	0.4	125	93.9	17	0	..	..	..	102	100	100	78	79	77
Luxembourg	..	..	..	..	..	0	..	..	..	..	..	..	58	57	59
Netherlands	3,170	0.2	114	100.4	13	3	..	..	..	97	99	99	91	93	88
New Zealand	3,580	0.4	131	104.7	12	..	..	..	..	102	100	100	94	91	96
Norway	3,230	0.3	120	98.6	15	..	..	..	..	99	99	99	92	92	93
Portugal	3,620	0.9	136	90.3	34	15	90	92	87	120	100	100	81	77	84
Spain	3,680	1.3	141	84.3	24	10	97	98	96	104	100	100	90	87	94
Sweden	2,960	0.1	111	91.1	13	0	..	..	..	100	100	100	82	81	84
Switzerland	3,380	-0.2	130	88.4	17	0	..	..	..	101	100	100	76	78	73
United Kingdom	3,280	0.0	130	98.4	12	0	..	..	..	112	100	100	86	85	86
United States	3,700	0.6	138	104.2	10	0	99x	..	..	107	96	97	96	93	98
World	**2,720**	**0.5**	**112**	**107.5**	..	**18**	**75**	**81**	**66**	**104**	**85**	**79**	**60**	**64**	**57**

a Territory.

b Central and Eastern European countries and the newly independent states of the former Soviet Union.

c Gaza, 80; West Bank, 115.

d Luxembourg included.

x Data refer to a period other than specified in the column heading, mostly more recent.

y Indicates net primary school data derived from household surveys

The number '0' (zero) means zero or less than half the unit shown.

TABLE 3: Hunger, Malnutrition and Poverty

	Undernourished population			Relative inadequacy of food supply: % below minimum required 1990-1992	% under-5 (1990-1997) suffering from:				% population with access to safe water 1990-1996			Population in Poverty (%)			
					Underweight		Wasting	Stunting				Below national poverty line 1984-1996			Below international poverty line ($1 a day; 1985 PPP$)
	Number of undernourished people (millions) 1990-1992	Proportion of population undernourished (%) 1969-1971	1990-1992		moderate & severe	severe	moderate & severe	moderate & severe	Total	Urban	Rural	National	Urban	Rural	1981-1996
Developing Countries	**841.0**	**35**	**20**	**4.7**	**32.0**	**10.0**	**9.0**	**39.0**	..	..	..	..	..	..	**32.0**
Africa (sub-Saharan)	**215.0**	**38**	**43**	..	**30.0**	**9.0**	**8.0**	**41.0**	**47**	..	..	..	..	..	**39.0h**
Angola	5.1	39	54	19.6	..	..	..	..	32	69	15	..	..	..	..
Benin	1.0	36	20	4.3	29.2	7.4	14.3	25.0	70	82	63	33.0	..	..	..
Botswana	0.4	34	29	7.3	15x	..	..	44x	70	100	53	..	..	..	34.7
Burkina Faso	3.8	66	41	12.4	32.7	9.3	13.2	33.3	78	..	..	..	..	..	..
Burundi	2.9	42	50	17.6	37.5	10.0	5.7	47.4	58	97	55	36.2	..	..	..
Cameroon	5.1	29	43	13.3	15.1	3.8	2.9	26.0	41	71	24	40.0	44.4	32.4	..
Cape Verde	..	..	..	..	18.8	..	3.3	25.8	52	75	34	44.0	..	..	..
Central African Republic	1.9	28	62	25.5	23.2	6.0	6.4	28.4	38	59	23	..	..	..	..
Chad	3.5	40	61	25.0	31.0	..	..	..	24	48	17	..	..	..	..
Comoros	..	..	..	..	25.8	7.9	8.3	33.8	48	..	..	..	..	..	..
Congo (Brazzaville)	0.8	42	34	9.2	23.9	4.7	5.5	27.5	60	94	8	..	..	..	..
Côte d'Ivoire	2.7	24	22	5.0	23.8	6.3	8.3	24.4	82	97	73	..	..	..	17.7
Djibouti	..	..	..	..	22.9	8.8	10.7	22.2	24	27	14	..	..	..	..
Equatorial Guinea	..	..	..	..	..	..	..	..	..	10	48	..	..	..	..
Eritrea	..	..	..	..	41.0	..	10.0	66.0	..	..	7	..	..	..	..
Ethiopia	31.2	59	65	28.0	47.7	16.0	8.0	64.2	27	90	20	..	..	..	33.8
Gabon	0.3	39	24	5.7	..	..	..	..	67	80	30	..	..	..	..
Gambia	0.3	36	29	7.5	..	..	..	..	61	87	86	64.0	..	..	..
Ghana	6.2	34	40	12.0	27.3	7.9	11.3	25.9	56	76	46	31.4	26.7	34.3	..
Guinea	1.5	35	25	5.8	26.0	9.0	12.0	32.0	49	78	51	..	..	..	26.3
Guinea-Bissau	..	..	..	..	23x	..	..	..	27	18	47	48.8	24.1	60.9	87.0
Kenya	11.3	33	46	15.1	22.5	5.6	7.8	33.6	49	74	43	42.0	29.3	46.4	50.2
Lesotho	0.6	49	35	10.0	21.4	2x	15.8	32.9	57	90	40	49.2	27.8	53.9	50.4
Liberia	1.6	34	59	23.0	..	..	..	..	46	79	13	..	..	..	..
Madagascar	3.8	20	31	8.0	34.1	9.9	7.4	49.8	32	55	10	59.0	..	..	72.3
Malawi	4.8	26	49	16.4	29.9	8.7	7.0	48.3	54	91	41	..	..	..	..
Mali	3.3	45	34	9.5	40.0	16.5	23.3	30.1	44	42	25	..	..	..	..
Mauritania	0.4	52	20	4.4	23.0	9.2	7.2	44.0	41	49	86	57.0	..	..	31.4
Mauritius	0.2	31	18	4.0	14.9	2.0	13.7	9.7	99	95	100	10.6	..	..	..
Mozambique	9.6	55	66	29.2	27.0	11.0	8.0	55.0	28	44	17	..	..	..	..
Namibia	0.5	36	35	9.6	26.2	5.8	8.6	28.5	57	97	37	..	..	..	..
Niger	2.9	48	37	10.4	42.6	15.0	15.0	39.5	57	58	54	..	..	..	61.5
Nigeria	42.9	26	38	11.1	35.3	11.8	8.9	42.7	43	69	11	34.1	30.4	36.4	28.9
Rwanda	3.4	35	47	14.5	29.4	6.0	3.8	48.7	..	..	79	51.2	..	..	45.7
Senegal	2.3	24	30	7.9	22.2	5.6	8.4	24.7	52	85	28	..	..	..	54.0
Sierra Leone	2.4	34	55	19.9	28.7	..	8.5	34.7	34	58	21	75.0	..	..	..
Somalia	6.4	59	72	35.1	..	..	..	..	31	..	28	..	..	..	..
South Africa	..	..	..	..	9.2	1.4	2.5	22.8	99	99	53	..	..	..	23.7
Sudan	9.7	36	37	10.9	33.9	11.0	13.1	34.3	60	84	41	..	..	..	..
Swaziland	0.1	26	13	2.5	9.7	..	0.9	30.3	60	80	42	..	..	..	..
Tanzania	10.3	60	38	11.1	28.9	7.2	6.0	43.2	49	65	45	51.1	..	..	16.4
Togo	1.1	30	30	7.8	24.5	5.9	5.3	29.2	67	64	54	32.3	..	..	..
Uganda	5.8	29	32	8.5	25.5	6.7	5.3	38.3	38	60	35	55.0	..	..	50.0
Zaire (Congo-Kinshasa)	14.9	36	39	11.2	34.4	10.2	9.6	45.2	42	89	26	..	..	..	..
Zambia	3.6	34	43	13.3	25.2	5.7	5.1	39.8	47	76	43	86.0	..	..	84.6
Zimbabwe	4.2	35	41	12.4	15.5	3.0	5.5	21.4	74	99	65	25.5	..	..	41.0
South Asia	**267.9e**	**33f**	**23e**	..	**52.0**	**20.0**	**16.0**	**53.0**	**63**	**84**	**80**	..	..	..	**43.0**
Afghanistan	12.9	37	73	34.2	..	..	..	..	10	38	17	..	..	..	..
Bangladesh	39.4	23	34	8.8	68.3	24.9	16.7	64.2	83	47	85	47.5	46.7	47.6	29.0
Bhutan	..	..	..	..	37.9	..	4.1	56.1	21	54	26	..	..	..	..
India	184.5	36	21	4.9	53.4	20.6	17.5	52.0	63	87	85	..	..	..	52.5
Maldives	..	..	..	..	39.0	8.3	16.0	30.1	69	57	85	..	..	..	..
Nepal	5.9	45	29	7.3	46.9	16.1	11.2	48.4	48	64	49	42.0	23.0	44.0	53.1
Pakistan	20.5	24	17	3.5	38.2	12.8	9.0	50.0	60	85	47	34.0	28.0	36.9	11.6
Sri Lanka	4.6	21	26	6.4	37.7	7.0	15.5	23.8	57	87	49	22.4	18.3	24.4	4.0
East Asia and the Pacific	**269.0**	**41**	**16**	..	**23.0**	**4.0**	**5.0**	**34.0**	**49**	..	..	..	..	..	**26.0**
Brunei	..	..	..	..	..	..	..	..	..	100	90	..	..	..	..
Burma (Myanmar)	5.2	34	12	2.3	42.9	15.8	8.0	45.0	39	38	36	..	..	..	..
Cambodia	2.5	13	29	7.1	40.0	7.0	8.0	38.0	13	20	12	..	..	..	..
China	188.9	45	16	3.5	17.4	2.9	3.4	31.4	67	97	56	8.6	0.4	11.5	29.4
Fiji	..	..	..	..	7.9	0.8	8.2	2.7	77	..	..	..	..	..	..

TABLE 3, continued: Hunger, Malnutrition and Poverty

	Undernourished population			Relative inadequacy of food supply:	% under-5 (1990-1997) suffering from:				% population with access to safe water 1990-1996			Population in Poverty (%)			
	Number of undernourished people (millions)	Proportion of population undernourished (%)		% below minimum required	Underweight		Wasting	Stunting				Below national poverty line 1984-1996			Below international poverty line ($1 a day; 1985 PPP$)
	1990-1992	1969-1971	1990-1992	1990-1992	moderate & severe	severe	moderate & severe	moderate & severe	Total	Urban	Rural	National	Urban	Rural	1981-1996
Hong Kong[a]	0.3	13	5	0.8	0.3	..	2.0	3.0	100	100	96	..	..	..	..
Indonesia	22.1	34	12	2.2	39.9	7.5	..	..	63	86	56	15.1	16.8	14.3	14.5
Korea, N.	2.0	20	9	1.6	..	..	..	..	100	100	100	..	..	..	..
Korea, S.	0.3	2	1	0.1	..	..	..	..	93	100	76	..	..	..	..
Laos	1.1	29	24	5.6	40.0	11.7	10.5	47.3	41	34	36	46.1	24.0	53.0	..
Malaysia	1.3	14	7	1.1	20.1	0.6	..	..	90	100	80	15.5	..	..	5.6
Mongolia	0.7	23	32	8.4	12.3	2.4	1.7	26.4	80	100	58	36.3	38.5	33.1	..
Papua New Guinea	0.4	27	10	1.9	29.9	6.4	5.5	43.2	31	97	18	..	..	..	..
Philippines	13.1	54	21	4.5	29.6	5.0	7.5	32.7	86	92	80	54.0	39.0	71.0	27.5
Singapore	..	..	..	..	..	..	..	..	100x	100x	..	..	..	..	..
Solomon Islands	..	..	..	..	21.3	3.6	6.6	27.3	..	80	62	..	..	..	..
Thailand	14.4	28	26	6.5	25.3	4.0	5.3	21.5	81	89	72	13.1	10.2	15.5	0.1
Vietnam	17.2	24	25	6.0	44.9	11.0	11.6	46.9	38	100	66	50.9	25.9	57.2	..
Latin America and the Caribbean	**64.0**	**19**	**15**	..	**11.0**	**2.0**	**3.0**	**20.0**	**80**	**89**	**57**	..	..	..	**24.0**
Argentina	2.9	4	9	1.6	1.9	0.0	1.1	4.7	64	73	17	25.5	..	..	..
Belize	..	..	..	..	6.2	1.3	..	..	82	95	53	35.0	..	..	..
Bolivia	2.9	43	40	11.9	14.9	3.4	4.2	26.8	60	82	21	..	..	..	7.1
Brazil	9.7	14	6	1.1	5.7	0.6	2.3	10.5	92	99	68	17.4	13.1	32.6	28.7
Chile	2.9	17	22	5.1	0.9	..	0.3	2.4	96	100	31	..	..	..	15.0
Colombia	5.9	38	18	3.9	8.4	0.9	1.4	15.0	96	90	90	18.8	9.9	31.2	7.4
Costa Rica	0.4	25	12	2.2	2.2	0.2	2.0	8.0	96	100	92	11.0	..	..	18.9
Cuba	1.0	15	9	1.7	1.5	0.1	0.4	3.1	94	100	91	..	..	..	..
Dominican Republic	2.4	44	32	8.6	10.3	1.7	1.4	16.5	79	75	40	20.6	..	..	19.9
Ecuador	2.0	32	19	4.1	16.5	0.0x	1.7	34.0	70	79	45	35.0	25.0	47.0	30.4
El Salvador	1.0	50	19	4.1	11.2	1.2	1.3	23.1	62	95	16	48.3	43.1	55.7	..
Guatemala	2.4	35	26	6.3	26.6	5.9	3.3	49.7	64	84	51	58.0	..	..	53.3
Guyana	0.2	22	24	5.6	18.3	2.2	..	..	83	100	75	43.0	..	..	..
Haiti	4.6	56	69	32.4	27.5	8.1	7.8	31.9	28	55	34	65.0	..	..	..
Honduras	1.1	27	21	4.6	18.3	3.2	2.0	39.6	70	90	54	50.0	56.0	46.0	46.5
Jamaica	0.6	21	23	5.6	10.2	2.7	3.5	9.6	70	92	48	34.2	..	..	4.7
Mexico	7.2	15	8	1.4	14.2	2.9	6.0	22.8	87	90	66	10.1	..	..	14.9
Nicaragua	1.0	22	25	5.9	11.9	1.0	1.9	23.7	57	74	30	50.3	31.9	76.1	43.8
Panama	0.5	12	19	4.1	7.0	1.0	1.0	9.0	82	..	..	..	..	..	25.6
Paraguay	0.6	12	15	2.9	3.7	0.5	0.3	13.9	42	70	10	21.8	19.7	28.5	..
Peru	10.7	20	49	15.9	10.7	1.7	1.7	31.8	60	76	24	54.0	50.3	68.0	49.4
Suriname	0.1	31	21	4.9	..	..	..	..	72	78	54	..	..	..	..
Trinidad and Tobago	0.1	15	11	2.1	6.5	0.4	3.8	4.8	82	83	80	21.0	..	..	..
Uruguay	0.3	3	8	1.5	4.4	0.7	1.4	9.5	83	93	5x	..	..	..	..
Venezuela	4.0	25	20	4.6	4.5	0.7	2.9	13.2	88	68	67	31.3	..	..	11.8
Middle East and North Africa	**24.1e**	**27g**	**8e**	..	**16.0**	**4.0**	**7.0**	**24.0**	**85**	**98**	**70**	..	..	..	**4.0h**
Algeria	2.4	52	9	1.6	12.8	3.4	8.9	18.3	78	91	64	..	..	..	1.6
Bahrain	..	..	..	..	7.2	0.8	5.5	9.9	100	100	100	..	..	..	..
Cyprus	..	..	..	..	..	..	..	..	100	100	99	..	..	..	..
Egypt	3.2	24	6	0.9	12.4	2.6	4.6	29.8	84	95	74	..	..	..	7.6
Iran	4.2	32	7	1.2	15.7	..	6.6	18.9	89	100	75	..	..	..	..
Iraq	4.0	21	21	4.8	11.9	2.3	3.4	21.8	45	100	85	..	..	..	..
Jordan	0.1	11	3	0.5	6.4	0.8	3.1	15.8	89	98	94	15.0	..	..	2.5
Kuwait	0.3	7	16	4.1	6.4	..	2.6	12.2	..	..	..	..	..	..	..
Lebanon	0.1	27	5	0.8	3.0	..	2.9	12.2	94	96	88	..	..	..	..
Libya	0.2	20	3	0.5	4.7	..	2.8	15.1	97	97	97	..	..	..	..
Morocco	2.6	23	10	1.8	9.5	2.0	2.2	24.2	59	100	18	13.1	7.6	18.0	1.1
Oman	..	..	..	..	14.1	0.9	9.1	15.7	56	98	56	..	..	..	..
Qatar	..	..	..	..	5.5	..	1.5	8.1	100	100	100	..	..	..	..
Saudi Arabia	1.9	51	12	2.4	..	..	..	..	93	98	54	..	..	..	..
Syria	0.4	20	3	0.4	12.1	3.0	8.1	26.6	87	95	77	..	..	..	..
Tunisia	0.2	23	3	0.4	9.0	2x	3.9	22.5	86	100	67	14.1	..	..	3.9
Turkey	1.8	9	3	0.5	10.3	3.4	3.0	21.0	92	100	85	..	..	..	..
United Arab Emirates	0.1	5	4	0.6	..	..	..	..	98	98	98	..	..	..	..
West Bank and Gaza[a]	..	..	..	..	..	..	..	..	..	..	..	..	..	..	..
Yemen	3.0	51	24	5.6	30.0	4.3	12.7	44.1	52	88	17	19.1	18.6	19.2	..
Countries in Transition[b]	..	..	..	..	..	..	..	..	..	..	..	..	..	..	..
Albania	..	..	..	..	..	..	..	..	..	..	..	19.6	..	..	..
Armenia	..	..	..	..	..	..	..	..	..	..	..	..	..	..	..

TABLE 3, continued: Hunger, Malnutrition and Poverty

	Undernourished population			Relative inadequacy of food supply: % below minimum required 1990-1992	% under-5 (1990-1997) suffering from:				% population with access to safe water 1990-1996			Population in Poverty (%)			
	Number of undernourished people (millions) 1990-1992	Proportion of population undernourished (%) 1969-1971	Proportion of population undernourished (%) 1990-1992		Underweight moderate & severe	Underweight severe	Wasting moderate & severe	Stunting moderate & severe	Total	Urban	Rural	Below national poverty line 1984-1996 National	Urban	Rural	Below international poverty line ($1 a day; 1985 PPP$) 1981-1996
Azerbaijan	..	..	..	..	10.1	2.3	2.9	22.2	..	..	..	..	..	..	..
Belarus	..	..	..	..	..	..	..	..	..	..	..	37.0	..	..	23.0d
Bosnia and Herzegovina	..	..	..	..	..	..	..	..	..	..	..	..	..	..	..
Bulgaria	..	..	..	..	..	..	..	..	..	..	..	..	..	..	2.6
Croatia	..	..	..	..	..	..	..	..	96	98	74	..	..	..	..
Czech Republic	..	..	..	..	1.0	0.0	2.1	1.9	..	..	..	..	..	..	3.1
Estonia	..	..	..	..	..	..	..	..	..	..	..	8.9	6.8	14.7	6.0
Georgia	..	..	..	..	..	..	..	..	..	..	..	30.0	..	..	..
Hungary	..	..	..	..	2.2	0.2	1.6	2.9	..	..	..	25.3	..	..	0.7
Kazakhstan	..	..	..	..	8.3	1.5	3.3	15.8	..	..	..	..	..	..	50.0d
Kyrgyzstan	..	..	..	..	..	..	7.0		75	84	..	45.4	32.0	52.2	18.9
Latvia	..	..	..	..	..	..	..	..	..	..	..	..	..	..	23.0d
Lithuania	..	..	..	..	..	..	..	..	..	..	..	..	..	..	2.1
Macedonia	..	..	..	..	..	..	..	..	..	..	..	..	24.0	28.0	..
Moldova	..	..	..	..	..	..	..	..	55	98	18	..	..	..	6.8
Poland	..	..	..	..	..	..	..	..	..	..	..	23.8	..	..	6.8
Romania	..	..	..	..	5.7	0.6	2.5	7.8	..	..	..	21.5	15.6	28.0	17.7
Russia	..	..	..	..	3.0	0.5	3.9	12.7	..	..	..	30.9	..	..	1.1
Slovakia	..	..	..	..	..	..	..	..	..	..	..	..	..	..	12.8
Slovenia	..	..	..	..	..	..	..	..	..	..	..	..	..	..	1.0d
Tajikistan	..	..	..	..	..	..	..	30.0	..	82	49	..	..	..	..
Turkmenistan	..	..	..	..	..	..	..	..	85	..	..	..	..	..	4.9
Ukraine	..	..	..	..	..	..	..	..	97	..	..	31.7	..	..	41.0d
Uzbekistan	..	..	..	..	..	..	..	..	62	82	49	..	..	..	29.0d
Yugoslavia	..	..	..	..	..	..	..	..	..	..	..	..	..	..	..
Industrial Countries	..	..	..	..	..	..	..	..	..	..	..	..	..	..	..
Australia	..	..	..	..	..	..	..	..	95	..	..	..	..	..	8.0c
Austria	..	..	..	..	..	..	..	..	..	..	..	..	..	..	..
Belgium	..	..	..	..	..	..	..	..	..	..	..	..	..	..	12.0c
Canada	..	..	..	..	..	..	..	..	100	..	..	..	..	..	6.0c
Denmark	..	..	..	..	..	..	..	..	100	..	100	..	..	..	8.0c
Finland	..	..	..	..	..	..	..	..	100	100	100	..	..	..	4.0c
France	..	..	..	..	..	..	..	..	100	100	100	..	..	..	12.0c
Germany	..	..	..	..	..	..	..	..	..	..	..	..	..	..	12.0c
Greece	..	..	..	..	..	..	..	..	..	..	..	..	..	..	..
Ireland	..	..	..	..	..	..	..	..	..	..	..	..	..	..	37.0c
Israel	..	..	..	..	..	..	..	..	99	..	..	..	..	..	..
Italy	..	..	..	..	..	..	..	..	..	..	..	..	..	..	2.0c
Japan	..	..	..	..	..	..	..	..	97	100	85	..	..	..	5.0c
Luxembourg	..	..	..	..	..	..	..	..	..	..	..	..	..	..	4.0c
Netherlands	..	..	..	..	..	..	..	..	100	100	100	..	..	..	14.0c
New Zealand	..	..	..	..	..	..	..	..	97	100	82	..	..	..	..
Norway	..	..	..	..	..	..	..	..	100	..	..	..	..	..	3.0c
Portugal	..	..	..	..	..	..	..	..	..	..	..	..	..	..	..
Spain	..	..	..	..	..	..	..	..	99	..	..	..	..	..	21.0c
Sweden	..	..	..	..	..	..	..	..	..	..	..	..	..	..	5.0c
Switzerland	..	..	..	..	..	..	..	..	100	100	..	..	..	..	..
United Kingdom	..	..	..	..	..	..	..	..	100	100	100	..	..	..	13.0c
United States	..	..	..	..	..	..	..	..	90	..	..	..	..	..	14.0c
World	..	..	..	..	28.7	9.0	8.5	35.3	76	..	..	..	..	..	..

.. Data not available.

a Territory.

b Central and Eastern European countries and the newly independent states of the former Soviet Union.

c Poverty line is $14.40 (1985 PPP$) per person per day.

d Poverty line is $4.00 (1990 PPP$) per person per day.

e Bread for the World Institute estimate.

f Afghanistan not included.

g Afghanistan included.

h Djibouti, Somalia and Sudan are included in Middle East and North Africa.

x Indicates data that refer to years or periods other than those specified in the column heading, differ from the standard definition or refer to only part of a country.

The number '0' (zero) means zero or less than half the unit of measure.

TABLE 4: Economic and Development Indicators

	GNP per capita			Human Development Index (HDI) rank[c] 1998	Distribution of income or consumption by quintiles[k] 1978-1995						Central government expenditure (% of GDP) 1995	Education and health[e] (% of central government expenditure) 1992-1995	Military expenditure (% of combined education and health expenditure) 1990-1991	Per capita energy consumption (kg. of oil equivalent) 1995	Annual deforestation[m] (% of total forest) 1990-1995
	US$ 1996	Purchasing Power Parity (PPP) , $ per capita 1996	Average annual growth % 1995-96		Lowest 20%	Second quintile	Third quintile	Fourth quintile	Highest 20%	Ratio of highest 20% to lowest 20%[e]					
Developing Countries	..	..	..	..	..	..	..	..	..	..	..	..	63	..	..
Africa (sub-Saharan)	490	1450.0	1.9		..	..	..	..	..	..	..	..	..	238	0.7e
Angola	270	1030.0	-1.7	156	..	..	..	..	..	..	..	..	208	89	1.0
Benin	350	1230.0	3.2	145	..	..	..	..	..	..	..	..	..	20	1.2
Botswana	3,020	7390.0	..	97	..	..	..	..	..	..	38.0	25.2	22	383	0.5
Burkina Faso	230	950.0i	3.3	172	..	..	..	..	..	..	..	24.2	30	16	0.7
Burundi	170	590.0	-11.1	170	..	..	..	..	..	..	24.9	..	42	23	0.4
Cameroon	610	1760.0	4.5	132	..	..	..	..	..	..	12.7	22.8	48	117	0.6
Cape Verde	960x	1870.0x	..	117	..	..	..	..	..	..	..	..	..	..	-24.0
Central African Republic	340x	1430.0i	-5.0	154	..	..	..	..	..	..	..	..	33	29	0.4
Chad	160	880.0	0.5	163	..	..	..	..	..	..	..	..	74	16	0.8
Comoros	470x	1320.0	..	141	..	..	..	..	..	..	..	..	..	..	5.6
Congo (Brazzaville)	670	1410.0	4.7	..	..	..	..	..	..	..	..	..	37	139	0.2
Côte d'Ivoire	660	1580.0	4.6	148	6.8	11.2	15.8	22.2	44.1	6.49	..	..	14	97	0.6
Djibouti	g	..	..	162	..	..	..	..	..	..	..	..	..	..	0.0
Equatorial Guinea	380x	..	..	135	..	..	..	..	..	..	..	..	..	..	0.5
Eritrea	f	..	..	168	..	..	..	..	..	..	..	..	..	..	0.0
Ethiopia	100	500.0	7.2	169	..	..	..	..	..	..	18.1x	13.8	190	21	0.5
Gabon	3,950	6300.0	-1.2	120	..	..	..	..	..	..	..	..	51	587	0.5
Gambia	f	1280.0i	..	165	..	..	..	..	..	..	21.5x	19.2	11	55	0.9
Ghana	360	1790.0i	2.3	133	7.9	12.0	16.1	21.8	42.2	5.34	22.1x	29.0	12	92	1.3
Guinea	560	1720.0	1.8	167	3.0	8.3	14.6	23.9	50.2	16.73	..	..	37	64	1.1
Guinea-Bissau	250	1030.0	3.7	164	2.1	6.5	12.0	20.6	58.9	28.05	..	..	..	37	0.4
Kenya	320	1130.0	3.1	137	3.4	6.7	10.7	17.0	62.1	18.26	29.8x	24.3	24	109	0.3
Lesotho	660	2380.0i	6.7	134	2.8	6.5	11.2	19.4	60.1	21.46	50.7x	33.4	48	..	0.0
Liberia	f	..	..	..	..	..	..	..	..	..	..	..	..	..	0.6
Madagascar	250	900.0	0.5	153	5.8	9.9	14.0	20.3	50.0	8.62	17.2	23.7	37	36	0.8
Malawi	180	690.0	13.0	161	..	..	..	..	..	..	..	..	24	38	1.6
Mali	240	710.0	1.2	171	..	..	..	..	..	..	..	..	53	21	1.0
Mauritania	470	1810.0	1.8	149	3.6	10.6	16.2	23.0	46.5	12.92	..	..	40	102	0.0
Mauritius	3,710	9000.0	4.5	61	..	..	..	..	..	..	22.6	25.8	4	388	0.0
Mozambique	80	500.0i	5.0	166	..	..	..	..	..	..	..	..	121	38	0.7
Namibia	2,250	5390.0i	0.3	107	..	..	..	..	..	..	38.5x	..	23	..	0.3
Niger	200	920.0i	-0.1	173	7.5	11.8	15.5	21.1	44.1	5.88	..	..	11	37	0.0
Nigeria	240	870.0	1.9	142	4.0	8.9	14.4	23.4	49.3	12.33	..	..	33	165	0.9
Rwanda	190	630.0	7.8	..	9.7	13.2	16.5	21.6	39.1	4.03	25.8x	..	25	33	0.2
Senegal	570	1650.0	3.2	158	3.5	7.0	11.6	19.3	58.6	16.74	..	..	33	104	0.7
Sierra Leone	200	510.0	7.6	174	..	..	..	..	..	..	16.4	22.9	23	72	3.0
Somalia	f	..	..	..	..	..	..	..	..	..	..	..	..	..	0.2
South Africa	3,520	7450.0i	1.0	89	3.3	5.8	9.8	17.7	63.3	19.18	33.7	..	41	2,405	0.2
Sudan	f	..	..	157	..	..	..	..	..	..	..	..	44	65	0.8
Swaziland	1,170x	2880.0x	..	115	..	..	..	..	..	..	..	..	11	..	0.0
Tanzania	170n	..	1.7	150	6.9	10.9	15.3	21.5	45.4	6.58	..	..	77	32	1.0
Togo	300	1650.0	4.3	144	..	..	..	..	..	..	..	..	39	45	1.4
Uganda	300	1030.0i	6.2	160	6.8	10.3	14.4	20.4	48.1	7.07	..	..	18	22	0.9
Zaire (Congo-Kinshasa)	130	790.0i	-0.1	143	..	..	..	..	..	..	7.6	1.3	71	47	0.7
Zambia	360	860.0	3.4	146	3.9	8.0	13.8	23.8	50.4	12.92	25.0	29.2	63	145	0.8
Zimbabwe	610	2200.0	5.8	130	4.0	6.3	10.0	17.4	62.3	15.58	34.1x	..	66	424	0.6
South Asia	380	1520.0	4.4		8.8	..	..	..	39.9	4.53	..	4.5	61	231	0.3e
Afghanistan	f	..	..	..	..	..	..	..	..	..	..	..	..	..	6.8
Bangladesh	260	1010.0	3.8	147	9.4	13.5	17.2	22.0	37.9	4.03	..	..	41	67	0.8
Bhutan	420x	1260.0x	5.5x	155	..	..	..	..	..	..	..	18.5	..	..	0.3
India	380	1580.0	5.1	139	8.5	12.1	15.8	21.1	42.6	5.01	16.4	3.7	65	260	0.0
Maldives	990x	3080.0x	..	95	..	..	..	..	..	..	..	..	..	..	..
Nepal	210	1090.0	1.8	152	7.6	11.5	15.1	21.0	44.8	5.89	17.5	15.5	35	33	1.1
Pakistan	480	1600.0	0.3	138	8.4	12.9	16.9	22.2	39.7	4.73	23.2	..	125	243	2.9
Sri Lanka	740	2290.0	0.5	90	8.9	13.1	16.9	21.7	39.3	4.42	29.3	17.0	107	136	1.1
East Asia and the Pacific	890	3370.0	7.4		6.9	..	..	..	44.3	6.42	11.5	..	..	657	0.5e
Brunei	h	..	..	35	..	..	..	..	..	..	..	..	125	..	0.6
Burma (Myanmar)	g	..	1.2x	131	..	..	..	..	..	..	10.6	20.0	222	50	1.4
Cambodia	300	..	3.9	140	..	..	..	..	..	..	..	..	..	52	1.6
China	750	3330.0	8.9	106	5.5	9.8	14.9	22.3	47.5	8.64	8.3	3.3	114	707	0.1
Fiji	2,440x	5780.0x	..	44	..	..	..	..	..	..	27.5x	27.8	37	..	0.4

TABLE 4, continued: Economic and Development Indicators

	GNP per capita			Human Development Index (HDI) rank[c] 1998	Distribution of income or consumption by quintiles[a] 1978-1995					Ratio of highest 20% to lowest 20%[a]	Central government expenditure (% of GDP) 1995	Education and health[e] (% of central government expenditure) 1992-1995	Military expenditure (% of combined education and health expenditure) 1990-1991	Per capita energy consumption (kg. of oil equivalent) 1995	Annual deforestation[m] (% of total forest) 1990-1995
	US$ 1996	Purchasing Power Parity (PPP), $ per capita 1996	Average annual growth % 1995-96		Lowest 20%	Second quintile	Third quintile	Fourth quintile	Highest 20%						
Hong Kong[a]	24,290	24260.0	2.2	25	5.4	10.8	15.2	21.6	47.0	8.70	..	..	10	..	..
Indonesia	1,080	3310.0	5.8	96	8.4	12.0	15.5	21.0	43.1	5.13	14.7	12.7	49	442	1.0
Korea, N.	g	..	..	75	..	..	..	..	..	..	..	..	..	1,113	0.0
Korea, S.	10,610	13080.0	5.6	30	..	..	..	..	..	..	17.7	20.9	60	3,225	0.2
Laos	400	1250.0	4.0	136	9.6	12.9	16.3	21.0	40.2	4.19	..	..	..	40	1.2
Malaysia	4,370	10390.0	5.8	60	4.6	8.3	13.0	20.4	53.7	11.67	22.9	27.4	38	1,655	2.4
Mongolia	360	1820.0	-0.1	101	7.3	12.2	16.6	23.0	40.9	5.60	21.5	10.4	..	1,045	0.0
Papua New Guinea	1,150	2820.0i	-2.4	129	4.5	7.9	11.9	19.2	56.5	12.56	29.4x	26.5	41	232	0.4
Philippines	1,160	3550.0	4.5	98	6.5	10.1	14.4	21.2	47.8	7.35	17.9	18.9	41	307	3.5
Singapore	30,550	26910.0	5.6	28	5.1	9.9	14.6	21.4	48.9	9.59	15.9	30.8	129	7,162	0.0
Solomon Islands	910x	2190.0x	..	123	..	..	..	..	..	..	..	..	..	..	0.2
Thailand	2,960	6700.0	4.4	59	5.6	8.7	13.0	20.0	52.7	9.41	15.8	29.2	71	878	2.6
Vietnam	290	1570.0	7.3	122	7.8	11.4	15.4	21.4	44.0	5.64	..	..	..	104	1.4
Latin America and the Caribbean	**3,710**	**6530.0**	**..**		**4.5**	**..**	**..**	**..**	**52.9**	**11.76**	**24.5x**	**..**	**29**	**969**	**0.6e**
Argentina	8,380	9530.0	2.7	36	..	..	..	..	..	..	14.5	12.2	51	1,525	0.3
Belize	2,630x	5400.0x	3.0x	63	..	..	..	..	..	..	31.1x	32.3	..	..	0.3
Bolivia	830	2860.0	2.6	116	5.6	9.7	14.5	22.0	48.2	8.61	23.1	25.6	57	396	1.2
Brazil	4,400	6340.0	6.7	62	2.5	5.7	9.9	17.7	64.2	25.68	37.4x	8.8	23	772	0.5
Chile	4,860	11700.0	8.5	31	3.5	6.6	10.9	18.1	61.0	17.43	19.2	26.1	68	1,065	0.4
Colombia	2,140	6720.0	-0.5	53	3.1	6.8	10.9	17.6	61.5	19.80	14.4x	24.4	57	655	0.5
Costa Rica	2,640	6470.0	-2.0	34	4.0	8.8	13.7	21.7	51.8	12.95	29.1	43.4	5	584	3.0
Cuba	g	..	..	85	..	..	..	..	..	..	..	..	125	949	1.2
Dominican Republic	1,600	4390.0	5.7	88	4.2	7.9	12.5	19.7	55.7	13.26	15.6	20.9	22	486	1.6
Ecuador	1,500	4730.0	1.2	73	5.4	8.9	13.2	19.9	52.6	9.74	15.7x	29.6	26	553	1.6
El Salvador	1,700	2790.0	0.0	114	..	..	..	..	..	..	13.7	21.5	66	410	3.3
Guatemala	1,470	3820.0	8.6	111	2.1	5.8	10.5	18.6	63.0	30.00	8.9	29.6	31	206	2.0
Guyana	590x	2420.0x	-2.6	100	..	..	..	..	..	..	..	..	21	..	0.0
Haiti	310	1130.0i	0.0	159	..	..	..	..	..	..	..	..	30	50	3.4
Honduras	660	2130.0	-0.3	119	3.4	7.1	11.7	19.7	58.0	17.06	..	..	92	236	2.3
Jamaica	1,600	3450.0	-1.9	84	5.8	10.2	14.9	21.6	47.5	8.19	..	..	8	1,191	7.2
Mexico	3,670	7660.0	4.7	49	4.1	7.8	12.5	20.2	55.3	13.49	15.9	15.8	5	1,456	0.9
Nicaragua	380	1760.0i	4.2	126	4.2	8.0	12.6	20.0	55.2	13.14	33.2	28.9	97	265	2.5
Panama	3,080	7060.0	4.1	45	2.0	6.3	11.6	20.3	59.8	29.90	24.7	40.2	34	678	2.1
Paraguay	1,850	3480.0	-1.5	91	5.9	10.7	18.7	62.4	46.6	7.90	13.0x	29.4	42	308	2.6
Peru	2,420	4410.0	0.0	86	4.9	9.2	14.1	21.4	50.4	10.29	17.2	..	39	421	0.3
Suriname	880x	2250.0x	4.3x	65	..	..	..	..	..	..	..	..	27	..	0.1
Trinidad and Tobago	3,870	6100.0	3.0	40	..	..	..	..	..	..	29.2	..	9	5,381	1.5
Uruguay	5,760	7760.0	6.8	38	..	..	..	..	..	..	31.5	12.3	38	639	0.0
Venezuela	3,020	8130.0	-3.7	46	4.3	8.8	13.8	21.3	51.8	12.05	18.8	..	33	2,158	1.1
Middle East and North Africa	**2,070**	**4530.0**	**..**		**6.9**	**..**	**..**	**..**	**45.4**	**6.58**	**..**	**..**	**..**	**1,178**	**0.4e**
Algeria	1,520	4620.0i	1.8	82	7.0	11.6	16.1	22.7	42.6	6.09	..	..	11	866	1.2
Bahrain	7,840x	13400.0x	-2.2x	43	..	..	..	..	..	..	..	20.6	41	..	0.0
Cyprus	h	..	..	23	..	..	..	..	..	..	..	17.2	17	..	0.0
Egypt	1,080	2860.0	3.5	112	8.7	12.5	16.3	21.4	41.1	4.72	37.4x	14.7	52	596	0.0
Iran	g	5360.0	0.6x	78	..	..	..	..	..	..	23.2	24.8	38	1,374	1.7
Iraq	g	..	..	127	..	..	..	..	..	..	..	..	271	1,206	0.0
Jordan	1,650	3570.0	2.8	87	5.9	9.8	13.9	20.3	50.1	8.49	31.6	23.4	138	1,031	2.5
Kuwait	17,390x	..	..	54	..	..	..	..	..	..	51.4	16.6	88	9,381	0.0
Lebanon	2,970	6060.0	0.6	66	..	..	..	..	..	..	32.5	..	..	1,120	7.8
Libya	h	..	..	64	..	..	..	..	..	..	..	..	71	3,129	0.0
Morocco	1,290	3320.0	10.4	125	6.6	10.5	15.0	21.7	46.3	7.02	..	20.9	72	311	0.3
Oman	4,820x	8680.0	..	71	..	..	..	..	..	..	42.4	18.9	293	1,880	0.0
Qatar	11,600x	11600x	-5.9	57	..	..	..	..	..	..	..	..	192	..	0.0
Saudi Arabia	7,040x	9700.0	..	70	..	..	..	..	..	..	..	..	151	4,360	0.8
Syria	1,160	3020.0	0.6	81	..	..	..	..	..	..	24.5	12.1	373	1,001	2.2
Tunisia	1,930	4550.0	-0.4	83	5.9	10.4	15.3	22.1	46.3	7.85	32.8	24.1	31	591	0.5
Turkey	2,830	6060.0	5.0	69	..	..	..	..	..	..	22.2	16.6	87	1,009	0.0
United Arab Emirates	17,400x	17000.0i	..	48	..	..	..	..	..	..	11.8x	24.4	44	11,567	0.0
West Bank and Gaza[a]	g	..	..	..	..	..	..	..	..	..	..	..	..	..	..
Yemen	380	790.0	-7.8	151	..	..	..	..	..	..	24.7	25.4	197	192	0.0

TABLE 4, continued: Economic and Development Indicators

| | GNP per capita | | | | Distribution of income or consumption by quintiles[k] 1978-1995 | | | | | | | | | | |
	US$ 1996	Purchasing Power Parity (PPP), $ per capita 1996	Average annual growth % 1995-96	Human Development Index (HDI) rank[c] 1998	Lowest 20%	Second quintile	Third quintile	Fourth quintile	Highest 20%	Ratio of highest 20% to lowest 20%[e]	Central government expenditure (% of GDP) 1995	Education and health[e] (% of central government expenditure) 1992-1995	Military expenditure (% of combined education and health expenditure) 1990-1991	Per capita energy consumption (kg. of oil equivalent) 1995	Annual deforestation[m] (% of total forest) 1990-1995
Countries in Transition[b]	..	..	..	..	8.8	..	..	..	37.8	4.30	30.9x	..	..	2,690	-0.1e
Albania	820	..	..	105	..	..	..	..	..	..	31.0	..	51	314	0.0
Armenia	630	2160.0	7.4	99	..	..	..	..	..	..	..	..	..	444	-2.7
Azerbaijan	480	1490.0	-1.3	110	..	..	..	..	..	..	..	..	..	1,735	0.0
Belarus	2,070	4380.0	2.9	68	11.1	15.3	18.5	22.2	32.9	2.96	..	20.1	..	2,305	-1.0
Bosnia and Herzegovina	f	..	..	..	..	..	..	..	..	..	..	..	..	364	0.0
Bulgaria	1,190	4280.0	-8.8	67	8.3	13.0	17.0	22.3	39.3	4.73	41.6	6.1	29	2,724	0.0
Croatia	3,800	4290.0	4.7	76	..	..	..	..	..	..	46.5	20.6	..	1,435	0.0
Czech Republic	4,740	10870.0	4.6	39	10.5	13.9	16.9	21.3	37.4	3.56	39.9	27.9	17	3,776	0.0
Estonia	3,080	4660.0	5.2	77	6.6	10.7	15.1	21.4	46.3	7.02	35.2	25.7	..	3,454	-1.0
Georgia	850	1810.0	..	108	..	..	..	..	..	..	..	..	..	342	0.0
Hungary	4,340	6730.0	2.6	47	9.5	14.0	17.6	22.3	36.6	3.85	..	11.2	18	2,454	-0.5
Kazakhstan	1,350	3230.0	1.8	93	7.5	12.3	16.9	22.9	40.4	5.39	..	..	..	3,337	-1.9
Kyrgyzstan	550	1970.0	4.1	109	..	..	..	..	..	..	..	..	..	513	0.0
Latvia	2,300	3650.0	3.5	92	9.6	13.6	17.5	22.6	36.7	3.82	32.2	20.6	..	1,471	-0.9
Lithuania	2,280	4390.0	2.7	79	8.1	12.3	16.2	21.3	42.1	5.20	25.5	11.7	..	2,291	-0.6
Macedonia	990	..	0.6	80	..	..	..	..	..	..	..	..	..	1,308	0.0
Moldova	590	1440.0	-9.7	113	6.9	11.9	16.7	23.1	41.5	6.01	..	..	..	963	0.0
Poland	3,230	6000.0	6.2	52	9.3	13.8	17.7	22.6	36.6	3.94	43.0	..	30	2,448	-0.1
Romania	1,600	4580.0	4.7	74	9.2	14.4	18.4	23.2	34.8	3.78	32.0x	17.8	25	1,941	0.0
Russia	2,410	4190.0	-5.0	72	3.7	8.5	13.5	20.4	53.8	14.54	24.0	4.6	132	4,079	..
Slovakia	3,410	7460.0	6.3	42	11.9	15.8	18.8	22.2	31.4	2.64	..	..	..	3,272	-0.1
Slovenia	9,240	12110.0	3.2	37	9.5	13.5	17.1	21.9	37.9	3.99	..	..	..	2,806	0.0
Tajikistan	340	900.0	-8.4	118	..	..	..	..	..	..	..	..	..	563	0.0
Turkmenistan	940	2010.0	-4.3	103	6.7	11.4	16.3	22.8	42.8	6.39	..	..	..	3,047	0.0
Ukraine	1,200	2230.0	-8.5	102	9.5	14.1	18.1	22.9	35.4	3.73	..	..	..	3,136	-0.1
Uzbekistan	1,010	2450.0	-0.8	104	..	..	..	..	..	..	..	..	..	2,043	-2.7
Yugoslavia	g	..	..	..	..	..	..	..	..	..	..	..	..	1,125	0.0
Industrial Countries	25,870	22390.0	2.0	..	..	..	..	..	..	..	31.3	..	..	5,123	-0.2e
Australia[l]	20,090	19870.0	2.6	15	4.4	11.1	17.5	24.8	42.2	9.59	27.4	20.7	24	5,215	0.0
Austria	28,110	21650.0	1.0	13	..	..	..	..	..	..	42.2	22.7	9	3,279	0.0
Belgium[l]	26,440	22390.0	1.4	12	7.9	13.7	18.6	23.8	36.0	4.56	49.4	..	20	5,167	0.0
Canada[l]	19,020	21380.0	0.5	1	5.7	11.8	17.7	24.6	40.2	7.05	24.6x	8.6	15	7,879	-0.1
Denmark[l]	32,100	22120.0	1.8	18	5.4	12.0	18.4	25.6	38.6	7.15	43.4	11.7	18	3,918	0.0
Finland[l]	23,240	18260.0	3.5	6	6.3	12.1	18.4	25.5	37.6	5.97	42.7	22.5	15	5,613	0.1
France[l]	26,270	21510.0	1.0	2	5.6	11.8	17.2	23.5	41.9	7.48	46.4	22.5	29	4,150	-1.1
Germany[l]	28,870	21110.0	0.9	19	7.0	11.8	17.1	23.9	40.3	5.76	33.9	17.6	29	4,156	0.0
Greece	11,460	12730.0	2.2	20	..	..	..	..	..	..	33.6	15.9	71	2,266	-2.3
Ireland	17,110	16750.0	8.7	17	..	..	..	..	..	..	40.3x	26.8	12	3,196	-2.7
Israel[l]	15,870	18100.0	..	22	6.0	12.1	17.8	24.5	39.6	6.60	44.7x	19.3	106	3,003	0.0
Italy[l]	19,880	19890.0	0.7	21	6.8	12.0	16.7	23.5	41.0	6.03	48.6	..	21	2,821	-0.1
Japan[l]	40,940	23420.0	3.6	8	8.7	13.2	17.5	23.1	37.5	4.31	23.7x	7.6	12	3,964	0.1
Luxemburg	41,210x	37930.0x	3.0x	26	..	..	..	..	..	..	..	11.5	10	..	0.0
Netherlands[l]	25,940	20850.0	3.9	7	8.2	13.1	18.1	23.7	36.9	4.50	50.8	24.4	22	4,741	0.0
New Zealand[l]	15,720	16500.0	-0.6	9	5.1	10.8	16.2	23.2	44.7	8.76	32.9	30.8	16	4,290	-0.6
Norway[l]	34,510	23220.0	4.6	3	6.2	12.8	18.9	25.3	36.7	5.92	39.0	19.9	22	5,439	-0.3
Portugal[l]	10,160	13450.0	2.4	33	..	..	..	..	..	..	44.1	..	32	1,939	-0.9
Spain[l]	14,350	15290.0	1.6	11	8.3	13.7	18.1	23.4	36.6	4.41	38.2x	10.6	18	2,639	0.0
Sweden[l]	25,710	18770.0	0.8	10	8.0	13.2	17.4	24.5	36.9	4.61	49.5	5.2	16	5,736	0.0
Switzerland[l]	44,350	26340.0	-1.2	16	5.2	11.7	16.4	22.1	44.6	8.58	26.6	..	14	3,571	0.0
United Kingdom[l]	19,600	19960.0	2.3	14	4.6	10.0	16.8	24.3	44.3	9.63	42.0	17.3	40	3,786	-0.5
United States[l]	5,760	28020.0	6.8	4	4.7	11.0	17.4	25.0	41.9	8.91	22.7	19.9	46	7,905	-0.3
World	..	6200.0	..	..	..	..	..	..	..	..	29.1	..	38	1,474	0.3e

.. Data not available.

a Territory.

b Central and Eastern European countries and the newly independent states of former Soviet Union.

c Regional ranking compares developing regions; 1 highest, 8 lowest.

d Preliminary.

e Bread for the World Institute estimate.

f Estimated to be low income ($785 or less)

g Estimated to be lower middle income ($785 to $3,115)

h Estimated to be high income($9386 or more)

i Estimate based on regression; others are extrapolated from the latest International Comparison Programme benchmark estimates

j GDP data.

k Income shares by percentiles of population, ranked by per capita income, excepted as noted.

l Income shares by percentiles of households; ranked by household income.

m Positive data indicate loss of forest; negative data indicate gain in forest.

x Data refer to a period other than specified in the column heading.

n Data refers to mainland Tanzania only

The number '0' (zero) means zero or less than half the unit of measure.

Table 5: Economic Globalization

	Trade — Exports of goods and services (% of GDP) 1970	Exports of goods and services (% of GDP) 1996	Manufactured exports (% of merchandise exports) 1996	Food Trade[e] — Food exports (% of merchandise exports) 1995	Food imports (% of total imports) 1996	Food imports (% of total consumption) 1995	Imports of goods and services (% of GDP) 1996	Gross domestic investment (GDI) (% of GDP)	Net private capital flows ($ millions)	Investment — FDI ($ million) 1996	Aid (% of GDI)	Foreign direct investment net inflows (% of GDI)	Foreign direct investment net inflows (% of GDP)	Debt — Total External debt (US $ billions) 1996	Debt service (% of exports of goods and services) 1996	Workers' remittances, receipts (US $ millions) 1996
Developing Countries	..	..	**77.0**	..	..		**27**	..	65,176	49,531	..	9.8	3.3	537.00	13.3	..
Africa (sub-Saharan)	**20.5**	**28.4**	..	..	..	..	**28**	**18**	4,376	3,271	27.8	6.0	1.1	227.20	14.2	..
Angola	..	73.9	..	0.12	15.4	14.7	40	11	753	300	72.0	39.7	4.5	10.60	13.3	..
Benin	22.1	..	..	..	..	..	33	17	2	2	77.5	0.5	0.1	1.65	6.8	84.00
Botswana	22.7	49.4	..	4.09	17.6	6.8	33	24	66	75	6.8	6.3	1.5	0.60	4.9	..
Burkina Faso	6.2	..	..	22.27	..	..	29	25	..	1	64.8	0.0	0.0	1.27	10.8	76.00
Burundi	10.7	12.4	..	40.15	25.1	3.8	14	9	..	1	203.2	1.0	0.1	1.10	54.6	0.00
Cameroon	26.2	25.9	8.0	22.36	6.1	2.3	13	16	(28)	35	28.4	2.4	0.4	9.50	23.6	67.00
Cape Verde	..	..	..	0.51	20.9	..	..	..	..	..	..	..	..	0.2x	4.0x	92.00
Central African Republic	28.0	18.5	43.0	1.27	9.8	2.9	22	6	5	5	280.7	8.4	0.5	0.94	6.3	6.00
Chad	23.1	..	..	15.42	13.3	..	44	19	18	18	134.9	8.0	1.5	1.00	9.5	1.00
Comoros	..	19.3	..	41.52	34.1	11.3	..	17	..	..	109.8x	5.1x	0.9x	0.2x	3.0x	17.00
Congo (Brazzaville)	34.7	61.8	2.0	1.31	19.4	5.3	97	61	(7)	8	29.6	0.6	0.3	5.20	21.3	..
Côte d'Ivoire	35.8	41.4	..	50.76	12.2	4.9	38	14	160	21	66.1	1.4	0.2	19.70	26.2	0.00
Djibouti	..	41.7	..	19.46	15.4	11.7	..	12	..	..	173.9x	6.7x	0.8x	0.3x	4.0x	1.00
Equatorial Guinea	35.7	..	..	9.92	6.4	..	..	..	..	..	..	..	0.6x	0.3x	2.0x	..
Eritrea	..	29.6	..	0.49	17.3	..	85	26	..	..	..	..	..	0.05	0.0	122.70
Ethiopia	..	14.7	..	68.58	13.8	4.7	27	21	(205)	5	67.6	0.4	0.1	10.01	42.2	0.00
Gabon	49.7	61.1	2.0	0.06	14.8	4.3	37	20	(114)	(65)	11.0	-5.7	-1.1	4.21	11.1	0.00
Gambia	33.1	53.4	..	7.82	26.9	..	74x	21x	11	11	62.6x	10.2	2.2	0.45	12.7	..
Ghana	21.3	25.0	..	41.24	11.7	3.6	38	19	477	120	55.2	10.1	1.9	6.20	26.4	27.50
Guinea	..	21.0	..	4.23	17.2	5.3	22	13	41	24	57.6	4.7	0.6	3.24	14.7	1.07
Guinea-Bissau	4.0	13.0	..	94.95	42.1	10.3	32	22	1	1	304.3	1.7	0.4	0.94	48.7	0.00
Kenya	29.8	32.6	..	45.16	4.2	3.7	37	20	(104)	13	32.4	0.7	0.1	6.89	27.5	..
Lesotho	10.8	20.8	..	1.47	12.7	10.4	114	104	38	28	11.6	3.0	3.2	0.65	6.1	0.00
Liberia	58.8	..	..	0.03	14.0	..	..	..	..	..	..	..	..	2.13x	3.0x	..
Madagascar	19.2	23.3	14.0x	43.87	12.2	2.4	24	10	5	10	87.8	2.4	0.2	4.18	9.4	6.10
Malawi	24.2	28.8	7.0x	16.14	14.9	6.8	27	17	(3)	1	132.4	0.3	0.0	2.31	18.6	0.00
Mali	13.2	22.3	..	26.23	12.2	3.7	36	27	23	23	71.7	3.3	0.9	3.02	17.9	105.00
Mauritania	40.8	50.4	..	6.95	51.4	12.7	62	22	25	5	113.8	2.1	0.5	2.36	21.7	6.00
Mauritius	43.2	58.4	68.0	27.40	12.6	8.0	65	26	112	37	1.8	3.3	0.9	1.82	7.2	0.00
Mozambique	..	..	17.0	14.03	20.4	..	56	48	23	29	111.5	3.5	1.7	5.84	32.3	0.00
Namibia	..	..	..	14.73	6.4	..	58	20	..	..	29.4	21.4	4.2	..	..	7.68
Niger	10.8	..	..	12.64	18.7	..	22	10	(24)	..	134.8	0.0	0.0	1.56	17.3	6.00
Nigeria	8.4	..	..	1.95	9.3	2.3	11	19	706	1,391	3.2	23.2	4.3	31.41	16.0	826.00
Rwanda	13.6	6.1	..	25.13	36.9	7.0	22	14	1	1	371.9	0.6	0.1	1.03	20.3	..
Senegal	27.4	31.6	..	1.54	27.5	9.2	36	17	34	45	68.3	5.3	0.9	3.66	15.9	86.00
Sierra Leone	30.1	12.7	..	13.33	62.4	14.6	31	9	5	5	223.2	5.7	0.5	1.17	52.6	0.00
Somalia	11.5	..	..	49.06	36.3	..	..	..	..	..	..	..	..	2.68x	1.0x	..
South Africa	22.0	22.1	49.0	5.87	4.6	1.2	26	18	1,417	136	1.6	0.6	0.1	23.59	11.1	0.00
Sudan	16.5	..	..	40.85	15.4	..	..	..	..	..	..	..	..	16.97	5.0	251.40
Swaziland	66.6	83.2	..	32.46	7.9	8.1	..	17	..	..	..	..	5.4x	0.25x	2.0x	..
Tanzania	..	29.8	..	37.68	7.1	4.1	36	18	143	150	84.8	14.2	2.6	7.41	18.7	0.00h
Togo	49.6	30.8	..	10.99	12.9	3.9	38	14	..	..	85.4	0.0	0.0	1.46	10.8	20.00
Uganda	22.2	12.0	..	67.69	4.2	1.1	22	16	114	121	68.3	12.1	2.0	3.67	20.0	0.00
Zaire (Congo-Kinshasa)	15.5	..	..	19.77	51.0	..	33	6	2	2	38.5	0.5	0.0	12.83	2.4	..
Zambia	53.6	31.5	..	3.62	6.1	1.3	45	15	33	58	120.2	11.4	1.7	7.11	24.6	0.00
Zimbabwe	..	..	30.0	13.34	6.1	..	41	18	42	63	27.6	4.7	0.8	5.01	21.2	0.00
South Asia	**5.4**	**13.9**	**76.0**	..	..	..	**17**	**25**	8,743	3,439	4.8x	2.9	0.7	152.10	22.0	..
Afghanistan	9.8	..	..	37.38	22.6	..	..	..	..	..	..	..	..	..	..	..
Bangladesh	8.3	14 2	..	1.67	7.2	3.4	24	17	92	15	23.2	0.3	0.0	16.08	11.7	1,217.00
Bhutan	..	..	..	29.70	13.7	..	..	..	..	..	..	..	0.0x	0.09x	8.0x	0.00
India	3.7	12.2	74.0x	12.74	2.0	0.6	15	27	6,404	2,587	2.1	2.7	0.7	89.83	24.1	7,840.00
Maldives	..	..	..	..	16.0	..	..	..	..	..	..	..	3.3x	0.20x	6.0x	0.00
Nepal	4.9	24.3	99.0x	14.23	5.7	2.6	37	23	9	19	38.8	1.9	0.4	2.41	7.7	77.60
Pakistan	7.8	16.4	84.0	8.34	7.4	3.3	21	19	1,936	690	7.3	5.7	1.1	29.90	27.4	1.46
Sri Lanka	25.5	35.9	73.0x	16.97	9.0	5.0	44	25	123	120	13.9	3.4	0.9	8.00	7.3	832.21
East Asia and the Pacific	**5.7**	**29.5**	**75.0**	..	..	..	**29x**	**39**	101,272	58,681	..	10.4	4.0	477.22	13.0	..
Brunei	..	..	..	0.75	10.1	..	..	..	..	..	..	..	..	..	..	..
Burma (Myanmar)	5.2	..	..	29.70	1.3	..	2	11	129	100	..	..	..	5.18	..	..
Cambodia	5.8	..	..	0.15	7.9	..	43	21	290	294	70.0	45.4	9.4	2.11	1.2	10.00

Table 5, continued: Economic Globalization

	Exports of goods and services (% of GDP) 1970	1996	Manufactured exports (% of merchandise exports) 1996	Food exports (% of merchandise exports) 1995	Food imports (% of total imports) 1996	Food imports (% of total consumption) 1995	Imports of goods and services (% of GDP) 1996	Gross domestic investment (GDI) (% of GDP) 1996	Net private capital flows ($ millions) 1996	FDI ($ million) 1996	Aid (% of GDI) 1996	Foreign direct investment net inflows (% of GDI) 1996	Foreign direct investment net inflows (% of GDP) 1996	Total External debt (US $ billions) 1996	Debt service (% of exports of goods and services) 1996	Workers' remittances, receipts (US $ millions) 1996
China	2.7	21.0	84.0	4.87	3.2	2.8	19x	42	50,100	40,180	0.8	11.6	4.9	128.82	8.7	1,672.00
Fiji	48.4	51.2	..	33.28	11.1	6.0	..	14		..	15.5x	24.0	3.2	0.25x	7.0x	
Hong Kong[a]	94.6	147.1	93.5	1.42	3.1	6.3	..	35		..		0.0		..	..	..
Indonesia	13.0	25.5	51.0	4.18	8.9	2.6	25	32	18,030	7,960	1.6	11.1	3.5	129.03	36.8	810.00
Korea, N.	..	..	..	4.02	16.1	..	..	..		..	..	..		..	..	
Korea, S.	13.9	33.2	92.0	0.93	134.3	1.7	36	38		2,325	-0.1	1.3	0.5	..	..	466.00
Laos	..	..	..	15.93	4.3	..	42	31	104	104	59.8	18.4	5.6	2.26	6.3	0.00
Malaysia	42.0	95.5	76.0	1.99	4.2	5.3	91	41	12,096	4,500	-1.1	11.0	4.5	39.78	8.2	0.00
Mongolia	..	..	10.0	4.01	17.2	..	46	22	(15)	5	93.0	2.3	0.5	0.52	9.7	0.00
Papua New Guinea	18.5	60.5	..	7.95	12.8	6.7	44	27	414	225	27.7	16.2	4.4	2.36	12.6	
Philippines	21.6	36.3	84.0	4.64	6.0	2.8	52	24	4,600	1,408	4.4	6.9	1.7	41.21	13.7	569.00
Singapore	102.1	..	84.0	1.38	2.3	8.2	169x	35		9,440	0.0	28.6	10.0	..	..	..
Solomon Islands	..	..	..	2.36	11.4	..	..	..		..	..	..	4.8x	0.16x	4.0x	..
Thailand	15.0	41.5	73.0x	11.94	2.4	1.0	44	41	13,517	2,336	1.1	3.1	1.3	90.82	11.5	..
Vietnam	..	35.9	..	12.08	4.3	2.3	55	28	2,061	1,500	14.2	23.0	6.4	26.76	3.5	..
Latin America and the Caribbean	**12.2**	**16.7**	**45.0**	**..**	**..**	**..**	**16**	**20**	**95,569**	**38,015**	**1.7**	**10.4**	**2.1**	**656.39**	**32.3**	**..**
Argentina	5.6	8.5	30.0	27.69	4.0	0.3	9	19	14,417	4,285	0.5	7.9	1.5	93.84	44.2	41.00
Belize	..	..	20.6	67.34	16.8	..	..	..		..	..		3.6x	0.26x	9.0x	14.00
Bolivia	24.7	..	16.0	15.77	9.4	..	27x	15x	571	527	71.6x	17.9	6.4	5.17	30.9	2.10
Brazil	7.0	7.0	54.0	22.20	7.5	0.9	8	19	28,384	9,889	0.3	6.8	1.3	179.05	41.1	2.16
Chile	14.6	29.3	15.0	13.50	5.7	1.6	29	28	6,803	4,091	1.0	19.9	5.5	27.41	32.3	..
Colombia	14.0	15.4	34.0	23.95	9.4	1.6	20	21	7,739	3,322	1.4	18.7	3.9	28.86	34.6	140.20
Costa Rica	28.2	40.9	24.0	58.31	8.0	3.7	46	23	387	410	-0.3	19.7	4.5	3.45	14.1	0.00
Cuba	..	..	..	58.43	14.9	..	..	..		..	..	..		..	..	..
Dominican Republic	17.2	25.9	77.0x	44.77	10.8	4.1	34	24	366	394	3.3	12.3	3.0	4.31	11.4	847.00
Ecuador	14.0	28.8	9.0	30.27	7.8	1.8	26	17	816	447	7.8	13.4	2.3	14.49	22.6	0.00
El Salvador	24.8	21.0	41.0	26.21	11.6	3.2	33	16	48	25	19.3	1.5	0.2	2.89	9.5	1.06
Guatemala	18.6	..	31.0	54.78	11.5	..	23	13	5	77	10.7	3.8	0.5	3.79	11.0	375.40
Guyana	56.5	73.0	..	23.60	7.5	..	..	..		..	..		0.5x	2.11x	17.0x	..
Haiti	13.8	..	..	23.09	32.9	..	28	2x	4	4	2117.2	0.0	0.2	0.90	13.8	..
Honduras	27.9	35.5	31.0	35.54	13.1	4.9	52	32	65	75	28.6	5.8	1.9	4.45	28.8	150.00
Jamaica	33.2	68.9	69.0	19.59	11.6	5.4	68	27	191	175	5.1	14.9	4.0	4.04	18.0	410.00
Mexico	6.4	25.5	78.0	7.70	8.1	2.0	20	21	23,647	7,619	0.4	10.9	2.3	157.13	35.4	4,223.70
Nicaragua	26.5	..	34.0	37.38	13.4	..	66	28	41	45	..	8.2	2.3	5.93	24.2	95.00
Panama	..	38.6	20.0	51.07	9.2	3.7	91	29	301	238	3.7	9.9	2.9	6.99	10.7	15.80
Paraguay	14.9	..	17.0	18.10	6.9	..	26	23	202	220	4.5	10.1	2.3	2.14	5.5	..
Peru	17.9	11.9	16.0	8.96	14.6	1.8	16	24	5,854	3,581	2.9	25.0	5.9	29.18	35.4	404.00
Suriname	60.3	..	..	11.34	17.1	..	..	..		..	..		4.5x	..	..	..
Trinidad and Tobago	42.8	39.5	39.0	4.41	9.6	5.9	42	15	343	320	2.0	38.1	5.9	2.24	15.6	30.00
Uruguay	14.4	19.1	36.0	55.33	11.9	1.3	20	12	499	169	2.3	7.7	0.9	5.90	15.6	0.00
Venezuela	20.9	26.7	12.0	1.10	9.3	2.1	24	17	4,244	1,833	0.4	16.3	2.7	35.34	16.8	..
Middle East and North Africa	**..**	**..**	**..**	**..**	**..**	**..**	**26x**	**26**	**1,979**	**614**	**..**	**3.3**	**0.7**	**212.39**	**11.4**	**..**
Algeria	22.0	26.7	4.0x	0.59	20.0	9.4	25	27	(72)	4	2.5	0.0	0.0	33.26	27.7	1,045.00
Bahrain	..	..	..	0.02	6.2	..	..	..		..	..	..		..	..	..
Cyprus	..	..	57.7x	12.52	8.0	..	..	..		..	..	..		..	..	..
Egypt	14.2	21.3	32.0	10.17	22.6	6.3	25	17	1,434	636	19.7	5.7	0.9	31.41	11.6	2,798.00
Iran	..	20.6	..	2.70	12.6	..	16x	29x	(352)	10	..	..	..	21.18	20.0x	..
Iraq	..	..	..	1.72	38.4	..	..	..		..	..		..	..	..	..
Jordan	..	..	49.0x	8.51	13.2	..	75	35	(119)	16	20.2	0.6	0.2	8.12	12.3	1,544.00
Kuwait	59.8	54.7	5.0x	0.40	13.8	4.7	49x	12x		..	0.2x	..		..	..	..
Lebanon	..	..	..	9.02	12.1	..	58	30	740	80	6.0	2.0	0.6	4.00	6.4	2,503.00
Libya	61.0	..	..	0.21	21.1	..	..	..		..	..		..	..	..	..
Morocco	17.6	27.3	50.0	15.89	14.4	4.7	30	21	388	311	8.6	4.1	0.8	21.77	27.7	2,009.70
Oman	73.7	..	14.0x	1.35	12.2	..	40x	17x	69	67	5.0x	4.0	0.4	3.42	9.9	39.01
Qatar	..	..	..	0.37	8.4	..	..	..		..	..		..	..	..	..
Saudi Arabia	66.3	..	..	0.52	1.5	..	30x	20x		..	0.1	-7.7	-1.5	..	..	0.00
Syria	17.5	..	..	11.71	13.1	..	..	..	77	89	..	..	0.6	21.42	3.8	0.00
Tunisia	22.0	44.8	80.0	2.55	6.9	5.7	44	24	697	320	2.7	6.8	1.6	9.89	16.5	735.56
Turkey	4.2	20.3	74.0	14.90	3.9	1.5	27	24	5,635	722	0.5	1.7	0.4	79.79	21.7	3,542.00
United Arab Emirates	..	..	..	1.37	6.5	..	69x	27x		..	..	..		..	..	..
West Bank and Gaza[a]	..	..	..	79.13	15.6	..	..	..		..	..	..		..	..	..
Yemen	..	..	1.0x	1.59	77.3	..	50	25	100	100	17.1	6.6	6.4	6.36	2.4	1,134.50

Table 5, continued: Economic Globalization

	Exports of goods and services (% of GDP) 1970	Exports of goods and services (% of GDP) 1996	Manufactured exports (% of merchandise exports) 1996	Food exports (% of merchandise exports) 1995	Food imports (% of total imports) 1996	Food imports (% of total consumption) 1995	Imports of goods and services (% of GDP) 1996	Gross domestic investment (GDI) (% of GDP)	Net private capital flows ($ millions)	FDI ($ million) 1996	Aid (% of GDI) 1996	Foreign direct investment net inflows (% of GDI) 1996	Foreign direct investment net inflows (% of GDP) 1996	Total External debt (US $ billions) 1996	Debt service (% of exports of goods and services) 1996	Workers' remittances, receipts (US $ millions) 1996
Countries in Transition[b]	..	..	..	..	..	..	33	23	35,005	14,941	2.3	5.7	1.3	370.17	11.4	..
Albania	..	13.8	..	1.33	24.3	6.1	40	21	92	90	40.2	16.3	3.4	0.78	3.5	499.60
Armenia	..	23.7	..	0.85	36.3	3.8	62x	10x	18	18	146.8x	9.4	1.0	0.55	10.7	11.12
Azerbaijan	..	27.0	..	1.75	40.6	8.1	42	24	601	601	11.9	67.3	16.5	0.44	1.3	..
Belarus	..	42.7	..	4.00	7.1	2.1	52	25	7	18	1.5	0.4	0.1	1.07	2.0	29.90
Bosnia and Herzegovina	..	..	..	..	..	..	..	..	..	..	..	..	..	..	..	..
Bulgaria	..	49.1	..	5.87	4.3	3.4	62	14	300	115	12.7	8.6	1.2	9.82	20.5	..
Croatia	..	40.3	72.0	8.02	9.4	3.8	53	15	915	349	4.7	12.4	1.8	4.63	5.5	..
Czech Republic	..	51.6	84.0	..	..	3.0	62	35	4,894	1,435	0.6	7.6	2.6	20.09	8.3	..
Estonia	..	75.5	68.0	13.36	17.0	0.5	86	27	191	150	5.4	12.9	3.5	0.41	1.3	0.05
Georgia	..	16.8	..	6.88	33.2	9.5	28x	4x	40	40	121.1x	4.6	0.2	1.36	..	..
Hungary	30.1	34.9	68.0	15.57	4.0	1.4	40	27	1,618	1,982	1.5	16.5	4.4	26.96	41.0	10.51
Kazakhstan	..	34.5	..	10.31	5.8	1.5	34	23	615	310	2.6	6.4	1.5	2.92	9.9	..
Kyrgyzstan	..	26.3	38.0	19.51	16.1	5.5	55	19	46	46	69.2	13.8	2.6	0.79	9.2	..
Latvia	..	42.7	61.0	3.65	5.7	2.5	55	19	331	328	8.4	34.9	6.5	0.47	2.3	..
Lithuania	..	57.8	60.0	12.16	4.2	2.5	62	21	469	152	5.5	9.3	2.0	1.29	2.9	1.85
Macedonia	..	37.3	..	5.07	13.3	13.2	49x	15x	8	8	26.0x	4.6	0.7	1.66	3.9	..
Moldova	..	35.2	23.0x	33.44	6.8	1.2	66	28	115	41	7.3	8.0	2.2	0.83	6.2	..
Poland	..	27.9	74.0	9.22	7.7	1.6	26	20	5,333	4,498	3.0	16.4	3.3	40.90	6.4	723.00
Romania	..	27.6	77.0	6.88	5.4	2.1	33	25	1,814	263	2.4	2.9	0.7	8.29	12.6	10.00
Russia	..	22.3	..	0.77	19.3	3.6	19	22	7,454	2,479	0.0	2.5	0.6	124.79	6.6	0.00
Slovakia	..	62.9	68.0	3.44	5.4	3.6	69	38	1,265	281	2.0	3.9	1.5	7.70	11.9	4.11
Slovenia	..	55.7	90.0	3.09	6.5	3.8	56	23	1,219	186	1.9	4.3	1.0	4.03	8.7	41.60
Tajikistan	..	114.3	..	2.76	25.6	10.5	114x	17x	16	16	20.3x	4.7	0.8	0.71	0.1	..
Turkmenistan	..	..	..	0.56	19.6	..	..	..	355	108	..	..	2.5	0.83	10.6	0.00
Ukraine	..	..	..	9.58	3.6	..	48	23	395	350	3.8	3.5	0.8	9.34	6.1	0.00
Uzbekistan	..	..	..	2.36	13.9	..	38	16	431	55	2.1	1.4	0.2	2.32	8.1	..
Yugoslavia	..	..	49.0	..	10.8	..	..	..	..	..	..	..	..	13.44i	..	..
Industrial Countries	..	..	81.0	..	..	..	20x	21x	..	195,736	..	5.4	0.9	..	..	..
Australia	14.5	19.8	30.0	19.54	3.0	0.6	21x	21x	..	6,321	..	18.9	1.6	..	..	..
Austria	31.1	38.1	88.0	3.62	4.9	1.7	39x	25x	..	3,826	..	1.1	1.7	..	..	321.84
Belgium	51.9	74.4	77.0	9.08	7.9	6.4	68x	18x	..	..	n/a	..	..	..	..	120.41
Canada	22.7	36.9	63.0	5.45	4.3	1.4	35x	18x	..	6,398	n/a	10.5	1.1	..	..	..
Denmark	27.9	34.9	59.0	15.92	6.7	1.7	30	17x	..	773	n/a	14.1	0.4	..	..	..
Finland	25.7	38.0	83.0	2.23	5.0	1.2	30x	16x	..	1,118	n/a	5.1	0.9	..	..	..
France	15.8	22.9	79.0	9.55	6.9	1.6	21x	18x	..	21,972	n/a	8.5	1.4	..	..	1.72
Germany	..	23.5	87.0	3.83	7.3	1.6	23x	23x	..	(3,183)	n/a	2.2	-0.1	..	..	..
Greece	10.0	22.4	50.0x	14.64	10.7	3.5	27x	14x	..	..	n/a	7.0	0.7	..	..	2.89
Ireland	35.5	75.5	82.0	12.91	6.9	4.2	59x	15x	..	2,456	n/a	23.6	3.5	..	..	..
Israel	25.0	29.4	91.0	4.26	4.9	1.6	40x	24x	..	2,110	1.6x	7.3	1.7	..	..	0.00
Italy	16.4	26.4	89.0	4.63	8.2	1.8	23x	18x	..	3,523	n/a	2.5	0.3	..	..	337.21
Japan	10.8	9.5	95.0	0.21	8.3	0.8	8x	29x	..	200	n/a	0.0	0.0	..	..	256.53
Luxembourg	87.7	96.3	..	9.08	7.8	..	19x	..	..	..	n/a	..	..	..	..	..
Netherlands	43.5	53.0	63.0	12.32	7.8	5.5	47x	19x	..	7,824	n/a	18.7	2.0	..	..	..
New Zealand	22.6	31.6	29.0	36.38	5.9	1.6	29x	22x	..	280	n/a	31.5	0.4	..	..	0.00
Norway	38.2	38.3	23.0	0.71	4.2	..	31	23x	..	3,960	n/a	..	2.5	..	..	..
Portugal	21.5	28.3	86.0	2.67	8.5	..	41x	25x	..	618	n/a	8.3	0.6	..	..	3,712.39
Spain	13.2	23.7	78.0	11.23	7.1	2.0	23x	21x	..	6,396	n/a	5.2	1.1	..	..	2.79
Sweden	23.8	40.6	80.0	1.63	4.8	1.3	33	15x	..	5,492	n/a	41.2	2.2	..	..	135.71
Switzerland	32.8	35.7	94.0	2.22	4.1	1.5	32	23x	..	3,512	n/a	..	1.2	..	..	169.90
United Kingdom	23.1	28.0	78.0	3.48	6.6	..	29x	16	..	32,347	n/a	..	2.8	..	..	..
United States	5.8	11.3	78.0	6.82	2.9	..	13x	18x	..	76,955	n/a	5.4	1.0	..	..	..
World	14.1	22.5	78.0	5.96	6.1	..	21x	23	..	552,616	..	8.1	1.1	..	..	..

a Territory.

b Central and Eastern European countries and the newly independent states of the former Soviet Union.

c Consumption is the sum of private (market value of all goods and services, including durable products, such as cars, washing machines and home computers) and general government consumption (current expenditures to purchase goods and services and capital expenditures on national defense and security).

d Net capital flows include net private capital flows (private debt and nondebt flows) and aid (official development assistance and official aid – including emergency aid).

e Bread for the World Institute estimate.

f Net private capital flows consist of private debt flows (commercial bank lending, bonds and other private credits) and nondebt private flows (foreign direct investment and portfolio equity investment).

g Luxembourg included.

h Data cover mainland Tanzania only.

i Data refers to the former Yugoslavia

n/a not applicable

The number '0' (zero) means zero or less than half the unit of measure.

TABLE 6: Global Communications

	Daily papers per 1,000 people 1994	TV sets per 1,000 people 1996	Mobile phones per 1,000 people 1996	Fax machines per 1,000 people 1996	Personal computers per 1,000 people 1996	Internet hosts per 10,000 per people July 1997
Developing Countries	**19**	**147**	**3**	**0.2x**	**2.3**	**0.12**
Africa (sub-Saharan)	**11**	**43x**	..	..	..	**2.03**
Angola	11	51x	0	..	..	0.02
Benin	2	73x	0	0.1x	..	0.02
Botswana	24	27	..	2.2	6.7	1.58
Burkina Faso	0	6	0	..	..	0.04
Burundi	3	2	0	0.5	..	0.01
Cameroon	4	75x	0	..	..	0.05
Cape Verde	..	..	..	..	..	..
Central African Republic	1	5x	0	0.0x	..	0.02
Chad	0	2x	..	0	..	0
Comoros	..	..	..	..	..	..
Congo (Brazzaville)	8	8x	..	..	..	0.02
Côte d'Ivoire	7	60x	1	..	1.4	0.17
Djibouti	..	..	..	..	..	..
Equatorial Guinea	..	..	..	..	..	..
Eritrea	..	7	..	0.2	..	0
Ethiopia	2	4x	..	0	..	0
Gabon	16	76x	6	0.3	6.3	0
Gambia	2	..	3	0.9x	..	0
Ghana	18	41x	1	0.3x	1.2x	0.15
Guinea	..	8x	0	..	0.3	0
Guinea-Bissau	6	..	..	0.5x	..	0.09
Kenya	13	19x	0	0.1x	1.6	0.16
Lesotho	7	13x	1	0.3x	..	0.08
Liberia	..	..	..	..	..	..
Madagascar	4	24x	0	..	..	0.03
Malawi	2	..	0	0.1	..	0
Mali	4	11	0	..	..	0.03
Mauritania	0	82	..	0.1	5.3	0
Mauritius	68	219x	18	17.7	31.9x	1.84
Mozambique	5	3x	..	0.4x	0.8	0.02
Namibia	102	29x	4	..	12.7	2.16
Niger	1	23x	..	0.0x	..	0.04
Nigeria	18	55x	0	..	4.1x	0
Rwanda	0	..	..	..	..	0.01
Senegal	6	38x	0	..	7.2x	0.31
Sierra Leone	2	17	..	0.2	..	0
Somalia	..	..	..	..	..	..
South Africa	33	123	22	2.4x	37.7	30.67
Sudan	23	80x	0	0.2	0.7	0
Swaziland	..	..	..	..	..	..
Tanzania	8	16x	0	..	..	0.02
Togo	2	14	..	2.4	..	0.01
Uganda	2	26	0	0.1	0.5	0.01
Zaire (Congo-Kinshasa)	3	41x	0	0.1x	..	0
Zambia	8	80	0	0.1	..	0.27
Zimbabwe	18	29x	..	0.4x	6.7	0.24
South Asia	..	**53**	**0**	**0.2x**	**1.5**	**0.06**
Afghanistan	..	..	..	..	..	..
Bangladesh	6	7	0x	0.0x	..	0
Bhutan	23	7	0	0	..	0
India	..	64	0	0.1x	1.5	0.05
Maldives	..	..	..	..	..	..
Nepal	8	4	..	0.0x	..	0.07
Pakistan	21	24	0	1.2x	1.2x	0.07
Sri Lanka	25	82	4	0.6x	3.3	0.33
East Asia and the Pacific	**29**	**228**	**7**	**0.4x**	**4.5**	**0.57**
Brunei	..	..	..	..	..	..
Burma (Myanmar)	23	7	0	0	..	0
Cambodia	..	9	2	0.1	..	0.01
China	23	252	6	0.2x	3	0.21
Fiji	..	..	..	..	..	..

TABLE 6, continued: Global Communications

	Daily papers per 1,000 people 1994	TV sets per 1,000 people 1996	Mobile phones per 1,000 people 1996	Fax machines per 1,000 people 1996	Personal computers per 1,000 people 1996	Internet hosts per 10,000 per people July 1997
Hong Kong[a]	719	388	216	46.3	150.5	74.84
Indonesia	20	232	3	0.4x	4.8	0.54
Korea, N.	213	115x	..	0.1	..	0
Korea, S.	404	326	70	8.9x	131.7	28.77
Laos	3	10	1	0.1x	1.1	0
Malaysia	124	228	74	5.0x	42.8	19.3
Mongolia	88	63	0	0.9	..	0.07
Papua New Guinea	15	4	1	0.2x	..	0.18
Philippines	65	125	13	0.7x	9.3	0.59
Singapore	364	361	141	25.1	216.8	196.3
Solomon Islands	..	..	..	..	..	..
Thailand	48	167	28	1.7	16.7	2.11
Vietnam	8	180	1	0.2	3.3	0
Latin America and the Caribbean	**83**	**216x**	**14**	**1.9x**	**23.2**	**3.48**
Argentina	138	347x	16	1.4	24.6x	5.32
Belize	..	..	..	..	..	..
Bolivia	69	202x	4	..	..	0.69
Brazil	45	289	16	1.7	18.4	4.2
Chile	100	280x	23	1.8x	45.1	13.12
Colombia	64	188x	13	2.6	23.3	1.81
Costa Rica	99	220x	14	0.7	..	12.14
Cuba	120	200x	0	..	..	0.06
Dominican Republic	34	84	8	0.3	..	0.03
Ecuador	72	148x	5	2.7	3.9x	0.9
El Salvador	50	250	3	..	..	0.34
Guatemala	23	122x	4	1.0x	2.8x	0.79
Guyana	..	..	..	..	..	..
Haiti	6	5x	..	..	..	0
Honduras	44	80	0	..	..	0.94
Jamaica	66	326	22	..	4.6	1.36
Mexico	113	193x	11	2.4x	29	3.72
Nicaragua	30	170x	1	..	..	1.6
Panama	62	229x	..	..	..	1.44
Paraguay	42	144x	7	..	..	0.47
Peru	86	142	8	0.6x	5.9x	2.63
Suriname	..	..	..	..	..	..
Trinidad and Tobago	135	318x	11	1.6	19.2x	3.24
Uruguay	237	305x	25	3.5x	22.0x	3.18
Venezuela	215	180x	35	1.1x	21.1	2.06
Middle East and North Africa	**37**	**144x**	**3**	**1.0x**	**17.1**	**0.2**
Algeria	46	68	0	0.2	3.4	0.01
Bahrain	..	..	..	..	..	..
Cyprus	..	..	..	..	..	..
Egypt	64	126x	0	0.4x	5.8	0.31
Iran	17	164	1	0.5x	32.7	0
Iraq	27	78x	..	..	..	0
Jordan	48	175x	3	7.3x	7.2	0.38
Kuwait	401	373	89	20.7	74.1	21.72
Lebanon	172	355	65	..	24.3	2.72
Libya	13	143	..	..	..	0.01
Morocco	13	145x	2	0.3	1.7x	0.32
Oman	30	591	6	1.3	10.9	0
Qatar	..	..	..	..	..	..
Saudi Arabia	54	263x	10	8.4x	37.2	0.15
Syria	18	91x	..	0.3	1.4	0
Tunisia	46	156x	1	2.8	6.7x	0.02
Turkey	44	309	13	1.6	13.8	3.6
United Arab Emirates	161	276	79	16.8	65.5	7.66
West Bank and Gaza[a]	..	..	..	..	..	..
Yemen	17	278x	1	0.2x	..	0

TABLE 6, continued: Global Communications

	Daily papers per 1,000 people 1994	TV sets per 1,000 people 1996	Mobile phones per 1,000 people 1996	Fax machines per 1,000 people 1996	Personal computers per 1,000 people 1996	Internet hosts per 10,000 per people July 1997
Countries in Transition[b]	**171**	**350**	**6**	**1.2x**	**17.4x**	**6.53**
Albania	54	173	1	..	..	0.32
Armenia	23	216	0	0.1x	..	0.88
Azerbaijan	28	212	2	0.3x	0	0.11
Belarus	187	292x	1	0.9x	..	0.44
Bosnia and Herzegovina	131	55	0	..	..	0.13
Bulgaria	..	361	3	1.8x	295.2	6.65
Croatia	575	251x	14	8.2	20.9x	14.08
Czech Republic	219	406x	19	7.1	53.2x	47.66
Estonia	242	449	47	8.8x	6.7x	45.35
Georgia	..	474x	0	0.1x	..	0.55
Hungary	228	444x	46	4.4x	44.1	33.29
Kazakhstan	..	275x	0	0.2x	..	0.7
Kyrgyzstan	11	238	..	..	..	0.23
Latvia	228	598	11	0.3x	7.9x	21.03
Lithuania	136	376	14	1	6.5x	7.46
Macedonia	21	170x	0	0.8	..	2.15
Moldova	24	307	0	0.1	2.6	0.39
Poland	141	418	6	1.4x	36.2	11.22
Romania	297	226	1	0.9x	5.3x	2.66
Russia	267	386	2	0.2	23.7	5.51
Slovakia	256	384	5	8.3	186.1	20.47
Slovenia	185	375x	20	7.8	47.8x	85.66
Tajikistan	13	279	0	0.2	..	0
Turkmenistan	..	163x	..	..	..	0
Ukraine	118	341	1	0	5.6x	2.09
Uzbekistan	7	190x	0	0.1	..	0.06
Yugoslavia	90	185x	..	1.4	..	2.72
Industrial Countries	**303**	**611x**	**131**	**47.5x**	**224.2**	**203.46**
Australia	258	666	208	26.3x	311.3	382.44
Austria	472	493	74	35.4x	148	108.25
Belgium	321	464x	47	17.8	167.3	84.64
Canada	189	709x	114	23.6	192.5x	228.05
Denmark	365	533	250	47.6x	304.1	259.73
Finland	473	605	292	31.5	182.1x	653.61
France	237	598x	42	32.7x	150.7	49.86
Germany	317	493	71	19.5	233.2	106.68
Greece	156	442x	53	2.9	33.4x	18.76
Ireland	170	469x	82	22.4	145.0x	90.89
Israel	281	303x	184	25.0x	117.6	104.79
Italy	105	436x	112	31.4x	92.3	36.91
Japan	576	700	214	102.2	128	75.8
Luxembourg	..	..	..	..	..	..
Netherlands	334	495x	52	32.3x	232	219.01
New Zealand	297	517	138	18.1x	266.1	424.34
Norway	607	569	287	30.1	273	474.63
Portugal	41	367	67	5.0x	60.5x	18.26
Spain	104	509	33	16.6	94.2	31
Sweden	483	476x	282	45.3	214.9	321.48
Switzerland	409	493	93	27.8	408.5	207.98
United Kingdom	351	612x	122	30.8x	192.6	149.06
United States	228	806x	165	64.6	362.4	442.11
World	**99**	**211**	**28**	**8.9**	**49.9**	**35.18**

.. Data not available.

a Territory.

b Central and Eastern European countries and the newly independent states of the former Soviet Union.

x Data refer to a period other than specified in the column heading

TABLE 7: U.S. National Hunger and Poverty Trends

	1970	1980	1982	1984	1985	1986	1987	1988	1989	1990	1991	1992	1993	1994	1995	1996	1997
Total population (millions)	**205.1**	**227.8**	**232.5**	**237.0**	**239.3**	**241.6**	**243.9**	**246.3**	**248.3**	**249.4**	**252.1**	**255.0**	**257.8**	**260.4**	**262.9**	**265.3**	**267.63**
Northeastern region population	..	..	..	..	..	..	..	..	..	50.9	51.0	51.1	51.3	51.4	51.5	51.6	51.59
Midwestern region population	..	..	..	..	..	..	..	..	..	59.8	60.2	60.6	61.0	61.3	61.7	62.1	62.46
Southern region population	..	..	..	..	..	..	..	..	..	85.7	86.9	88.2	89.5	90.7	92.0	93.1	94.18
Western region population	..	..	..	..	..	..	..	..	..	53.0	54.1	55.1	56.0	56.8	57.7	58.5	29.63
Total food insecure population (millions)	..	..	..	..	**20.0**	..	..	..	..	..	**30.0**	..	..	..	..	..	
Children under 12 hungry (millions)	..	..	..	..	..	..	..	..	..	..	5.5	..	..	..	4.0	..	
Children under 12 at risk of hunger (millions)	..	..	..	..	..	..	..	..	..	..	6.0	..	..	..	9.6	..	
Percent of federal budget spent on food assistance[a]	**0.5**	**2.4**	**2.1**	**2.1**	**2.0**	**1.9**	**1.9**	**1.9**	**1.9**	**1.9**	**2.0**	**2.3**	**2.5**	**2.47**	**2.48**	**2.43**	**1.94**
Total infant mortality rate (per 1,000 live births)	**20.0**	**12.6**	**11.5**	**10.8**	**10.6**	**10.4**	**10.1**	**10.0**	**9.7**	**9.1**	**8.9**	**8.5**	**8.4**	**8.0**	**7.6**	..	
White infant mortality rate	17.8	11.0	10.1	9.4	9.3	8.9	8.6	8.5	8.5	7.7	7.3	6.9	6.8	6.6	6.3	..	
African American infant mortality rate	32.6	21.4	19.6	18.4	18.2	18.0	17.9	17.6	17.6	17.0	17.6	16.8	16.5	15.8	15.1	..	
Hispanic infant mortality rate	..	..	..	..	..	..	7.9	8.1	8.5	7.8	7.5	6.8	..	..	..	..	
Total poverty rate (%)	**12.6**	**13.0**	**15.0**	**14.4**	**14.0**	**13.6**	**13.4**	**13.1**	**12.8**	**13.5**	**14.2**	**14.8**	**15.1**	**14.5**	**13.8**	..	
Northeastern region poverty rate	..	..	..	..	..	..	..	..	10.2	10.2	11.3	12.6	13.3	12.9	12.5	12.7	
Midwestern region poverty rate	..	..	..	..	..	..	..	..	12.0	11.9	12.8	13.3	13.4	13.0	11.0	10.7	
Southern region poverty rate	..	..	..	..	..	..	..	..	15.6	15.9	16.2	17.1	17.1	16.1	15.7	15.1	
Western region poverty rate	..	..	..	..	..	..	..	..	12.8	11.6	12.4	14.8	15.6	15.3	14.9	15.4	
White poverty rate	9.9	10.2	12.0	11.5	11.4	11.0	10.4	10.1	10.0	10.7	11.3	11.9	12.2	11.7	11.2	11.2	
African American poverty rate	33.5	32.5	35.6	33.8	31.1	31.1	32.6	31.6	30.7	31.9	32.7	33.4	33.1	30.6	29.3	28.4	
Hispanic poverty rate	..	25.7	29.9	28.4	29.0	27.3	28.1	26.8	26.2	28.1	28.7	29.6	30.6	30.7	30.3	29.4	
Elderly poverty rate	24.6	15.7	14.6	12.4	12.6	12.4	12.5	12.0	11.4	12.2	12.4	12.9	12.2	11.7	10.5	11.5	
Female-headed households poverty rate	38.1	36.7	40.6	38.4	37.6	38.3	38.3	37.2	32.2	33.4	39.7	39.0	38.7	34.6	32.4	32.6	
Total child poverty rate (%)	**15.1**	**18.3**	**21.9**	**21.5**	**20.7**	**20.5**	**20.5**	**19.7**	**19.6**	**20.6**	**21.1**	**22.3**	**22.7**	**21.8**	**20.8**	..	
White child poverty rate	..	13.9	17.0	16.7	16.2	16.1	15.4	14.6	14.8	15.9	16.1	17.4	17.8	16.9	16.2	..	
African American child poverty rate	..	42.3	47.6	46.6	43.6	43.1	45.6	44.2	43.7	44.8	45.6	46.6	46.1	43.8	41.9	..	
Hispanic child poverty rate	..	33.2	39.5	39.2	40.3	37.7	39.6	37.9	36.2	38.4	39.8	40.0	40.9	41.5	40.0	..	
Unemployment rate (%)	**4.9**	**7.1**	**9.7**	**7.5**	**7.2**	**7.0**	**6.2**	**5.5**	**5.3**	**5.6**	**6.8**	**7.5**	**6.9**	**6.1**	**5.6**	**5.4**	
White unemployment rate	4.5	6.3	8.6	6.5	6.2	6.0	5.3	4.7	4.5	4.8	6.1	6.6	6.1	5.3	4.9	4.7	
African American unemployment rate	..	14.3	18.9	15.9	15.1	14.5	13.0	11.7	11.4	11.4	12.5	14.2	13.0	11.5	10.4	10.5	
Hispanic unemployment rate	..	10.1	13.8	10.7	10.5	10.6	8.8	8.2	8.0	8.2	10.0	11.6	10.8	9.9	9.3	8.9	
Household income distribution (per quintile in %)																	
All races																	
Lowest 20 percent	4.1	4.2	4.0	4.0	3.9	3.8	3.8	3.8	3.8	3.9	3.8	3.8	3.6	3.6	3.7	3.7	
Second quintile	10.8	10.2	10.0	9.9	9.8	9.7	9.6	9.6	9.5	9.6	9.6	9.4	9.0	8.9	9.1	9.0	
Third quintile	17.4	16.8	16.5	16.3	16.2	16.2	16.1	16.0	15.8	15.9	15.9	15.8	15.1	15.0	15.2	15.1	
Fourth quintile	24.5	24.8	24.5	24.6	24.4	24.3	24.3	24.3	24.0	24.0	24.2	24.2	23.5	23.4	23.3	23.3	
Highest 20 percent	43.3	44.1	45.0	45.2	45.6	46.1	46.2	46.3	46.8	46.6	46.5	46.9	48.9	49.1	48.7	49.0	
Ratio of highest 20 percent to lowest 20 percent[e]	10.6	10.5	11.3	11.3	11.7	12.1	12.2	12.2	12.3	11.9	12.2	12.3	13.6	13.6	13.2	13.2	
White																	
Lowest 20 percent	4.2	4.4	4.2	4.3	4.1	4.1	4.1	4.1	4.1	4.2	4.1	4.1	3.9	3.8	4.0	3.9	
Second quintile	11.1	10.5	10.3	10.2	10.1	10.0	10.0	10.0	9.8	10.0	9.9	9.7	9.3	9.2	9.3	9.2	
Third quintile	17.5	17.0	16.6	16.5	16.4	16.3	16.3	16.2	16.0	16.0	16.0	15.9	15.3	15.1	15.3	15.2	
Fourth quintile	24.3	24.6	24.4	24.4	24.3	24.2	24.2	24.1	23.8	23.9	24.1	24.1	23.3	23.2	23.3	23.2	
Highest 20 percent	42.9	43.5	44.4	44.6	45.1	45.4	45.5	45.6	46.3	46.0	45.8	46.2	48.2	48.6	48.1	48.4	
Ratio of highest 20 percent to lowest 20 percent[e]	10.2	9.9	10.6	10.4	11.0	11.1	11.1	11.1	11.3	11.0	11.2	11.3	12.4	12.8	12.0	12.4	
African American																	
Lowest 20 percent	3.7	3.7	3.6	3.6	3.5	3.1	3.3	3.3	3.2	3.1	3.1	3.1	3.0	3.0	3.2	3.1	
Second quintile	9.3	8.7	8.6	8.4	8.3	8.0	7.9	7.7	8.0	7.9	7.8	7.8	7.7	7.9	8.2	8.0	
Third quintile	16.3	15.3	15.3	15.0	15.2	14.9	14.8	14.6	15.0	15.0	15.0	14.7	14.3	14.3	14.8	14.5	
Fourth quintile	25.2	25.2	25.3	24.7	25.0	25.0	24.4	24.7	24.9	25.1	25.2	24.8	23.7	24.3	24.2	23.7	
Highest 20 percent	45.5	47.1	47.1	48.4	48.0	49.0	49.7	49.7	48.9	49.0	48.9	49.7	51.3	50.5	49.6	50.7	
Ratio of highest 20 percent to lowest 20 percent[e]	12.3	12.7	13.1	13.4	13.7	15.8	15.1	15.1	15.3	15.8	15.8	16.0	17.1	16.8	15.5	16.4	
Hispanic origin																	
Lowest 20 percent	..	4.3	4.2	3.9	4.1	3.9	3.7	3.7	3.8	4.0	4.0	4.0	3.9	3.7	3.8	3.8	
Second quintile	..	10.1	9.6	9.5	9.4	9.5	9.1	9.3	9.5	9.5	9.4	9.4	9.1	8.7	8.9	9.0	
Third quintile	..	16.4	16.1	16.2	16.1	15.8	15.5	15.6	15.7	15.9	15.8	15.7	15.1	14.8	14.8	14.7	
Fourth quintile	..	24.8	24.6	24.9	24.8	24.8	24.1	24.2	24.4	24.3	24.3	24.1	23.1	23.3	23.3	23.1	
Highest 20 percent	..	44.5	45.5	45.5	45.6	46.1	47.6	47.2	46.6	46.3	46.5	46.9	48.7	49.6	49.3	49.5	
Ratio of highest 20 percent to lowest 20 percent[e]	..	**10.3**	**10.8**	**11.7**	**11.1**	**11.8**	**12.9**	**12.8**	**12.3**	**11.6**	**11.6**	**11.7**	**12.5**	**13.4**	**13.0**	**13.0**	

.. *Data not available.*
a *Data refer to fiscal year.*
e *Bread for the World Institute estimate.*

TABLE 8: United States – State Hunger and Poverty Statistics

	Total population (millions) July 1997	% children under 12 hungry 1993	% children under 12 hungry or at risk		Infant mortality rate per 1,000 live births 1995			% population in poverty 1995	Unemployment rate (%) (seasonally adjusted) June 1998[a]
			1991	1993	Total	White	African American		
Alabama	4.32	8.6	35.0	29.5	9.8	7.1	15.2	20.1	3.8
Alaska	0.61	5.5	17.7	20.3	7.7	6.1	..	7.1	6.4
Arizona	4.55	9.0	25.8	30.4	7.5	7.2	17.0	16.1	4.0
Arkansas	2.52	10.0	38.5	36.1	8.8	7.2	14.3	14.9	4.8
California	32.27	11.8	27.8	37.1	6.3	5.8	14.4	16.7	5.8
Colorado	3.89	6.0	21.0	21.0	6.5	6.0	16.8	8.8	3.4
Connecticut	3.27	6.1	16.2	19.4	7.2	6.5	12.6	9.7	3.8
Delaware	0.73	5.9	21.8	21.8	7.5	6.0	13.1	10.3	4.0
District of Columbia	0.53	11.3	33.7	40.0	16.2	..	19.6	22.2	8.2
Florida	14.65	11.8	27.5	39.5	7.5	6.0	13.0	16.2	4.5
Georgia	7.49	7.3	27.1	24.5	9.4	6.5	15.1	12.1	4.1
Hawaii	1.19	5.4	23.7	19.1	5.8	..	..	10.3	6.0
Idaho	1.21	8.2	34.4	30.6	6.1	5.8	..	14.5	5.0
Illinois	11.90	7.9	28.0	26.3	9.4	7.2	18.7	12.4	4.5
Indiana	5.86	7.2	25.3	28.1	8.4	7.3	17.5	9.6	2.8
Iowa	2.85	6.4	31.7	23.2	8.2	7.8	21.2	12.2	2.5
Kansas	2.59	8.1	22.8	29.1	7.0	6.2	17.6	10.8	3.5
Kentucky	3.91	9.2	29.8	33.7	7.6	7.4	10.7	14.7	4.4
Louisiana	4.35	12.1	32.1	39.1	9.8	6.2	15.3	19.7	5.2
Maine	1.24	9.9	24.3	35.0	6.5	6.3	..	11.2	4.0
Maryland	5.09	5.9	16.4	19.9	8.9	6.0	15.3	10.1	4.5
Massachusetts	6.12	6.5	19.3	22.5	5.2	4.7	9.0	11.0	3.4
Michigan	9.77	8.4	27.6	29.9	8.3	6.2	17.3	12.2	3.6
Minnesota	4.69	6.7	21.2	24.4	6.7	6.0	17.6	9.2	2.6
Mississippi	2.73	10.3	38.7	37.3	10.5	7.0	14.7	23.5	4.6
Missouri	5.40	9.2	26.9	32.4	7.4	6.4	13.8	9.4	4.2
Montana	0.88	7.9	31.5	30.3	7.0	7.0	..	15.3	5.4
Nebraska	1.66	6.9	28.6	24.8	7.4	7.3	..	9.6	1.7
Nevada	1.68	6.7	27.9	22.9	5.7	5.5	..	11.1	4.4
New Hampshire	1.17	6.3	12.6	22.8	5.5	5.5	..	5.3	2.7
New Jersey	8.05	7.1	20.3	22.7	6.6	5.3	13.3	7.8	4.8
New Mexico	1.73	8.7	36.1	31.4	6.2	6.1	..	25.3	6.7
New York	18.14	9.5	29.7	30.7	7.7	6.2	13.9	16.5	5.5
North Carolina	7.43	8.3	26.3	29.5	9.2	6.7	15.9	12.6	3.1
North Dakota	0.64	5.3	27.9	21.2	7.2	6.7	..	12.0	2.2
Ohio	11.18	7.1	24.3	26.5	8.7	7.3	17.5	11.5	4.5
Oklahoma	3.32	10.6	28.7	38.7	8.3	8.0	15.1	17.1	4.0
Oregon	3.24	6.9	24.1	25.2	6.1	5.9	..	11.2	5.4
Pennsylvania	12.02	7.6	25.6	28.1	7.8	6.2	17.6	12.2	4.4
Rhode Island	0.99	6.9	25.6	25.8	7.2	7.0	..	10.6	4.1
South Carolina	3.76	10.0	31.3	35.8	9.6	6.7	14.6	19.9	3.2
South Dakota	0.74	8.0	28.6	29.9	9.5	7.9	..	14.5	2.7
Tennessee	5.37	10.6	30.7	36.8	9.3	6.8	17.9	15.5	3.9
Texas	19.44	10.1	28.6	30.6	6.5	5.9	11.7	17.4	5.0
Utah	2.06	7.0	25.5	24.7	5.4	5.3	..	8.4	3.2
Vermont	5.89	5.2	20.5	21.9	6.0	6.2	..	10.3	3.5
Virginia	6.73	5.8	20.5	20.7	7.8	5.7	15.3	10.2	3.1
Washington	5.61	7.4	22.7	27.5	5.9	5.6	16.2	12.5	4.7
West Virginia	1.82	10.2	38.6	37.3	7.9	7.6	..	16.7	6.9
Wisconsin	5.17	7.8	24.7	28.6	7.3	6.3	18.6	8.5	3.0
Wyoming	0.48	8.9	22.6	28.9	7.7	6.8	..	12.2	4.7
United States	**265.18**	**8.9**	**26.8**	**29.0**	**7.6**	**6.3**	**15.1**	**13.8**	**4.5**

.. Data not available.
a Preliminary.

SOURCES FOR TABLES

TABLE 1: Global Hunger – Life and Death Indicators

Total population, projected population, projected growth rate, projected total fertility rate, life expectancy: United Nations Population Fund (UNFPA), *The State of World Population 1998* (New York: UNFPA, 1998).

Population under age 15: Statistics Division and Population Division of the United Nations Secretariat, "Indicators on Youth and Elderly Populations," posted at http://www.un.org/Depts/unsd/social/youth.htm

Infant mortality rate, low birthweight infants, under-5 mortality rate, children immunized, maternal mortality, population urbanized: U.N. Children's Fund (UNICEF), *The State of the World's Children 1998* (New York: Oxford University Press, 1998 – "SWC")

Refugees: U.S. Committee for Refugees, *World Refugee Survey 1998* (Washington: Immigration and Refugee Services of America, 1998).

TABLE 2: Food, Nutrition and Education

Per capita dietary energy supply, annual growth rate: Food and Agriculture Organization of the United Nations (FAO), *The Sixth World Food Survey* (Rome: FAO, 1996).

Food production per capita: FAO, FAOSTAT TS software, 1996.

Goiter rate, adult literacy rates: *SWC*, 1998.

Primary, secondary and tertiary enrollment. *SWC*, 1997.

TABLE 3: Hunger, Malnutrition and Poverty

Undernourished population: FAO, *Mapping Undernutrition – An Ongoing Process* (Rome: FAO, 1996).

Relative inadequacy of food supply: FAO, *The Sixth World Food Survey*.

Underweight, wasting, stunting, access to safe water: *SWC*, 1998.

Population in poverty: The World Bank, *1997 World Development Indicators* (Washington: The World Bank, 1997 – "WDI"); U.N. Development Programme, *Human Development Report 1997* (New York: Oxford University Press, 1997 – "HDR").

TABLE 4: Economic and Development Indicators

GNP per capita, distribution of income or consumption, central government expenditure, per capita energy consumption: *WDI*, 1998.

HDI rank: *HDR*, 1998.

Education and health, military expenditure: *HDR*, 1997.

Annual deforestation: FAO, *State of the World's Forests 1997* (Rome: FAO, 1997).

TABLE 5: Economic Globalization

Exports of goods and services, imports of goods and services, gross domestic investment, international capital flows, debt, workers' remittances: *WDI*, 1998.

Food as percent of total merchandise exports and imports, food imports as percent of consumption: FAO, data posted at http://www.fao.org

TABLE 6: Global Communications

Daily newspapers, television sets, mobile phones, fax machines, personal computers, Internet hosts: WDI, 1998.

TABLE 7: U.S. National Hunger and Poverty Trends

Total population, poverty data, household income distribution: U.S. Bureau of the Census, data posted at http://www.census.gov

Total food insecure population: Center on Hunger, Poverty and Nutrition Policy, Tufts University.

Children under 12 hungry, at risk of hunger: Food Research and Action Center (FRAC), data posted at http://www.frac.org

Percent of federal budget spent on food assistance: Congressional Budget Office.

Infant mortality: National Center for Health Statistics, *Monthly Vital Statistics Report* 45:11, Supplement 2 (June 12, 1997).

Unemployment: U.S. Bureau of Labor Statistics, data posted at http://stats/bls.gov.news.release/laus.t03.htm

TABLE 8: United States – State Hunger and Poverty Statistics

Population, population in poverty: U.S. Bureau of the Census.

Unemployment: U.S. Bureau of Labor Statistics.

Infant mortality: National Center for Health Statistics.

Children under 12 hungry, at risk of hunger: FRAC.

ABBREVIATIONS

ADMARC – Agricultural Development and Marketing Corporation (Malawi)

AFDC – Aid to Families with Dependent Children

BFW – Bread for the World

BFWI – Bread for the World Institute

BWP – Bank Watchers' Project

CAS – Country Assistance Strategy

CBI – Caribbean Basin Initiative

CBPP – Center on Budget and Policy Priorities

CDF – Children's Defense Fund

CNN – Cable News Network

DAC – OECD Development Assistance Committee

DHR – Department of Human Resources, State of Alabama

DPRK – Democratic People's Republic of Korea (North Korea)

EBT – Electronic Benefits Transfer

EITC – Earned Income Tax Credit

ETAN – East Timor Action Network

EU – European Union

FAO – Food and Agriculture Organization of the United Nations

FBI – U.S. Federal Bureau of Investigation

FIAN – Food First Information and Action Network

FRAC – Food Research and Action Center

G-7/G-8 – Group of Seven/Group of Eight (United States, Great Britain, Germany, France, Canada, Japan, Italy and Russia)

G-24 – Intergovernmental Group of Twenty Four

GAO – U.S. General Accounting Office

GATT – General Agreement on Tariffs and Trade

GDP – Gross Domestic Product

GNP – Gross National Product

HIPC – Highly Indebted Poor Country

HHS – U.S. Department of Health and Human Services

HUD – U.S. Department of Housing and Urban Development

ICESCR – International Covenant on Economic, Social and Cultural Rights, 1966

IDB – Inter-American Development Bank

IFAD – International Fund for Agricultural Development

IFPRI – International Food Policy Research Institute

IFST – International Food Security Treaty

IMF – International Monetary Fund

LICO – Low Income Cut-Off

LIFDC – Low-Income Food Deficit Country

MAI – Multilateral Agreement on Investment

MFA – Multi-Fiber Arrangement

NATO – North Atlantic Treaty Organization

NGO – Nongovernmental Organization

NIEO – New International Economic Order

NIS – Newly Independent States

NOVIB – Oxfam Netherlands Co-operation

OECD – Organization for Economic Cooperation and Development

OL – Offering of Letters

OPEC – Organization of Petroleum Exporting Countries

PRWORA – Personal Responsibility and Work Opportunity Reconciliation Act, 1996

SSI – Supplemental Security Income

TAHL – Transforming Anti-Hunger Leadership

TANF – Temporary Assistance for Needy Families

U.N. – United Nations

UNHCR – U.N. High Commissioner for Refugees

UNCTAD – U.N. Conference on Trade and Development

UNDP – U.N. Development Programme

UNICEF – U.N. Children's Fund

U.S. – United States

USAID – U.S. Agency for International Development

USDA – U.S. Department of Agriculture

WFP – World Food Programme

WHY – World Hunger Year

WIC – Special Supplemental Nutrition Program for Women, Infants and Children

WIN – Work Incentive Program

WTO – World Trade Organization

GLOSSARY

Absolute poverty – The income level below which a minimally nutritionally adequate diet plus essential non-food requirements are not affordable.

Anemia – A condition in which the hemoglobin concentration (the number of red blood cells) is lower than normal due to disease or as a result of a deficiency of one or more essential nutrients such as iron.

Block grants – Federal government lump-sum payments to the states, which then have wide discretion over the use of these funds.

Campaign finance reform – Reform of the laws governing the kinds and amounts of donations that may be made to political campaigns.

Civil society – The sphere of civic action outside of the government comprised of citizens' groups, non-governmental organizations, religious congregations, labor unions and foundations.

Coalition – A set of actors (e.g., NGOs, public interest groups, foundations) that coordinate shared strategies and tactics to influence public policy and social change broadly.

Cold War – The global state of tension and military rivalry that existed from 1945 to 1990 between the United States and the former Soviet Union and their respective allies.

Cyber – Information processor mediated by an on-line computer network. Cyberspace is the continuum of on-line computer networks in which Internet communication takes place.

Daily calorie requirement – The average number of calories needed to sustain normal levels of activity and health, taking into account age, sex, body weight and climate; on average, about 2,350 calories per person per day.

Debt relief – Measures to reduce the debt owed by developing-country governments to either private lenders (commercial banks like Citibank), governments (like the United States or Germany), or international financial institutions (like the World Bank or IMF).

Declining terms of trade – See "Terms of trade."

Democratization – The process by which political systems move toward democratic principles and practices, such as open multi-party regime with regular and fair elections, universal suffrage, freedom of the press and other civil liberties (freedom of expression, freedom of organization).

Developing countries – Countries in which most people have a low economic standard of living. Also known as the "Third World," the "South" and the "less-developed countries."

Dietary energy supply (DES) – The total daily food supply, expressed in calories, available within a country for human consumption.

Earned income tax credit – A U.S. federal government program that reduces or eliminates taxes for many low-income working people and, in some cases of very low incomes, provides funds.

Empowerment – The process by which people gain greater economic and political voice and power over the decisions affecting their lives.

Famine – A situation of extreme scarcity of food, potentially leading to widespread starvation.

Food security – Assured access for every person, primarily by production or purchase, to enough nutritious food to sustain an active and healthy life with dignity. Includes food availability, food access and appropriate food utilization.

Food self-reliance – A strategy where countries boost yields, employing sustainable and efficient farming practices, and diversify their agricultural production, some for export and some for domestic consumption.

Food self-sufficiency – A strategy whereby countries, communities or regions rely exclusively on their own food production.

Food stamps – Coupons for low-income people to buy food in retail stores.

Foreign direct investment (FDI) – Investment from abroad in ownership and control of productive activities, as opposed to more passive stock and bond investment.

Free trade agreements – Agreements between two countries (bilateral), or among several (multilateral), to eliminate or reduce practices that distort trade. These may include tariffs (taxes on traded goods and services) and/or non-tariff barriers such as quotas (limits on the amount traded).

General Agreement on Tariffs and Trade (GATT) – An agreement established at the 1948 Geneva conference on multilateral trade and providing the ground rules for trade policy by its member nations. Successive negotiating rounds at the GATT culminated in the **Uruguay Round** that concluded in 1994. In 1995, the GATT was replaced by the **World Trade Organization** (WTO).

Global communications revolution – The growing interconnection of people around the world through communications technologies such as television, satellites, celluar phones, computers and the Internet.

Globalization – In economic terms, the process of increasing integration of national economies at the global level.

Gross domestic product (GDP) – The value of all goods and services produced within a nation during a specified period, usually a year.

Gross national product (GNP) – The value of all goods and services produced by a country's citizens, wherever they are located.

Human Development Index (HDI) – As used by the United Nations Development Programme, a measure of well-being based on economic growth, educational attainment and health.

Human rights – The basic rights and freedoms due all human beings, including the right to food and other basic necessities, the right to life and liberty, freedom of thought and expression and equality before the law.

Hunger – A condition in which people do not get enough food to provide the nutrients (carbohydrate, fat, protein, vitamins, minerals and water) for fully productive, active and healthy lives.

Industrial countries – Countries in which most people have a high economic standard of living (though there are often significant poverty populations). Also called the "developed countries" or the "North."

Infant mortality rate (IMR) – The annual number of deaths of infants under 1 year of age per 1,000 live births.

International Monetary Fund (IMF) – An international organization that makes loans to countries with short-term foreign exchange and monetary problems. These loans are conditioned upon the borrowing country's willingness to adopt IMF-approved economic policies.

Internet – The global communication network formed by the interconnection of all the Internet Protocol computer networks linking nearly 200 countries.

Jubilee 2000 – A worldwide movement calling for cancellation of the unpayable foreign debt of heavily indebted poor countries (HIPC) by the year 2000.

Jubilee 2000 USA – A movement in the United States, working in collaboration with Jubilee 2000

(see above), calling for cancellation of poor-country debt. That cancellation includes acknowledgment of responsibility by both lenders and borrowers, as well as mechanisms to prevent recurrence of such debts.

Livelihood security – The ability of a household to meet *all* its basic needs – for food, shelter, water, sanitation, health care and education.

Living wage – The wage level necessary for ensuring that a person earns enough to live at an adequate standard of living.

Macroeconomic policies – Policies related to general levels of production and income, and the relationship among economic sectors. "Microeconomics" deals with individual units of activity, such as a firm, household or prices for a specific product.

Malnutrition – A condition resulting from inadequate consumption (undernutrition) or excessive consumption of a nutrient; can impair physical and mental health, and can be the cause or result of infectious diseases.

Market economy – An economy in which prices for goods and services are set primarily by private markets rather than by government planning or regulation.

Medford Group – The group of national anti-hunger organizations that formed in the early 1990s to promote *The Medford Declaration to End Hunger in the United States.*

Microcredit – Small, short-term loans to low-income people, too poor to borrow from commercial banks, to help them start their own businesses, generate income and raise their standard of living.

Minimum caloric requirements – See "Daily calorie requirement."

Minimum wage – The lowest acceptable level of hourly wages set by law.

Multilateral trade negotiations – Trade negotiations among more than two countries. Since the postwar period, multilateral trade has been governed by agreements negotiated in successive rounds of the **General Agreements on Tariffs and Trade** (see **Uruguay Round**), which was replaced in 1995 by the **World Trade Organization**.

Non-governmental organizations (NGOs) – Voluntary, non-profit organizations that support community development, provide social services, protect the environment and promote the public interest.

North-South – Pertaining to relations between the rich countries of the North and the poor countries of the South.

Poverty line – An official measure of poverty defined by national governments. In the United States, it is calculated as three times the cost of the U.S. Department of Agriculture's "Thrifty Food Plan," which provides a less-than-adequate diet. In 1997, the poverty line was $12,515 for a family of three, $16,036 for a family of four.

Privatization – The transfer of ownership of companies and delivery of services from government to private firms or agencies.

Public policy advocacy – Citizen political action focused on the policies, programs and practices of governments, international financial institutions and corporations.

Purchasing Power Parity (PPP) – An estimate of the amount of money required to purchase comparable goods in different countries, usually expressed in U.S. dollars.

Repatriation – The return to their country of origin by persons who have been involuntarily displaced from it by war, famine, persecution, or other extreme circumstances.

Right-to-Food Resolution – Legislation enacted by the United States Congress in 1976 declaring "the right of every person in this country and throughout the world to food and a nutritionally adequate diet."

Social safety nets – Government and private charitable programs to meet the basic human needs (health, education, nutrition) of low-income, disabled and other vulnerable people.

Starvation – Suffering or death from extreme or prolonged lack of food.

Structural adjustment program (SAP) – Economic policy changes, often negotiated as a condition for loans, intended to stimulate economic growth. These measures generally involve reducing the role of government in the economy and increasing exports.

Stunting – Failure to grow to normal height caused by chronic undernutrition during the formative years of childhood.

Sustainable development – The reduction of hunger and poverty in environmentally sound ways. It includes: meeting basic human needs, expanding economic opportunities, protecting and enhancing the environment, and promoting pluralism and democratic participation.

Terms of trade – The relative price at which a country trades, measured as the price of exports divided by the price of imports. Declining terms of trade occur when imports become increasingly expensive relative to exports. In developing countries this typically means increasingly expensive manufactured goods (imports), relative to raw materials or to products that are not highly processed (exports).

Trade deficit – The difference between the value of a country's imports and the value of its exports when the former is greater than the latter.

Under-5 mortality rate – The annual number of deaths of children under 5 years of age per 1,000 live births. A high rate correlates closely with hunger and malnutrition.

Uruguay Round – The eighth round of global trade negotiations under the **General Agreement on Tariffs and Trade (GATT)** to reduce tariffs and non-tariff barriers, launched in that South American country in 1986. The resulting agreement, approved in 1994, establishes the **World Trade Organization (WTO)**, calls for significant cuts in industrial tariffs, sets down new rules for trade in services and agriculture, and adds protections for intellectual property.

Vulnerability to hunger – Individuals, households, communities or nations who have enough to eat most of the time, but whose poverty makes them especially susceptible to hunger due to changes in the economy, climate, political conditions or personal circumstances.

Wasting – A condition in which a person is seriously below the normal weight for her or his height due to acute undernutrition or a medical condition.

Welfare – Financial and other assistance provided by government and private charitable organizations to people in need in the areas of nutrition, education, health care and employment.

World Bank – An intergovernmental agency that makes long-term loans to the governments of developing nations.

World Trade Organization (WTO) – An international organization, headquartered in Geneva, established in 1995 to enforce the **Uruguay Round** global trade agreement.

NOTES

Introduction

1 International Fund for Agricultural Development, *Annual Report 1997*, Rome: IFAD, 1998, 26-27.

2 School of Nutrition Science and Policy, Tufts University, September 16, 1997, summary of the U.S. Department of Agriculture Food Security Measurement.

3 "Famine: The Man-Made Disaster," *New York Times*, July 26, 1998, 14.

4 Barbara Crossette, "Where the Hunger Season Is Part of Life," *New York Times,* August 16, 1998, Section E, 1, 5.

5 Thomas B. Edsall, "Issue Coalitions Take On Political Party Functions," *Washington Post*, August 8, 1996, and Michael Weisskopf, "Small Business Lobby Becomes a Big Player in Campaigns," *Washington Post,* August 9, 1996.

6 Letter from Carol Capps, Church World Service/Lutheran World Relief.

7 John W. Lynch, George A. Kaplan, Elsie R. Pamuk, Richard D. Cohen, Katherine E. Heck, Jennifer L. Balfour and Irene H. Yen, "Income Inequality and Mortality in Metropolitan Areas of the United States," *American Journal of Public Health*, 88(7), July 1998, 1074-1080.

Chapter 1

1 Peter Berger, *Pyramids of Sacrifice*, New York: Doubleday, 1976.

2 Kathryn Sikkink and Margaret Keck, *Activists Beyond Borders,* Ithaca: Cornell University Press, 1998; Paul Ekins, *A New World Order: Grassroots Movements for Global Change,* London: Routledge, 1992.

3 UNICEF, *State of the World's Children 1998*, New York: Oxford University Press, 31-34.

4 Aaron Sachs, "Dying for Oil," *Worldwatch*, May/June 1996, 10-21.

5 Richard J. Barnet and John Cavanagh, *Global Dreams: Imperial Corporations and the New World Order,* New York: Simon & Schuster, 1994, 229-230.

6 For various definitions of democracy, see Larry Diamond, *Promoting Democracy in the 1990s: Actors and Instruments, Issues and Imperatives*, A Report to the Carnegie Commission on Preventing Deadly Conflict, Washington, DC: Carnegie Council on Preventing Deadly Conflict, December 1995, 9-10.

7 James V. Riker, "Linking Development from Below to the International Environmental Movement: Sustainable Development and State-NGO Relations in Indonesia," *Journal of Business Administration*, Vol. 22-23, 1994/1995, 157-188.

8 Mathias Stiefl and Marshall Wolfe, *A Voice for the Excluded: Popular Participation in Development*, London: Zed, 1994.

9 Anne Marie Goetz and David O'Brien, "Governing for the Common Wealth? The World Bank's Approach to Poverty and Governance," *IDS Bulletin*, vol. 26(2), 1995, 17-26.

10 "Food for Cuba," *Washington Post*, September 3, 1998, A-20.

11 Jean Drèze and Amartya Sen, *Hunger and Public Action*, Oxford: Clarendon Press, 1989, 212.

12 Paul Nelson, "The *Movimiento Pro-Tierra* of Guatemala as a Case of Grassroots Empowerment," unpublished paper, 1988.

13 S. Slesinger and S. Kinzer, *Bitter Fruit,* London: Sinclair Browne, 1982.

14 Peace Brigades International, *Organizing in the Maquilas of Guatemala*, New York: Peace Brigades International, 1996.

15 Peter Uvin, *Development, Aid and Conflict: Reflections from the Case of Rwanda,* Geneva: United Nations University, 1996, 34.

16 *Ibid.,* 34.

17 UNICEF, *State of the World's Children 1998,* New York, Oxford University Press, 41-44.

18 *Ibid.,* 43.

19 John C. Quinley and Timothy D. Baker, "Lobbying for International Health: The Link between Good Ideas and Funded Programs: Bread for the World and the Agency for International Development," *American Journal of Public Health* 76:7, 795.

20 UNICEF, *The State of the World's Children 1998,* 39.

21 For background, see Marc J. Cohen, ed., *The Causes of Hunger: Hunger 1995,* Silver Spring, MD: Bread for the World Institute, 1994.

Chapter 2

1 Bread for the World Institute, *Hunger 1998: Hunger in a Global Economy*, Silver Spring: Bread for the World Institute, 1998, 3.

2 UNDP, *Human Development Report 1997*, New York: Oxford University Press, 1997, 7.

3 "The Perils of Global Capital," *Economist*, April 11, 1998, 52.

4 Maurice Williams, personal communication, February 1998.

5 *Trade and Development Report, 1997*, UNCTAD, IV.

6 "Opening Address by the President of the General Assembly for the Overall Review and Appraisal of the Implementation of Agenda 21," United Nations, New York, June 23, 1997.

7 See Jeffrey J. Schott, *The Uruguay Round: An Assessment,* Washington, DC: Institute for International Economics, 1994, 55.

8 See Bernard M. Hoekman, "Developing Countries and the Multilateral Trading System after the Uruguay Round," In: *Global Development Fifty Years after Bretton Woods: Essays in Honour of Gerald K. Helleiner,* New York: St. Martin's Press, 1997, 252-279.

9 GDP – the value of all goods and services produced within a nation during a specified period, usually a year.

10 James D. Wolfensohn, "The Challenge of Inclusion," World Bank and IMF Annual Meetings Address, Hong Kong, September 23, 1997.

11 The coalition was led by Australia and included Argentina, Brazil, Canada, Chile, Colombia, Fiji, Hungary, Indonesia,

Malaysia, New Zealand, the Philippines, Thailand and Uruguay.

12 Diana Tussie, "Holding the Balance: The Cairns Group in the Uruguay Round," In: Diana Tussie and David Glover, eds., *The Developing Countries in World Trade,* Boulder, CO: Lynne Rienner Publishers, 1993, 181-203.

13 Ann Weston calculates that 33 least-developed countries and six low-income countries will be negatively affected in the short run by Uruguay Round provisions. See "The Uruguay Round – Costs and Compensation for Developing Countries," *International Monetary and Financial Issues for the 1990s,* Vol. VII, U.N. Conference on Trade and Development, New York and Geneva, 1996, 84-85. Other reports suggest that the negative impacts may be exaggerated because implementation of the new rules is proceeding very slowly, if at all.

14 As Canadian economist Gerry Helleiner argues, "[International financial policy-making has been] tortuously slow, insufficiently participatory, overly influenced by powerful lobbies from the financial sector and constrained by jurisdictional ambiguities and turf struggles," Presentation to the Second Committee of the U.N. General Assembly, October 15, 1997.

15 James H. Michel, *Development Cooperation: Efforts and Policies of the Members of the Development Assistance Committee,* Paris: OECD, 1997.

16 GNP – the value of all goods and services produced by a country's citizens, wherever they are located.

17 The DAC is a specialized committee of the OECD, "whose members have agreed to secure an expansion of aggregate volume of resources made available to developing countries and to improve their effectiveness." Alexander R. Love, *Development Co-operation,* Paris: OECD, 1994.

18 George Psacharopoulos, "Building Human Capital for Better Lives," *Directions in Development Series,* Washington, DC: The World Bank, July 1995, 40. However, some experts debate the bank's criteria for poverty-targeted programs and note extensive problems of leakage in bank projects to higher income groups.

19 Maurice Williams, "United Nations Reform and Performance," Memorandum, February 1998.

20 For further discussion on country-level aid coordinating bodies, and more general obstacles to aid coordination, see author's draft, "National Programming for the New Global Development Agenda: What Role for Civil Society?" Prepared for Bread for the World and Friedrich Ebert Foundation Workshop on "Managing Aid for National Development – Moving Towards Ownership, Participation and Results," May 14, 1996.

21 Ngaire Woods, Executive Summary, "Governance in International Organizations: The Case for Reform in the Bretton Woods Institutions," Prepared for the G-24, draft, (undated) 1.

22 See, for example, Development Bank Watchers' Project, *Who Shapes Your Country's Future? A Guide to Influencing the World Bank's Country Assistance Strategies,* Silver Spring, MD: Bread for the World Institute, January 1998. For more information about the Development Bank Watchers' Project, see Bread for the World's Web site at: <http://www.bread.org>

23 See Paul J. Nelson, *The World Bank and Non-Governmental Organizations: The Limits of Apolitical Development,* New York: St. Martin's Press, 1995; Nancy C. Alexander, "Accountable to Whom? The World Bank and Its Strategic Allies," Silver Spring, MD: Bread for the World Institute, Development Bank Watchers' Project.

24 Social Watch's Web address is: <http://www.chasque.apc.org/socwatch>.

25 See especially, Jonathan L. Fox and L. David Brown, "Conclusions: Assessing the Impact of NGO Advocacy Campaigns on World Bank Projects and Policies," In: *The Struggle for Accountability: The World Bank, NGOs and Grassroots Movements,* Cambridge, MA: MIT Press, Forthcoming 1998, Chapter 13. See also, Patti L. Petesch, et al., "A Portfolio Review of Environmental Grantmaking to Reform the International Financial Institutions," Charles Stewart Mott Foundation, Flint, MI, August 22, 1997.

26 The World Bank, *The Handbook on Good Practices for Laws Relating to Non-Governmental Organizations,* discussion draft, Washington, DC, May 1997.

27 Commitment 2 of the "Copenhagen Declaration on Social Development," World Summit for Social Development, United Nations, March 1995. Nearly 190 heads of state signed this document.

28 Jessica T. Mathews, "Power Shift," *Foreign Affairs,* January-February 1997, 66.

Chapter 3

1 The Commission on Global Governance, *Our Global Neighborhood: The Report of the Commission on Global Governance,* New York: Oxford University Press, 1995, 31.

2 Margaret R. Biswas, "Conference Report: The World Food Summit, Rome, 13-17 November, 1996," *Food Policy,* 22(4), 1997, 374.

3 Bernard Cohen, "A View from the Academy," In: *Taken by Storm: The Media, Public Opinion, and U.S. Foreign Policy in the Gulf War,* Chicago: University of Chicago Press, 1994, 9-10.

4 Cited in Larry Minear, Colin Scott and Thomas G. Weiss, *The News Media, Civil War, & Humanitarian Action,* Boulder, CO: Lynne Rienner, 1996, 4.

5 Charles Bierbauer, "Foreword," In: Larry Minear, Colin Scott and Thomas G. Weiss, *The News Media, Civil War, & Humanitarian Action,* Boulder, CO: Lynne Rienner Press, 1996, viii.

6 Nancy Birdsall, "Life is Unfair: Inequality in the World," *Foreign Policy,* No. 111, Summer 1998, 77.

7 The Commission on Global Governance, *Our Global Neighborhood: The Report of the Commission on Global Governance,* New York: Oxford University Press, 1995, 31.

8 UNESCO, *World Communication Report: The Media and Challenges of the New Technologies,* Paris: UNESCO Publishing, 1997, 94.

9 Claude Moisy, "Myths of the Global Information Village," *Foreign Policy,* No. 107, Summer 1997, 79.

10 UNESCO, *World Communication Report,* 46, 48, 49.

11 Cited in Neil Munro, "For Richer and Poorer," *National Journal,* 30(29), July 18, 1998, 1677.

12 *Ibid.,* 1680.

[13] The Economist, "Here Is the News," *Economist*, July 4, 1998, 13.

[14] The Pew Research Center for the People & the Press, "Event-Driven News Audiences: Internet News Takes Off," July, Washington, DC, 1998, accessible at <http://www.people-press.org>; and Claude Moisy, 82.

[15] Robin Pogrebin, "Foreign Coverage Less Prominent in News Magazines," *New York Times*, September 23, 1996, D-2.

[16] The Pew Research Center for the People & the Press, "Opinion Leaders Say, Public Differs: More Comfort with Post-Cold War Era," Washington, DC, 1997, accessible at <http://www.people-press.org>.

[17] Cited in Howard Kurtz, "Going Weak in the Knees for Clinton," *Washington Post*, July 6, 1998, C-3.

[18] The Economist, "The News Business: Stop Press," *Economist*, July 4, 1998, 17.

[19] *Ibid.*, 17.

[20] David Callahan, "Ballot Blocks: What Gets the Poor to the Polls?," *The American Prospect*, July-August, 1998, 70.

[21] *Ibid.*, 70.

[22] The Pew Research Center for the People & the Press, "One-in-Ten Voters Online for Campaign '96," Washington, DC, 1996, accessible at <http://www.people-press.org>.

[23] The Commission on Global Governance, *Our Global Neighborhood,* 31.

[24] Jack Lule, "The Power and Pitfalls of Journalism in the Hypertext Era," *The Chronicle of Higher Education*, August 7, 1998, B-7.

[25] Cited in Peter J. Boyer, "The People's Network," *The New Yorker*, August 3, 1998, 28.

[26] The Pew Research Center for the People & the Press, "Politics, Morality, Entitlements Sap Confidence: The Optimism Gap Grows," Washington, DC, December 1996.

[27] See Lule, *op. cit.*, B-7; Alex M. Freeman and Rekha Balu, "Story of a Story: How Cincinnati Paper Ended Up Backing Off Chiquita Series," *The Wall Street Journal*, July 17, 1998, A-1, A-8.

[28] See Edward S. Herman and Robert W. McChesney, *The Global Media: The New Missionaries of Corporate Capitalism*, London: Cassell Academic, 1997; Robert McChesney, Ellen Meiskins Wood and John Bellamy Foster, eds., *Capitalism and the Information Age: The Political Economy of the Global Communication Revolution*, New York: Monthly Review Press, 1998.

[29] Gary Rodan, "The International Press and Reporting in Asia," Paper Presented at the International Studies Association 37th Annual Convention, March 18-22, 1997, Toronto, Canada, 23.

[30] *Ibid.*

[31] UNESCO, *World Communication Report,* 240-241; Robert O. Keohane and Joseph Nye, Jr., "Power and Interdependence in the Information Age," *Foreign Affairs*, 77(5), September-October 1998, 93.

[32] See Kevin A. Hill and John E. Hughes, *Cyberpolitics: Citizen Activism in the Age of the Internet*, New York: Rowman and Littlefield, 1998; Michael Ryan, "He Fights Dictators with the Internet," *Parade Magazine (Washington Post* edition*)*, August 23, 1998, 12; Alvin and Heidi Toffler, *Creating a New Civilization: The Politics of the Third Wave*, Washington, DC: Progress and Freedom Foundation, 1994.

[33] See Barbara Crossette, "Where the Hunger Season Is Part of Life," *New York Times*, August 16, 1998, Section 4, 1, 5.

[34] See Margaret E. Keck and Kathryn Sikkink, *Activists Beyond Borders: Advocacy Networks in International Politics*, Ithaca, NY: Cornell University Press, 1998.

Chapter 4

[1] J. Larry Brown, director, Tufts University School of Nutrition Science and Policy, "Release of National Food Security Measurement Study Results by USDA," September 16, 1997. The figures measure households over the 12-month period immediately preceding April 1995.

[2] Estimates according to the annual survey of 29 cities by the U.S. Conference of Mayors.

[3] Physicians for Human Rights, press release, May 7, 1998.

[4] Nick Kotz, *Hunger In America: The Federal Response*, New York: The Field Foundation, 1979.

[5] Nick Kotz, *Let Them Eat Promises: The Politics of Hunger*, Newark, NJ: Prentice-Hall, 1969.

[6] *Ibid.*

[7] Barbara Howell, "Ending Hunger in the United States," Silver Spring, MD: Bread for the World, Background Paper, May 1996.

[8] Kotz, *Hunger in America: The Federal Response.*

[9] Janet E. Poppendieck, *Sweet Charity? Emergency Food and the End of Entitlement*, New York: Viking Penguin, 1998.

[10] Personal interview.

[11] Personal interview.

[12] Peter Edelman, *Atlantic Monthly*, March 1997.

[13] *The Wall Street Journal*, June 1, 1998.

[14] See Marc J. Cohen, *Hunger in a Global Economy: Hunger 1998*, Silver Spring, MD: Bread for the World Institute, 1997.

[15] U.S. Census.

[16] "Poverty Matters: The Cost of Child Poverty in America," Children's Defense Fund, Washington, DC, 1998.

[17] "Young Child Poverty in the States," National Center for Children in Poverty, Columbia School of Public Health, New York, 1998.

[18] Rebecca Blank, *It Takes a Nation: A New Agenda for Fighting Poverty*, Princeton, NJ: Princeton University Press, 1997, 54.

[19] Center on Budget and Policy Priorities (CBPP), Washington, DC, October 1997.

[20] AFL-CIO, "Executive Pay Watch."

[21] Michael Parenti, *dollars and sense*, May/June 1998.

[22] CBPP.

[23] *Economist*, June 21, 1997.

[24] *Business Week*, April 20, 1998.

[25] Robert B. Reich, "Broken Faith: Why We Need to Renew the Social Compact," *The Nation*, February 1998.

[26] *Washington Post*, April 29, 1998.

[27] CBPP.

[28] Leon Howell, "Picking a Protest: Mushroom Workers Organize," *Christian Century*, March 4, 1998.

29 Pew Research Center on the People & the Press, March 10, 1998.

30 The Center on Budget and Policy Priorities has released two major studies on the subject: "The Safety Net Delivers: The Effects of Government Benefit Programs in Reducing Poverty," November 1996, Wendell Primus, Kathryn Porter, Margery Ditto and Mitchell Kent; "Social Security Reduces Elderly Poverty Sharply, But Study Shows Safety Net for Children Weakened in 1996," March 8, 1998, Wendell Primus and Kathryn Porter.

31 E. J. Dionne Jr., "Up From the Bottom," *Washington Post*, July 21, 1998, citing a study by Rebecca Blank.

32 Thomas and Mary Edsall, *Chain Reaction: The Impact of Race, Rights and Taxes on American Politics*, New York: W.W. Norton & Co., 1991.

33 Michael Cromartie, ed., *Disciples & Democracy: Religious Conservatives and the Future of American Politics*, Grand Rapids, MI: Eerdmans, 1994.

34 Leon Howell, *Funding the War of Ideas*, Cleveland, OH: United Church of Christ, 1995.

35 Lisbeth B. Schorr, *Common Purpose: Strengthening Families and Neighborhoods to Rebuild America*, New York: Doubleday, 1998.

36 Janet E. Poppendieck, *Sweet Charity? Emergency Food and the End of Entitlement*, New York: Viking Penguin, 1998.

37 Pat Kutzner, "Thirty Years of Anti-Hunger Advocacy," In: Marc J. Cohen, ed., *Hunger 1994: Transforming the Politics of Hunger*, Silver Spring, MD: Bread for the World Institute, 1993, 96.

Chapter 5

1 ADC was later renamed Aid to Families with Dependent Children (AFDC).

2 Congress provided only $1 billion, which was to be matched by the states, to pay for welfare-to-work initiatives.

3 Between 1979 and 1995 a steady erosion – from 23 percent to under 16 percent – of manufacturing jobs occurred in the United States. The United States lost more than 2.5 million manufacturing jobs between 1979 and 1995. These higher-paying jobs were replaced with lower-paying service and retail jobs – the least likely of all jobs to include affordable health benefits. This contributed to an increase in the number of working poor families. (Center for Community Change)

4 It was later leaked that President Clinton's pollsters predicted a drop in the polls of only 5 percent, which still would have left him with a wide margin over former Senator Robert Dole. *Time Magazine*.

5 These benefits were restored for immigrants who arrived in the United States before the welfare law was signed and who are or become disabled.

6 The Social Security Act was amended in 1962 giving the Secretary of Health and Human Services the authority to waive federal welfare laws in order to allow state flexibility for experimental welfare pilot programs. Committee on Ways and Means, U.S. House of Representatives, *1997 Green Book*, Washington: U.S. Government Printing Office, 1997.

7 Alabama has the second lowest benefit level in the country.

8 Former Bread for the World organizer.

9 Mary D. Janney, "Off Welfare, On to College," *Washington Post*, July 15, 1998, A17.

10 Carla Rivera, "Too Few Jobs May Imperil Welfare Reform Plan," *New York Times*, May 20, 1998.

11 Ann Scott Tyson, "Off Welfare, Yes. But No Job," *Christian Science Monitor*, April 9, 1998. To date, 36 states have increased their most severe sanction to a full-family termination of benefits. Seven states have enacted a lifetime ban on benefits for their most severe sanction.

12 *Ibid.*

13 The funding formula for the block grant was based on previous fiscal year participation, which happened to be at a record high, and when states received their first funding stream, caseloads had been down by 26 percent over the previous three years.

14 Ron Scherer, "Creative Outlets for Welfare Windfall," *Christian Science Monitor*, December 10, 1997.

15 *Are States Improving the Lives of the Poor?* Center on Hunger, Poverty and Nutrition Policy, Tufts University, 1998.

16 Jason DeParle, "Welfare Rolls Show Growing Racial and Urban Imbalance," *New York Times*, July 27, 1998.

17 Bruce Katz, Brookings Institution, cited in "Welfare Reform Success Cited in L.A.," *Washington Post*, August 19, 1998.

18 Mary D. Janney, "Off Welfare, On to College," *Washington Post*, July 15, 1998, A17.

19 NETWORK, Welfare Reform Watch Project, Phase One Report, April 7, 1998.

20 *Ibid.*

21 *Washington Post*, July 15, 1998, *op. cit.*

Chapter 6

1 United Nations Development Programme, *Human Development Report, 1994*, New York: UNDP, 1994.

2 Food deficit countries are defined as those that import more cereals than they export. "1997 Food Aid Flows – Priority Country Groups," posted at <www.wfp.org/reports/faf/97/priorcountr.htm>. Low-income food deficit countries (LIFDCs) are those food deficit countries with a per capita income "below the level used by the World Bank to determine eligibility for [highly concessional] assistance." Africa Report No. 2, August 1998, posted at <www.fao.org>.

3 Food and Agriculture Organization (FAO) from FAO Website: <www.fao.org/news> "New Record number of countries facing shortfalls in food supplies and will need emergency assistance."

4 International Food Policy Research Institute (IFPRI) news release, "Food gap widening in developing countries." <http://www.cgiar.org/ifpri/pressure/102697.html>.

5 *Ibid.*

6 FAO/GIEWS – Food Outlook No. 3, June 1998, 4 <http://www.fao.org>.

7 World Food Programme, "1997 Food Aid Flows – Priority Country Groups," <http://www.wfp.org/reports/faf/97/priorcountr.htm>.

8 "With Crops Up and Prices Down, Farmers are Looking East," *Washington Post*, September 20, 1998, A3.

9 U.S. Census Bureau, *Poverty 1997 – Poverty Estimates by Selected Characteristics*, <www.census.gov>.

10 Committee on Ways and Means, U.S. House of Representatives, *1998 Green Book*, Washington, DC: US GPO, 1998, 1305.

11 Eurostat Survey of 13 Member States. <http://europa.eu.int>.

12 "Questions and Answers About the USDA Food Security Management Study" Center on Hunger, Poverty and Nutrition Policy: September 16, 1997.

13 *1998 Green Book*, *op. cit.*, 934.

14 *Hunger 1997: The Faces & Facts*, Chicago: Second Harvest, 1997, 3

15 Toronto Daily Bread Food Bank, *The Daily Bread News*, Summer 1997 <http://www.dailybread.ca/news.html#4>.

16 Canadian Association of Food Banks, "Hunger Count 1997: A Report on Emergency Food Assistance in Canada," October 8, 1997.

17 National Anti-Poverty Organization. <www.napo-anpo.ca/napohome.htm>.

18 Campaign 2000 Report Card, *Child Poverty in Canada*.

19 Eurostat Survey of 13 Member States. <http://europa.eu.int>.

20 For a discussion of possible future European Monetary Union (EMU) policy and its effects on different sectors, see "The Euro: Who Wins, Who Loses?" *Foreign Policy*, Washington: Carnegie Endowment for International Peace, Fall 1998, 24–40.

21 FAO/GIEWS: Africa Report No. 2, August 1998.

22 *Ibid.*

23 Food and Agriculture Organization (FAO) from FAO Website: <www.fao.org>, "Foodcrops and Shortages No. 2, June 1998, 5.

24 FAO/GIEWS, May 15, 1998.

25 Francis Deng, "...And Ending Its Cruel War," *Washington Post*, August 2, 1998.

26 J. Brian Atwood, "Saving Sudan's People.. ." *Washington Post*, August 2, 1998.

27 FAO/GIEWS Special Alert No. 285 on the Democratic Republic of Congo, <http::/www.fao.org/WAICENT>.

28 *Ibid.*

29 "FAO/WFP Crop and Food Supply Assessment Mission to the Democratic People's Republic of Korea" GIEWS November 25, 1997.

30 FAO/GIEWS, *Special Report: Floods Cause Extensive Crop Damage in Several Parts of Asia*, August 27, 1998, 1-2.

31 *Ibid.*

32 IFPRI, "The World Food Situation: Recent Developments, Emerging Issues, and Long-term Prospects" Washington, DC: IFPRI, 1997.

33 WFP Website, "WFP Appeals for Emergency Food Aid for 615,000 victims of El Niño-Induced Drought in Eastern Cuba," <http://www.wfp.org/prelease>.

34 FAO NEWS <www.fao.org.news> "New record number of countries..." *op. cit.*

35 World Food Programme, "1997 Food Aid Flows," <http://www.wfp.org>.

36 FAO GIEWS Special Alert No. 283, Brazil, May 21, 1998. "No Way Without Water," by Kathleen Bond, Maryknoll lay missioner.

37 FAO/GIEWS Food Outlook No. 3, June 1998, 4.

38 USDA Food Security Assessment Situation and Outlook Series GFA-9, November 1997.

39 Food Outlook FAO GIEWS volumes 10/11/12 October/Nov./Dec. 1997.

40 Relief Web <www.reliefweb.int/dha-01>

41 World Food Programme Emergency Report, June 12, 1998; FAO/GIEWS Special Alert No. 281, March 17, 1998.

42 FAO Website, <www.fao.org> Press Release 98/43.

43 "Hunger-War Tools: Hi-Tech, Media," *Christian Science Monitor*, June 4, 1998.

44 FAO/GIEWS: Africa Report No. 2, August 1998, 4.

Chapter 7

1 See "Bellagio Declaration: Overcoming Hunger in the 1990s," In: David Beckmann and Richard Hoehn, *Transforming the Politics of Hunger*, Occasional Paper No. 2, Silver Spring, MD: Bread for the World Institute, 1992, 54-58.

2 United Nations Development Programme, "Eradicating Human Poverty Worldwide – An Agenda for the 21st Century," *Human Development Report 1997*, New York: Oxford University Press, 1997, 107.

3 To address the problem of underage workers, for example, Nike announced that it was "increasing the minimum age of footwear factory workers to 18, and the minimum age for all other light-manufacturing workers (apparel, accessories, equipment) to 16." See Nike, "Nike CEO Philip H. Knight Announces New Labor Initiatives," Washington, DC, May 12, 1998, accessible at: <www.nikeworkers.com>.

4 Anita Franklin, "50,000 Protest in UK to Cancel Third World Debt," *Review of African Political Economy*, 25(76), June 1998, 287-288.

5 To learn more about the Jubilee 2000 campaign, see the Web site at: <http://www.j2000usa.org>.

6 International Fund for Agricultural Development, *Annual Report 1997*, Rome: IFAD, 1998, 130-131.

7 Christian Aid, "The Global Supermarket," London: Christian Aid, October 28, 1996, 29.

8 *Ibid.*, 28-9.

9 Nadine Gordimer, "Dare to Dream of Eradicating Poverty," *New York Times*, August 1, 1998.

10 See Alison Van Rooy, "The Frontiers of Influence: NGO Lobbying at the 1974 World Food Conference, the 1992 Earth Summit and Beyond," *World Development*, 25(1):93-114, 1997; United Nations Non-Governmental Liaison Service, "The World Food Summit," *NGLS Roundup*, New York, January 1997, 1-8; Linda Elswick, "The World Food Summit: Perspectives from Civil Society," *Development*, Rome: Society for International Development, 1996(4), 62-69.

11 International Baby Food Action Network (IBFAN), "Governments Under Pressure to Abandon WHO Marketing Code," *Third World Resurgence*, July 1998, 6-7.

12 Gordimer, *op. cit.*

SPONSORS

Bread for the World Institute seeks to inform, educate, nurture and motivate concerned citizens for action on policies that affect hungry people. Based on policy analysis and consultation with poor people, it develops educational resources and activities, including its annual report on the state of world hunger, policy briefs and study guides, together with workshops, seminars, briefings and an anti-hunger leadership development program. Contributions to the Institute are tax deductible. It works closely with Bread for the World, a Christian citizens' movement of 44,000 members who advocate specific policy changes to help overcome hunger in the United States and overseas.

> 1100 Wayne Avenue, Suite 1000
> Silver Spring, MD 20910
> Phone: (301) 608-2400
> Fax: (301) 608-2401
> E-mail: institute@bread.org
> Website: www.bread.org

Brot für die Welt is an association of German Protestant churches that seeks to overcome poverty and hunger in developing countries, as an expression of their Christian faith and convictions, by funding programs of relief and development. Founded in 1959, Brot has funded more than 18,000 programs in over 100 nations in Africa, Latin America and Asia. The emphasis of the programs that Brot funds has shifted from relief to development and empowerment. Brot's programs of education in Germany are intended to lead to changes – in understanding and lifestyle at the personal level, and to policy changes at the national, European Community and international levels.

> Stafflenbergstrasse 76; Postfach 10 11 42
> D-70010 Stuttgart, Germany
> Phone: 011 49 7 11 2159 0
> Fax: 011 49 7 11 2159 110
> E-mail: bfdwinformation@brot-fuer-die-welt.org

Catholic Relief Services-USCC (CRS) is the overseas relief and development agency of the U.S. Catholic community. Founded in 1943, CRS provides over $200 million in development and relief assistance in more than 80 nations around the world. Working in partnership with the Catholic Church and other local institutions in each country, CRS works to alleviate poverty, hunger and suffering, and supports peacebuilding and reconciliation initiatives. Assistance is given solely on the basis of need. Even while responding to emergencies, CRS supports over 2,000 development projects designed to build local self-sufficiency. CRS works in conjunction with Caritas Internationalis and CIDSE, worldwide associations of Catholic relief and development agencies. Together, these groups build the capacity of local nonprofit organizations to provide long-term solutions. In the United States, CRS seeks to educate and build awareness on issues of world poverty and hunger and serve as an advocate for public policy changes in the interest of the poor overseas.

> 209 West Fayette Street
> Baltimore, MD 21201-3443
> Phone: (410) 625-2220
> Fax: (410) 685-1635
> E-mail: webmaster@catholicrelief.org
> Website: www.catholicrelief.org

Christian Children's Fund, founded in Richmond, VA, in 1938, is one of the world's oldest and most respected nonprofit child sponsorship charities. Christian Children's Fund is dedicated to providing long-term sustainable development assistance to approximately 2.5 million needy children and their families in more than 30 countries around the world, including the United States. Services are provided without regard to religion, gender or race.

> 2821 Emerywood Parkway, P.O. Box 26484
> Richmond, VA 23261-6484
> Phone: (804) 756-2700
> Fax: (804) 756-2718
> Website: www.christianchildrensfund.org

The **Evangelical Lutheran Church in America World Hunger Program** is a 25-year-old ministry that confronts hunger and poverty through emergency relief, long-term development, education, advocacy and stewardship of financial resources. Seventy-two percent of the program works internationally and 28 percent within the United States. Lutheran World Relief (New York City) and Lutheran World Federation (Geneva, Switzerland) are key implementing partners in international relief and development. Twelve percent is used for domestic relief and development, 10 percent for education and advocacy work in the United States and 6 percent for fundraising and administration.

> 8765 West Higgins Road
> Chicago, IL 60631-4190
> Phone: (800) 638-3522, ext. 2709
> Fax: (773) 380-2707
> E-mail: jhalvors@elca.org

LCMS World Relief (The Lutheran Church – Missouri Synod) provides relief and development funding for domestic and international projects. Based under the Synod's Department of Human Care Ministries, LCMS World Relief provides domestic grants for Lutheran congregations and social ministry organizations as well as other groups with Lutheran involvement which are engaged in ministries of human care. Domestic support is also provided to Lutheran Disaster Response and Lutheran Immigration and Refugee Service. International relief and development assistance is channeled through the Synod's mission stations and partner churches as well as Lutheran World Relief.

> 1333 So. Kirkwood Road
> St. Louis, MO 63122-7295
> Phone: (800) 248-1930, ext. 1392
> Fax: (314) 965-0541
> E-mail: ic_schroepj@lcms.org

Lutheran World Relief (LWR) acts on behalf of U.S. Lutherans in response to natural disasters, humanitarian crises and chronic poverty in some 50 countries of Asia, Africa, Latin America and the Middle East. In partnership with local organizations, LWR supports over 150 community projects to improve food production, health care, environment and employment, with special emphasis on training and gender. LWR monitors legislation on foreign aid and development, and advocates for public policies which address the root causes of hunger and poverty. LWR values the God-given gifts that each person can bring to the task of promoting peace, justice and human dignity. LWR began its work in 1945.

> Lutheran World Relief
> 390 Park Avenue South
> New York, NY 10016
> Phone: (212) 532-6350
> Resources: (800)LWR-LWR2
> Fax: (212) 213-6081
> E-mail: lwr@lwr.org
> Website: www.lwr.org

> LWR/CWS Office on Development Policy
> 110 Maryland Avenue, N.E.
> Building Mailbox #45
> Washington, DC 20002-5694
> Phone: (202) 543-6336
> Fax: (202) 546-6232
> E-mail: csw/lwr@igc.apc.org

For 28 years, the **Presbyterian Hunger Program** has provided a channel for congregations to respond to hunger in the United States and around the world. With a commitment to the ecumenical sharing of human and financial resources, the program provides support for programs of direct food relief, sustainable development and public policy advocacy. A network of 100 Hunger Action Enablers leads the Presbyterian Church (USA) in the study of hunger issues, engagement with communities of need, advocacy for just public policies, and the movement toward simpler corporate and personal lifestyles.

> 100 Witherspoon Street
> Louisville, KY 40202-1396
> Phone: (502) 569-5816
> Fax: (502) 569-8963
> Website: www.pcusa.org\pcusa\wmd\hunger

The **United Methodist Committee on Relief** (UMCOR) was formed in 1940 in response to the suffering of people during World War II. It was a "voice of conscience" expressing the concern of the church for the disrupted and devastated lives churned out by the war. UMCOR has expanded its ministry into more than 70 countries to minister with compassion to "persons in need, through programs and services which provide immediate relief and long-term attention to the root causes of their need." Focusing on refugee, hunger and disaster ministries, the work of UMCOR, a program department of the General Board of Global Ministries of the United Methodist Church, is carried out through direct services and a worldwide network of national and international church agencies that cooperate in the task of alleviating human suffering.

> 475 Riverside Drive, Room 330
> New York, NY 10115
> Phone: (212) 870-3816
> Hotline: (800) 841-1235
> Fax: (212) 870-3624
> E-mail: umcor@gbgm-umc.org

CO-SPONSORS

The **United Nations Development Programme** (UNDP) is the United Nations' largest provider of technical cooperation grants and the main coordinator of U.N. development assistance. It works with governments, U.N. agencies, organizations of civil society and individuals in 175 countries and territories to build national capacities for sustainable human development. Activities focus on poverty eradication, creation of jobs and sustainable livelihoods, advancement of women, protection and regeneration of the environment, and good governance. UNDP's central resources, totaling about $1 billion (U.S.) a year, are derived from the voluntary contributions of governments. UNDP also administers several special purpose funds (U.N. Capital Development Fund, U.N. Development Fund for Women, U.N. Volunteers) and, with the World Bank and the U.N. Environment Programme, the $2 billion Global Environment Facility.

> 1 United Nations Plaza
> New York, NY 10017
> Phone: (212) 906-5000
> Fax: (212) 906-5001
> E-mail: HQ@undp.org
> Web: www.undp.org

The **United Nations World Food Programme** is the food aid arm of the United Nations system. Food aid is one of the many instruments that can help promote food security, which is defined as access of all people at all times to the food needed for an active and healthy life. The policies governing the use of World Food Programme food aid must be oriented toward the objective of eradicating hunger and poverty. The ultimate objective of food aid should be the elimination of the need for food aid.

> Via Cesare Giulio Viola, 68
> Parco dei Medici
> Rome 00148
> Phone: (39-06) 6513-1
> Fax: (39-06) 6590-632/637
> Web: www.wfp.org

The **Academy for Educational Development** (AED), founded in 1961, is an independent, nonprofit service organization committed to addressing human development needs in the United States and throughout the world. Under contracts and grants, the Academy operates programs in collaboration with policy leaders; nongovernmental and community-based organizations; governmental agencies; international multilateral and bilateral funders; and schools, colleges and universities. In partnership with its clients, the Academy seeks to meet today's social, economic and environmental challenges through education and human resource development; to apply state-of-the-art education, training, research, technology, management, behavioral analysis and social marketing techniques to solve problems; and to improve knowledge and skills throughout the world as the most effective means for stimulating growth, reducing poverty, and promoting democratic and humanitarian ideals. AED is registered with the U.S. Agency for International Development as a private voluntary organization. The Academy is exempt from federal income taxes under Section 501(c)(3) of the Internal Revenue Code. Contributions to the Academy are tax deductible.

> 1875 Connecticut Avenue, N.W.
> Washington, DC 20009-1202
> Phone: (202) 884-8000
> Fax: (202) 884-8400
> E-mail: admindc@aed.org
> Website: www.aed.org

Adventist Development and Relief Agency International (ADRA) is the worldwide agency of the Seventh-day Adventist church set up to alleviate poverty in developing countries and respond to disasters. ADRA works on behalf of the poor in more than 150 developing countries spanning Africa, Asia, the Middle East, and Central and South America, without regard to ethnic, political or religious association. ADRA's projects include working to improve the health of mothers and children, developing clean water resources, teaching agricultural techniques, building and supplying clinics, hospitals and schools training people in vocational skills, and feeding people in countries where hunger is a long-term problem. When disasters strike, ADRA sends emergency supplies and stays in the disaster area to help rebuild.

> 12501 Old Columbia Pike
> Silver Spring, MD 20904
> Phone: (301) 680-6380
> Fax: (301) 680-6370
> Website: www.adra.org

Baptist World Aid (BWAid) is a division of the Baptist World Alliance, a fellowship of almost 200 Baptist unions and conventions around the world, comprising a membership of over 42 million baptized believers. This represents a community of over 100 million Baptists ministering in more than 200 countries. For over 75 years Baptists have been working in partnership to entrust, empower and enable the indigenous Baptist leadership to carry out programs of emergency relief, sustainable development and fellowship assistance.

> 6733 Curran Street
> McLean, VA 22101-6005
> Phone: (703) 790-8980
> Fax: (703) 790-5719
> E-mail: bwaid@bwanet.org
> Website: www.bwanet.org

The **Board of World Mission of the Moravian Church (BWM)** represents the Moravian Church in America in overseas ministries. BWM nourishes formal mission partnerships with Moravian Churches in Alaska, the eastern Caribbean, Guyana, Honduras, Labrador, Nicaragua and Tanzania, and with the Evangelical Church of the Dominican Republic. BWM supports medical clinics in Honduras and Nicaragua and has a long tradition of supporting educational efforts of all kinds. In addition, as a missionary sending agency, BWM is involved in evangelistic witness among people who have had little opportunity to hear the gospel. Offices are in Bethlehem, Pennsylvania and Winston-Salem, North Carolina.

> Reverend Hampton Morgan Jr., Executive Director
> 1021 Center Street
> Bethlehem, PA 18018
> Phone: (610) 868-1732
> Fax: (610) 866-9223
> E-mail: hampton@mcnp.org

Call to Action is a Catholic organization of over 18,000 lay people, religious, priests and bishops working together to foster peace, justice and love in our world, our church and ourselves in the spirit of the Second Vatican Council and the U.S. Catholic Bishops' Call to Action (1976). Programs include publications each month (*CTA News*, *ChurchWatch* and *Spirituality/ Justice Reprint*); annual *We Are the Church* national conference, 40 local chapters, a *Church Renewal Directory* of 400 national and local faith groups committed to church and societal renewal; the Future of Priestly Ministry Dialogue Project and a speakers and Artists Referral Service.

> 4419 N. Kedzie
> Chicago, IL 60625
> Phone: (773) 604-0400
> Fax: (773) 604-4719
> E-mail: ctaIL@igc.apc.org
> Website: call-to-action.org

Canadian Foodgrains Bank is a specialized food programming agency established and operated by 13 church-related relief and development organizations. It collects substantial amounts of foodgrain donations directly from Canadian farmers using an extensive network of grain elevators. The Foodgrains Bank uses donated cash and grain matched by cost-sharing funds from CIDA to procure and ship food assistance to food deficit countries, and to provide related services to partner agencies. Using food assistance to build and reconcile relationships with and within communities and countries such as Cuba, North Korea, Iran, Afghanistan, Rwanda and Guinea is a key interest. Other program involvements include monetization, food security reserves and household food security monitoring. Canadian Foodgrains Bank staff and partners also take a very active interest in food security policy issues. To support this policy dialogue, the Foodgrains Bank has a number of discussion papers related to the relationship between food security and peace, human rights, economic sanctions, gender, humanitarian action and international action.

> Box 747, 400-280 Smith Street
> Winnipeg, MB, Canada R3C 2L4
> Phone: (204) 944-1993
> Fax: (204) 943-2597

CARE is one of the world's largest and most effective private relief and development organizations. Each year, CARE reaches more than 35 million people in over 60 nations in Africa, Asia and Latin America. The organization's work began in 1946, when CARE packages helped Europe recover from World War II. Today, CARE provides famine and disaster victims with emergency assistance, improves health care, helps subsistence farmers and small-business owners produce more goods, addresses population and environmental concerns, and helps to develop economies and societies in a sustainable manner. The scope of CARE's work is broad, but its vision focuses on a single concept – helping people help themselves.

> 151 Ellis Street
> Atlanta, GA 30303
> Phone: (404) 681-2552
> Fax: (404) 577-5977

Catholic Charities USA is the nation's largest network of independent social service organizations. The 1,400 agencies and institutions work to reduce poverty, support families and empower communities. Catholic Charities organizations provide social services ranging from adoption and counseling to emergency food and housing. More than 12 million people of all religious, national, racial, social and economic backgrounds received services in 1996. Catholic Charities USA promotes public policies and strategies that address human needs and social injustices. The national office provides advocacy and management support for agencies. The Disaster Response Office organizes the Catholic community's response to U.S. disasters.

1731 King Street, Suite 200
Alexandria, VA 22314
Phone: (703) 549-1390
Fax: (703) 549-1656
E-mail: info@catholiccharitiesusa.org
Website: www.catholiccharitiesusa.org

The **Christian Reformed World Relief Committee**
(CRWRC) is a ministry of the Christian Reformed
Church in North America. CRWRC shows God's love
to people in need through **development** – working with
families and communities in food production, income
earning, health education, literacy learning, spiritual
and leadership skills – through **relief** – working with
disaster survivors by providing food, medicines, crisis
counseling, rebuilding and volunteer assistance – and
through **education** – working with people to develop
and act on their Christian perspective of poverty,
hunger and justice. CRWRC works with communities
in North America and in over 30 countries worldwide
to create permanent, positive change in Christ's name.

CRWRC U.S.
2850 Kalamazoo Avenue, S.E.
Grand Rapids, MI 49560-0600
Phone: (800) 552-7972
Fax: (616) 246-0806
E-mail for U.S. & Canada: CRWRC@crcna.org

CRWRC CANADA
3475 Mainway
P.O. Box 5070 STN LCD1
Burlington, ON L7R 3Y8
Phone: (800) 730-3490
Fax: (905) 336-8344

Church World Service (CWS) is a global relief, development and refugee-assistance ministry of the 34
Protestant and Orthodox communions that work
together through the National Council of the Churches
of Christ in the U.S.A. Founded in 1946, CWS works in
partnership with local church organizations in more
than 70 countries worldwide, supporting sustainable
self-help development of people which respects the
environment, meets emergency needs, and addresses
root causes of poverty and powerlessness. Within the
United States, CWS resettles refugees, assists communities in responding to disasters, advocates for justice in
U.S. policies which relate to global issues, provides educational resources, and offers opportunities for communities to join a people-to-people network of global and
local caring through participation in a CROP WALK.

The Rev. Dr. Rodney Page, Executive Director
475 Riverside Drive, Suite 678
New York, NY 10115-0050
Phone: (212) 870-2257 or 2175
Fax: (212) 870-3523
Website: www.ncccusa.org/cws

Congressional Hunger Center (CHC) was formed in
1993 by Democratic and Republican Members of
Congress after the House Select Committee on Hunger
was eliminated. Now in its fifth year, CHC is training
over 100 leaders at the community, national, and international levels annually. *Beyond Food* team members
work at the community level in the Mississippi Delta,
rural Vermont, and in the urban centers of Milwaukee
and Washington, DC, providing nutrition education,
designing and planting community gardens, and
strengthening the work of food banks. The *Mickey
Leland Hunger Fellows* work six months at direct service sites across the nation, then return to Washington,
DC where they help shape national food security policy
at a broad spectrum of host sites. The *International
Crisis Response Program* of the CHC trains existing
leaders at U.N. and U.S. Disaster Response agencies,
and non-governmental humanitarian workers in coordination strategies during acute crises such as those in
Rwanda, Bosnia, Sudan and North Korea. We are proud
to be accomplishing our original mission: "To lead,
speak, and act on behalf of the poor, the hungry, and the
victims of humanitarian crises by developing leaders at
the community, national, and international levels."

229^1/2 Pennsylvania Avenue, S.E.
Washington, DC 20003
Phone: (202) 547-7022
Fax: (202) 547-7575
E-mail: NOHUNGR@aol.com
Website: www.hungercenter.org

Covenant World Relief is the relief and development
arm of The Evangelical Covenant Church. Dr. Timothy
Ek is Vice President of the Covenant and Director of
Covenant World Relief. The Evangelical Covenant
Church has its national offices in Chicago, IL.
Covenant World Relief was formed in response to the
Covenant's historic commitment to being actively
involved in Christ's mission to respond to the spiritual
and physical needs of others.

5101 North Francisco Avenue
Chicago, IL 60625-3611
Phone: (773) 784-3000
Fax: (773) 784-4366
E-mail: 102167.1330@compuserve.com
Website: www.covchurch.org

EuronAid is a European association of nongovernmental
organizations (NGOs) which facilitates dialogue with
the Commission of the European Union in the areas of
food security and food aid. EuronAid cooperates with
the Commission in programming and procuring food
aid for the NGOs, then arranges and accounts for delivery to Third World NGOs for distribution. In recent
years, triangular operations (purchases within Third
World nations) have accounted for half of EuronAid's
food aid, which meets mainly development purposes.
EuronAid assimilates the experiences of NGOs
involved in food aid and employs this knowledge in its
dialogue with the Commission and the European

Parliament to achieve improved management of food aid. EuronAid was created in 1980 by major European NGOs in cooperation with the Commission of the European Union. The association has at present 29 member agencies and services an additional 60 European and Southern NGOs on a regular basis.

P.O. Box 12
NL-2501 CA Den Haag
The Netherlands
Phone: 31 70 330 57 57
Fax: 31 70 362 17 39
E-mail: euronaid@euronaid.nl

Food for the Hungry International (FHI) is an organization of Christian motivation committed to working with poor people to overcome hunger and poverty through development and, where needed, as appropriate relief. Founded in 1971, FHI is incorporated in Switzerland and works in over 30 countries of Asia, Africa and Latin America. As its name implies, FHI focuses on poverty needs that relate to food and nutrition. Its primary emphasis is on long-term development among the extremely poor, recognizing their dignity, creativity and ability to solve their own problems. The international staff numbers more than 1,300 persons. Autonomous Food for the Hungry National Organizations (N.O.s) in many different countries such as Food for the Hungry (USA) contribute resources.

7807 East Greenway Road, Suite 3
Scottsdale, AZ 85260
Phone: (602) 951-5090
Fax: (602) 951-9035
E-mail: general@fhi.net
Website: www.fhi.net

Founded in 1946, **Freedom from Hunger** fights chronic hunger with two of the most powerful and flexible resources ever created: money and information. Operating in rural regions of ten developing nations, our *Credit with Education* program builds on the success of village banking by integrating basic health, nutrition, family planning, and microenterprise management education into group meetings. Results from recent studies show beneficial impacts, not only on income and income-generating activities, but also on the health and nutrition of participants and their children. Freedom from Hunger's goal is to bring *Credit with Education* to 2.2 million women by the year 2005.

1644 DaVinci Court
Davis, CA 95617
Phone: (800) 708-2555
Fax: (530) 758-6241
E-mail: info@freefromhunger.org

Heifer Project International

In response to God's love for all people, the mission of Heifer Project International is to alleviate hunger and poverty in all parts of the world. HPI does this by:
– Providing food-producing animals, training and related assistance to families and communities.

– Enabling those who receive animals to become givers by "passing on the gift" of training and offspring to others in need.
– Educating people about the root causes of hunger.
Heifer Project International is supported by contributions from churches, individuals, corporations and foundations.

Heifer Project International
P.O. Box 808
Little Rock, AR 72203
Phone: (800) 422-0474
Fax: (501) 376-8906
Website: www.heifer.org

The **International Fund for Agricultural Development** (IFAD) is an international financial institution headquartered in Rome, Italy. Established in 1977 as a result of the 1974 World Food Conference, IFAD is a Specialized Agency of the United Nations with an exclusive mandate to provide the rural poor of the developing world with cost-effective ways of overcoming hunger, poverty and malnutrition. IFAD advocates a targeted, community-based approach to reducing rural poverty. The Fund's task is to help poor farmers raise their food production and improve their nutrition by designing and financing projects which increase their incomes. Since 1978, IFAD has mobilized $5.6 billion for 489 projects in 111 developing countries. The governance and funding of the institution are the result of a unique partnership among developed and developing countries. With the recent additions of South Africa and Croatia, IFAD now has 160 Member States.

Via del Serafico, 107
00142 Rome, Italy
Phone: 39 6 54591
Fax: 39 6 5043463
E-mail: ifad@ifad.org

1775 K Street, N.W., Suite 410
Washington, DC 20006
Phone: (202) 331-9099
Fax: (202) 331-9366
Website: www.ifad.org

MAZON: A Jewish Response to Hunger has granted more than $15 million since 1986 to nonprofit organizations confronting hunger in the United States and abroad. MAZON (the Hebrew word for "food") awards grants principally to programs working to prevent and alleviate hunger in the United States. Grantees include emergency and direct food assistance programs, food banks, multi-service organizations, anti-hunger advocacy/education and research projects, and international hunger-relief and agricultural development programs in Israel and impoverished countries. Although responsive to organizations serving impoverished Jews, in keeping with the best of Jewish tradition, MAZON responds to all who are in need.

12401 Wilshire Boulevard, Suite 303
Los Angeles, CA 90025-1015
Phone: (310) 442-0020
Fax: (310) 442-0030
Website: www.shamash.org/soc-action/mazon

Mennonite Central Committee (MCC), founded in 1920, is an agency of the Mennonite and Brethren in Christ churches in North America, and seeks to demonstrate God's love through committed women and men who work among people suffering from poverty, conflict, oppression and natural disaster. MCC serves as a channel for interchange between churches and community groups where it works around the world and North American churches. MCC strives for peace, justice and dignity of all people by sharing experiences, resources and faith. MCC's priorities include disaster relief and refugee assistance, rural and agricultural development, job creation, Ten Thousand Villages (formerly known as SELFHELP Crafts), health education and peace building.

21 South 12th Street
Akron, PA 17501-0500
Phone: (717) 859-1151
Fax: (717) 859-2171
E-mail: mailbox@mcc.org
Website: www.mennonitecc.ca.mcc

The mission of the **National Association of WIC Directors** (NAWD) is to provide leadership to the WIC community to promote quality nutrition services, serve all eligible women, infants and children and assure sound and responsive management of the Special Supplemental Nutrition Program for Women, Infants and Children (WIC). The purpose of the association is to link state WIC directors, local WIC directors, nutrition services coordinators and others in a national forum to act collectively on behalf of the program to include the following functions: A) To promote the improved health, well-being and nutritional status of women, infants and children; B) To provide a national resource network through which ideas, materials and procedures can be communicated to persons working in the WIC community; C) To promote good management practices and to assist WIC program directors at the state and local levels; D) To act as a resource at the request of governmental bodies and individual legislators regarding issues particular to the health and nutrition of women, infants and children and to assist WIC clients; and E) To do whatever is necessary to promote and sustain the WIC program.

P.O. Box 53355
2001 S Street, N.W., Suite 580
Washington, DC 20009-3355
Phone: (202) 232-5492
Fax: (202) 387-5281
E-mail: nawd@tomco.net
Website: www.nawd.com

Oxfam America fights global poverty and hunger by working in partnership with grassroots organizations promoting sustainable development in Africa, Asia, the Caribbean and the Americas, including the United States. In order to foster an environment supportive of long-term development, Oxfam America also advocates for policy change and produces educational materials for the U.S. public on poverty and hunger issues.

Oxfam America is a member of Oxfam International, which comprises 10 autonomous Oxfams around the world.

26 West Street
Boston, MA 02111
Phone: (800) 77-OXFAM
Fax: (617) 728-2594
E-mail: oxfamusa@igc.apc.org
Website: www.oxfamamerica.org

The **RLDS World Hunger Committee** was established in 1979 to engage the membership of the Reorganized Church of Jesus Christ of Latter Day Saints in a corporate response to the needs of hungry persons throughout the world. Included in the charge to the committee is a three-fold purpose: to provide assistance for those who are suffering from hunger, to advocate for the hungry, and to educate about the causes and alleviation of hunger in the world. The committee meets several times a year to consider applications for funding. The majority of the proposals considered by the committee originate with Outreach International and World Accord, both of which are recognized by the church as agencies engaged in comprehensive human development on a global scale. Projects that support food production or storage, economic development, the providing of potable water, nutrition or food preparation information, the providing of animals for transportation or cultivation are among those that receive favorable consideration by the committee.

P.O. Box 1059
Independence, MO 64051-0559
Phone: (816) 833-1000
Fax: (816) 521-3096
E-mail: ritasmck@rlds.org
Website: www.rlds.org

Save the Children Federation/U.S. works to make lasting, positive change in the lives of children in need in the United States and 40 countries around the world. International programs in health, education, economic opportunities and humanitarian response place children at the center of activities and focus on women as key decision-makers and participants. Key principles are child centeredness, women focus, participation and empowerment, sustainability, and maximizing impact. Programs in the United States emphasize youth and community service.

54 Wilton Road
Westport, CT 06880
Phone: (203) 221-4000
Fax: (203) 454-3914
Website: www.savethechildren.org

Second Harvest is the largest domestic charitable hunger-relief organization in the United States. Through a nationwide network of 187 food banks, Second Harvest distributes more than one billion pounds of donated food and grocery products annually to nearly 50,000 local charitable agencies. These food pantries, soup kitchens, women's shelters, Kid's Cafes and other feeding programs serve more than 26 million hungry Americans each year, including 8 million children and four million seniors.

116 South Michigan Avenue, Suite 4
Chicago, IL 60603-6001
Phone: (312) 263-2303
Fax: (312) 263-5626
Website: www.secondharvest.org

Share Our Strength (SOS) works to alleviate and prevent hunger and poverty in the United States and abroad. By supporting food assistance, treating malnutrition and other consequences of hunger, and promoting economic independence among people in need, Share Our Strength meets immediate demands for food while investing in long-term solutions to hunger and poverty. To meet its goals, SOS both mobilizes industries and individuals to contribute their talents to its anti-hunger efforts and creates community wealth to promote lasting change. Since 1984, Share Our Strength has distributed more than $45 million in grants to more than 1,000 anti-hunger, anti-poverty organizations worldwide. SOS's Operation Frontline is a food and nutrition education program that trains volunteer culinary professionals to teach six-week cooking, nutrition and food budgeting classes to low-income individuals in 90 communities nationwide. SOS's Taste of the Nation, presented by American Express and Calphalon, is the nation's largest culinary benefit to fight hunger, with 100 events each spring. SOS's Writers Harvest: The National Reading, is the nation's largest literary benefit. Every fall, thousands of writers read in bookstores and on college campuses to fight hunger and poverty. Corporate partnerships and publishing ventures also provide substantial support for SOS's anti-hunger, anti-poverty efforts.

1511 K Street, N.W., Suite 940
Washington, DC 20005
Phone: (202) 393-2925
Fax: (202) 347-5868
E-mail: info@strength.org
Website: www.strength.org

United Church Board for World Ministries (UCBWM) is the instrumentality of the United Church of Christ for the planning and conduct of its program of global missions, development and emergency relief. The UCBWM's fundamental mission commitment is to share life in partnership with global church partners and ecumenical bodies. Through service, advocacy and mission programs, the UCBWM sends as well as receives persons in mission; is committed to the healing of God's creation; engages in dialogue, witness and common cause with people of other faiths; and seeks a prophetic vision of a just and peaceful world order so that all might have access to wholeness of life.

475 Riverside Drive, Fl. 16
New York, NY 10115
Phone: (212) 870-2637
Fax: (212) 932-1236
E-mail: petrucel@ucc.org

U.S. Committee for UNICEF works for the survival, protection and development of children worldwide through education, advocacy and fund raising. UNICEF is currently in over 160 countries and territories providing needed assistance in the areas of health, nutrition, safe water and sanitation, girls' and women's issues, education, emergency relief, and child protection.

U.S. Committee for UNICEF
333 East 38th Street, 6th Floor
New York, NY 10016
Phone: (212) 686-5522
Fax: (212) 779-1679
E-mail: information@unicefusa.org
Website: www.unicefusa.org

World Hope International, Inc. seeks to mobilize individuals and organizations to exercise their specific gifts and abilities (personally and fiscally) by working in active partnership with persons around the world for the purpose of relief, economic and social development. World Hope is currently active in 15 countries around the world as well as communities in North America.

714 First Street
P.O. Box 31
Warrenton, MO 63383
Phone: (314) 456-4257
Fax: (314) 456-7817
E-mail: LyonJA@aol.com
Website: www.worldhopeintl.org

The mission of **World Relief** as set forth in our mission statement is: "to work with the church in alleviating human suffering worldwide in the name of Christ. For more than 50 years, World Relief – the international assistance and refugee resettlement arm of the National Association of Evangelicals – has enabled U.S. churches to be a lifeline to evangelical churches around the world. Representing more than 75 denominations, their missionaries and counterpart agencies, World Relief serves local U.S. congregations as they provide emergency relief, refugee care, urban ministries and long-term help to families in 19 countries.

P.O. Box WRC
Wheaton, IL 60189-8004
Phone: (800) 535-LIFE
Fax: (630) 665-0129
E-mail: worldrelief@wr.org